❧ RURAL ❧
RIDES

No 1: West Surrey

Country cycle rides
of adventure & discovery
for all the family

compiled & written
by
Ron Strutt

To Charles,
the best pal I could ever have had

Credits: Text, photographs, and sketch maps are by Ron Strutt, except photographs on pages 25, 106, 115, 127, 130, 136, 165, 166, and 167, which are by Lia Morreale.

Vintage line drawings are by the late Duncan Moul from *Picturesque Surrey*, published in 1902 by F E Robinson & Co.

ISBN 1 85284 272 5

Published by Cicerone Press, 2 Police Square, Milnthorpe, Cumbria LA7 7PY

**Ron
Strutt**

Welcome!

There is no better way of enjoying the incredibly beautiful and varied scenery that Surrey has to offer than on a bike. You can really appreciate the sights and sounds of the country and become part of the surroundings through which you're passing, instead of simply driving past it.

Anyone who has done it will know there is little to compare with the exhilaration of bowling along quiet lanes or freewheeling down a hill with the breeze in your face. With a bike you can stop wherever and whenever you like, without the worry of finding somewhere to park the car. And you can go further into the depths of the country than time or your feet might allow if you were walking.

From a bike you are certain to see more of nature than most other people will see in half a lifetime: deer, foxes, squirrels, countless rabbits, and many other creatures – not in an artificial setting, not at a distance, but close to, in their natural habitat.

The idea of these guides is to help you get the most from cycling in the countryside. Our rides will take you to places that you will almost certainly never have been before, and will give you a whole new view of the rural landscape which is so close at hand.

So get on your bike and go for it!

About the
original Rural Rides...

Rural Rides was the name given by William Cobbett to an account of his series of journeys on horseback across much of southern England in the years between 1821 and 1830. Cobbett was a countryman – he was born at Farnham, in Surrey – as well as a leading radical politician. He was deeply distrustful of the findings of a government commission on agriculture, and decided to find out for himself the state of things in the countryside. His *Rural Rides* were the result. They first appeared as a series of reports in Cobbett's own periodical *The Weekly Political Register* and were later published as a book.

Cobbett particularly chose to go on horseback and to keep away from the main roads:

> "*...my object was, not to see inns and turnpike-roads, but to see the country: to see the farmers at home, and to see the labourers in the fields; and to do this you must go either on foot or on horse-back. With a gig you cannot get about amongst bye-lanes and across fields, through bridleways and hunting-gates; and to tramp it is too slow, leaving the labour out of the question, and that is not a trifle.*"

written at Chilworth,
near Guildford, Surrey
Wednesday, 25th September, 1822

If Cobbett were alive today and repeating his travels, we think he would have chosen to use a bike, for that would be the ideal way for him to see today's countryside.

And although motorways and trunk roads with their service areas and Happy Eaters may have taken over from the turnpike-roads and their coaching inns, Cobbett would still recognise the quiet country lanes, the byways, and bridleways which he travelled then and which you will follow on the rides in this guide.

Acknowledgements

In writing these guides I have been fortunate in having the help and support of many friends.

In particular, I would like to express my gratitude to Martin Smethurst, whose offer to edit my work I accepted with alacrity. His guidance and suggestions have enhanced the readability of my original text immeasurably. Much of the credit for the final result is due to him.

From the moment I talked to him about my ideas for these books, Keith Dean was characteristically enthusiastic and not only drove me on to complete them, but also route-tested many of the rides. No-one could have been more generous with their praise and encouragement.

I also owe so much to the author Eric Parker who, through his wonderful writings about the beauties of Surrey, inspired me to seek them out.

Finally, these books could not have come to fruition without the love and support of my wife Liz, with whom it has been my good fortune to have shared both the joys and the tribulations of the task.

Contents

Introduction and Notes

    Key to Rides   page vi

    About the rides   page vii

        For newcomers

        Getting to the Rides

        Cycling on and off the road

        Off-road cycling

        Following the routes

        The Maps

        Facilities

    Useful Information   page xii

        When to go cycling

        What to wear

        Weather protection

        What to take

        Rights of Way

        The Law for cyclists

        Insurance

        Safety

        The Country Code

        Cycling and animals

        Find out more about Surrey

    Key to Maps   opposite page 21

The Rides

Key to Rides

Ride		Start at	Miles	Grade	Page
A	A Journey through Three Villages	Send	12	Easy	21
B	Wey Valley Wanderings	Newark	10–26	Moderate	31
C	Basingstoke Canal and Congo Stream	St Johns	19	Moderate	51
D	Highways, Byways, and a Wayward Stream	Bisley	11–16	Easy	67
E	Forest, Wood and Heath	Peaslake	9–13	Vigorous	79
F	Ups and Downs	Newlands Corner	24	Strenuous	95
G	Cobbett Country	Tilford	8	Moderate	113
H	Hymns, Ponds and a Devilish Murder	Tilford	15	Vigorous	123
I	Fold Villages of the Surrey Weald	Dunsfold	9½–21	Vigorous	141
J	Thameside Travels	Chertsey	4–24	Easy	161
K	Monks' Tracks and Gravel Pits	Chertsey	11	Easy	179

Abbreviations used

FL	Fork left		BW	Bridleway
FR	Fork right		BY	Byway
L	Left		CP	Car park
R	Right		FP	Footpath
SO	Straight on		SP	Signpost(ed)
THL	Turn hard left		TJ	T-Junction
THR	Turn hard right		XR	Cross roads
TL	Turn left		XT	Cross tracks
TR	Turn right		XW	Cross ways

About the Rides

The Rural Rides series of cycling guides are for people who want to go cycling for leisure and enjoyment. Our aim in writing them has been to introduce greater numbers of ordinary people, including families with children, to the joys of exploring the countryside on a bike.

These rides are not intended to be races or endurance tests – there are no prizes for completing them in the least possible time. We want you to get out into the countryside, to explore it, and to enjoy all it has to offer. There is absolutely nothing to be gained (but much to be missed) by rushing along, so don't worry if you find that your speed is averaging only a few miles an hour. That's about right on these rides!

For newcomers

If you are taking up cycling for the first time, or coming back to it after a long absence, start with a few rides of four or five miles near to home and then begin with some of the shorter rides in this guide. Don't put yourself off by trying to do too much at first. Give yourself time and, with a little practice, you'll soon be ready and eager to tackle longer routes.

Some of the rides involve hill climbing, but don't let that deter you. Surrey has magnificent scenery to offer, especially in the south of the county, but the best views are to be had from the tops of hills! You have to put a bit of effort into getting up there, but it's worth it. Don't worry about hills – if you want to get off and walk up, then do so. Relax and enjoy it. Take time to appreciate the scenery unfolding around you and to anticipate the exhilarating downhill ride to come. It's no admission of defeat to walk up a hill; there are few cyclists who haven't had to do it at one time or another, and besides, walking with your bike as well as riding it is good exercise.

Getting to the Rides

By car

Cycle carriers designed to fit onto the backs or roofs of cars mean you are no longer restricted to rides which start in your immediate locality. If you don't have one of your own, some cycle shops now hire them. You can also buy cycle carriers which fit onto roof bars; look for a set designed for your make of car.

All of our rides begin at places where you can park your car while you go cycling. However, since the rides are circular, you can start from almost any point on the route. But if you do, please don't leave your car where it might cause inconvenience; remember that you could be away for some time. In particular, don't park in front of gates leading into farm fields or woodlands, even if they look as if they're rarely used. If you want to park in a pub car park, or on any other private land, ask the owner for permission first.

By train

Once upon a time the favourite way of cycling in distant parts was to travel there by train with your bike in the guard's van, and this is still the most environmentally-friendly way of doing it. Our directions and maps show the location of stations which are on or close to the rides. However, it is a sad fact that some of the latest designs of trains have either limited or non-existent facilities for bikes. For example, the trains operated by South West Trains on the Waterloo–Salisbury–Exeter line, most InterCity and some Regional Railways trains will take only two bikes at a time, and you must make reservations in advance at a cost of £3 each per single journey. This is hardly ideal for families or groups, or for a spur-of-the-moment outing!

Furthermore, the railways are in a state of major change at present, and we advise prospective rail-users to check the up-to-date situation in advance. In addition, if you are travelling at the weekend, check to see if trains are diverted because of work on the lines – bikes are not carried on replacement buses. For peak-hour journeys within the commuter area (roughly 30 miles from London) bikes are not allowed on London-bound trains in the morning and back in the evening.

On the plus side, where there are no restrictions, bikes normally travel free (at the time of writing). Just label them with your name and destination. For all rail enquiries telephone 0345 48 49 50.

Cycling on and off the road

The rides in this book make use of both surfaced roads and unmade tracks. Properly surfaced roads obviously make for easier and faster cycling, but most people find little fun in riding in the midst of traffic. On the other hand, cycling through deep mud isn't everyone's idea of the perfect day out, so we have tried to reach a reasonable compromise.

Our rides use country roads and lanes wherever possible, but we have tried to avoid those which are too busy or where the traffic tends to be very fast-moving. In the main, we have followed the cyclist's old maxim "Stick to the yellow", referring to the minor roads coloured yellow on Ordnance Survey maps. These roads are normally fairly quiet, but you must still take care because they can get busy at certain times.

We have used paths and tracks to bypass busy stretches of road or to take you into scenic or peaceful areas of countryside which are inaccessible by car. In Surrey, which has one of the highest rates of car ownership in the UK, few roads are ever completely peaceful in the way that byways and bridleways can be.

However, off-road tracks can sometimes be in poor condition. Some people will not mind this but others will – one person's nightmare of mud and filth is another's excitement and challenge!

The route details tell you where problems are most likely to arise and, where possible, we suggest diversions along surfaced roads so that you have a choice.

Off-road cycling

Most off-road tracks are unsurfaced and their condition can vary enormously. Some can be muddy after wet weather, but in summer they should give few problems. Conversely, there are parts of Surrey where the ground is very sandy, and the going can be hard when it is dry. In both cases, tracks which are regularly used by horses can be challenging.

If a particular path is very bad, it may be worth contacting the County Council to see if they can make repairs. Budgets for this kind of work are limited, but something may be done if enough people complain. (Better still, volunteer to spend the odd weekend helping to look after Surrey's rights of way; contact the Environment Unit, Planning Dept, County Hall, Kingston-upon-Thames, KT1 2DT).

We have checked the rides in this guide in a variety of conditions, and most of the off-road tracks should not give you any problems in reasonable weather. There are a few places where you may have to walk your bike, but there is always a good reason for the ride being routed that way.

The majority of bikes sold today are all-terrain or 'mountain' bikes and can cope with some fairly difficult off-road conditions. On the other hand, there is no reason why you shouldn't use a road bike providing you're sensible. You may have to get off and push more often, and you must be careful not to damage your bike. If your own bike is not suitable for these rides you can hire one designed for off-road use. You must decide whether conditions are too difficult for the bike you are using. We cannot accept any responsibility for damage done to a bike as a result of using it on one of the rides in this guide.

Riding on off-road tracks means keeping in a low gear so you can cope with sudden problems or changes in conditions. Keep both hands on the handlebars at all times, make sure you are totally in control of your bike, and keep your speed down. Be especially careful of dry sand or gravel surfaces which can cause you to skid or lose your balance; mud and wet chalk can also be treacherously slippery. If mud builds up under your mudguards (if you have them) it can jam your wheels solid, so make sure you clear it out before that happens.

The simple answer is that if conditions become too difficult, get off and walk. Just as with climbing hills, there is nothing to say that you have to stay in the saddle all the time. Walking with your bike will allow you to enjoy the countryside all the more, and you will certainly see more wildlife. In any case, we happen to think

Studying the route

that walking with a bike can be as much fun as riding it (and good exercise), so be prepared for a little footwork on our rides!

The other point to remember about off-road tracks is that in summer they're often lined with nettles, brambles, and other unsociable vegetation. It's a good idea to cover bare skin with sleeves, long trousers and socks; you may not want to wear them all the time, but having them with you in case you need them may save a lot of discomfort. It also makes sense to carry ointment to treat stings.

Following the routes

For each ride there is a 'Route in Brief' opposite the map, followed by a more complete and readable description of the ride and the places of interest along the way. You can choose which you prefer to use as your guide.

The distances in the text give you a rough idea of how far you've cycled. They are approximate and are for interest, not precise navigation. In a few places where we think you might have problems with the route, we have put up small 'Rural Rides' waymark signs.

We have taken a great deal of care to ensure that our information is as accurate as possible but changes do happen with great regularity and surprising speed. If you discover any that have taken place since this guide went to press we would be delighted to hear from you.

The Maps

The sketch maps in this guide are intended to give basic information about the routes and the places along the way. To get the most out of your ride we recommend that cyclists and walkers should use the Ordnance Survey maps.

These come in two types: the Landranger series in illustrated red card covers at a scale of 1:50000 (roughly 1¼ inches to the mile) and the green-coloured Path-finder series at a scale of 1:25000 (or 2½ inches to the mile). The Landranger maps cover a wider area on each sheet, which can be useful on long trips, but the Pathfinder maps give you much more detailed information.

(The new Explorer series of maps, in orange covers, is gradually replacing the Pathfinders. They use the same 1:25000 scale but cover a much greater area.)

Facilities

Pubs, shops, refreshment facilities, toilets, and public telephones are shown on the maps in those areas where they are not very plentiful. In most towns and larger villages, readers should be able to find them without difficulty.

Pubs, Inns and Hotels

There are some absolutely delightful pubs and inns along the routes of these rides, and it can often be very difficult deciding which one (or ones) to call into.

The recent liberalisation of the licensing laws should increasingly prove a boon to the cyclist. Quite a few of the pubs referred to in these rides are now opening their doors from 11am through to 11pm (10.30pm on Sundays), so you don't have to ride with one eye on your watch if you're looking forward to that refreshing pint halfway round.

Although many pubs are sticking to the 'standard' opening times for the time being, a good number are experimenting with longer hours, and a steady trade from the cycling fraternity at a nice rural pub may well help to influence the situation in the long term. In the meantime, we have given times of opening and food service in the pub entries only if they differ substantially from the 'standard' hours of 11am to either 2.30 or 3pm, 6pm to 11pm (noon to 3pm, 7pm to 10.30pm on Sundays).

Many rural pubs pride themselves on a variety of real ales and a high standard of homemade food, several serving excellent Sunday lunches, though if you want to be certain a pub is open or that food is available we advise you to telephone in advance. And do remember, the cyclist is subject to the same laws on alcohol consumption as any other road-user.

The codes relating to pub facilities are as follows:

C: has a Children's Certificate or a room where children under 14 are allowed
G: has a garden
Food: serves bar meals or snacks – can be anything from sandwiches to full meals

Rest: has a restaurant with waiter/waitress service
Acc: provides accommodation

Shops

In rural areas, general shops and off-licences, where you can at least buy a can of drink or snacks, are shown on the maps or listed in the text. However, most rural shops have closed in recent years and there is no guarantee that those shown on the maps will still be there (although your custom will help those which remain). Bear in mind that many rural shops close at 5.30pm, have half-day closing, and don't open on Sundays.

Most petrol stations now include a small shop. They are usually open until late and on Sundays, and often provide toilet facilities as well. Where they provide the only such facilities in an area we have marked them on the maps.

Enjoying the countryside

Useful information

When to go cycling

Cycling isn't just a summer activity – the rest of the year has much to offer. Indeed, the cooler weather of spring and autumn can be more comfortable for cycling than the heat of summer, and even winter cycling can be great fun providing you dress appropriately and the roads are free from ice.

The countryside is beautiful whatever the time of year, so why not get out and enjoy it. In winter when the trees and hedges are bare of leaves you can see much more of the view. In spring the clear air is perfect for distant vistas, and the ground becomes a carpet of fresh green growth and flowers. In autumn the colours of the leaves can add a spectacular new dimension to many familiar scenes.

What to wear

There are two key rules as to what to wear on a bike. The first is to wear layers of clothes so that you can easily add or take off just the right amount for comfort; the choice between a thin cotton shirt and a thick woollen sweater is really no choice at all.

If you set out on a warm summer's day in just a T-shirt, always have a couple of extra layers with you. A hot day can turn very cool if it clouds over, and even in Surrey there are places where it can become quite inhospitable in bad weather.

The second rule is to ensure that what you wear below the waist is not going to chafe the more delicate parts of your anatomy. If you cycle only occasionally, the cost of lycra cycling shorts may seem excessive, but they really do have benefits. They have no rough seams, they move with the body rather than rub against it, and they dry quickly if they get wet. Worn without underwear, they are lined with chamois (the best) or a synthetic material (cheaper) which absorbs perspiration, prevents chafing, and provides extra padding between you and the saddle. They are definitely recommended. Their only drawback is that they don't protect your legs against nettles and the like. You can get long 'tights', but wearing light cotton trousers over lycra shorts, while not ideal, is better than getting your legs stung.

In winter your legs can get very cold. One solution is to wear thermal long johns under trousers, but we have found that a pair of light cotton pyjama trousers worn as under-trousers provides an excellent added layer of insulation which can cope with quite cold temperatures. Jeans are totally unsuitable for cycling. They are stiff and unyielding, with prominent seams in all the wrong places, and if they get wet they can be extremely heavy and uncomfortable.

You will need gloves more often than you may think. Hands can get cold and numb very quickly on a bike, even if the rest of you is warm. Special cycling gloves with shock-absorbing pads are available, but ordinary thermal gloves offer good protection in all but the coldest weather and are thin enough not to be cumbersome.

There has been much debate about the value and desirability of wearing cycle helmets. There is evidence to suggest they may give a feeling of security to wearers which encourages them to take more risks. Many wearers also seem to think that helmets give them more protection than they actually do. If you ride in heavy traffic, where the risk to you from other people's mistakes is much greater, you should probably wear a helmet. Children and novices, who have not yet developed their cycling skills and their ability to handle potentially dangerous situations, should always wear helmets. However, they must still learn to ride sensibly and not to take risks.

If you don't wear a helmet, you'll need a hat most of the time. On hot days you'll want one to prevent your head burning, but it mustn't make your head too warm. In cool weather you want a hat which will not only keep your head warm but your ears too. Whatever type of headgear you wear, make sure it will stay securely on your head. You won't be able to control your bike properly if you're trying to hang on to a hat.

Eye protection is vital, not just for bright sun but also to keep insects out of your eyes. Fashionable, if expensive, reflective visors can be bought from any cycle shop, but a good pair of sunglasses will do as well, provided their frames do not block your peripheral vision. You may want to wear them even in low light (there are a lot of insects at dusk on summer evenings), so consider glasses which adjust to match the light.

Rain need not be a problem on one-day rides like those in this guide. If heavy or continuous rain seems likely, we suggest you postpone your ride, but light showers need not bother you if there is some form of shelter nearby, and it can even be refreshingly pleasant to ride through light rain on a hot day. The problem comes if you want (or have) to push on through heavier showers.

Ordinary rainwear is excellent at keeping moisture out, but it is also very good at keeping it in. If you are prepared to stop for the duration of the rain (even if there is little shelter), ordinary cheap rainwear such as a light nylon jacket will suffice. Otherwise, you will need a waterproof of a type which allows sweat to escape (they can be quite expensive) or a traditional cycling cape.

Capes cost less, are naturally ventilated, and roll up into a fairly small space for carrying. Their main drawback is that wind or the draught of passing traffic can make the bike hard to control.

Never wear a rain garment with a hood while cycling. They dangerously restrict your ability to see to the side and rear and can muffle the sound of approaching vehicles.

Weather protection

In summer, and sometimes even in spring and autumn, you'll need to make sure your bare arms, legs and face are well-coated with suntan lotion. It is sometimes easy to forget that you can be out in the open sun for a long time on a bike ride, and the cooling breeze can be deceptive. Exposed skin can get burned before you realise it. Take the suntan lotion with you to top up your protection during the day.

What to take

If you are going out on any length of ride, you will want some means of carrying spare clothing, waterproofs, and other essential items. Small rucksacks or backpacks can be bought quite cheaply, but they are not ideal. Apart from the fact that the weight of the contents can soon mount up, your back will get unpleasantly hot under a pack. The answer is a set of front or back panniers, or a saddlebag. You don't want to look as if you're setting off on an expedition to the upper reaches of the Amazon, but there are a few things it is sensible to take with you in addition to spare clothing:

- a small first aid kit with a couple of plasters and some antiseptic cream to treat minor cuts and grazes
- a basic repair kit, including a puncture repair outfit, a set of tyre levers, an adjustable spanner, small screwdrivers and a cycle pump with connectors to fit the valves on all the group's bikes. Many people take a spare inner tube to save fixing a puncture out on the road
- food and drink: you always feel hungry and thirsty when you're miles from the nearest source of supplies; on a hot day you will be surprised how much liquid you need, and if it's cold you will need to eat more to keep warm
- a wet cloth in a plastic bag, a dry rag, and a few tissues
- a roll of insulating tape – it seems the kind of thing which is sure to come in handy one day
- a notebook and pen

A group of cyclists can, of course, divide some of these things between them.

Rights of Way

Cyclists have a legal right to ride on all public roads (except motorways and places where traffic signs indicate otherwise) and on those rights of way (but only those) which are classified as:

- bridleways (but not Permissive Horse Rides)
- byways open to all traffic (BOATs)
- roads used as public paths (RUPPs)
- the delightfully-named 'Carriage Roads used mainly as Bridleways' (CRBs)
- designated cycle tracks
- cross-country footpaths or tracks in Scotland

Rights of way are sometimes indicated by coloured arrows or waymarks to indicate their status; blue for bridleways and red for byways or RUPPs. (Yellow arrows indicate footpaths.) Even when you have a right of way as a cyclist, you must always give way to walkers and horses, for your safety as much as theirs.

Cycling is allowed on most canal and river towpaths – check the bylaws of the relevant navigation authority. On British Waterways' canals you need a BW Cycling Permit.

Except in Scotland, cyclists and horse riders have no right to use public footpaths. *Nor* do they have the right to ride across areas such as heaths, commons and woods, even on the tracks which cross them, unless those tracks are bridleways or byways, or when permission has been specifically given. The fact that the public has access to an area makes no difference to this; access is for walking only. Cycling on footpaths and open areas constitutes trespass, and the landowner could sue you. This might sound far-fetched, but it could be a serious possibility if you cause damage.

Beyond that, a local council can ban cyclists from particular footpaths, or even bridleways, if it feels that they are causing a nuisance, and it is then an offence to ignore the ban. In the past, few people were ever prosecuted for this offence but, with the introduction of fixed penalty 'on-the-spot' fines, the police in many areas are beginning to crack down. It is also usually an offence under local bylaws to cycle on public open areas such as commons or the tracks that cross them (if they are not rights of way).

Bikes can do tremendous damage to the countryside, so please, never ride on unauthorised paths or open areas, and even if you are on a bridleway, if you think you might be damaging the path or its surroundings, dismount and walk.

This may sound like an awful lot of legal dos and don'ts aimed at restricting your enjoyment of the countryside, but there is a serious point to it. Cyclists won the right to use bridleways only through the 1968 Countryside Act. Many ramblers, horse riders, and country residents would like to see that right taken away, with cyclists being limited to the roads once more, and the pressure groups which represent these people have a lot of influence.

The actions of a small number of stupid or inconsiderate cyclists who refuse to stick to reasonable rules could result in off-road cycling being banned for everyone.

In one or two instances, our routes do follow footpaths, but only where they offer the only realistic alternative to riding on busy roads. Where this happens you must dismount and walk; in most cases only short distances are involved.

Rights of way matters are generally the responsibility of county councils (or, where they exist, unitary councils), although in some cases they may be handled by borough, district, or even parish councils. If you find a right of way in Surrey that is blocked, is in poor condition, which is not signposted where it meets a public road, or which needs waymarking along its route, contact Surrey County Council Rights of Way Section on 0181-541 9331 or 01483 519331 in the first instance.

Rights of way are shown on most Ordnance Survey maps, but there may occasionally have been changes since the map was printed.

The Law for Cyclists

Traffic restrictions such as one-way systems, prohibited turns, and many other requirements of the law and the Highway Code apply as much to cyclists as to drivers of motor vehicles. Strictly speaking, the restrictions apply even if you are wheeling your bike, but a dismounted cyclist acting in a sensible manner is unlikely to get into trouble.

The situation is less clear if you're riding your bike though. In some places cyclists are expected (even by the police) to ignore restrictions clearly not aimed at them. In other places the law is rigidly enforced. The main problem, though, is one of safety. Other road-users may not expect you to make a banned movement – such as riding the wrong way in a one-way street – and an accident could result.

It is an offence under the 1972 Road Traffic Act to ride recklessly, carelessly, or under the influence of drink or drugs. This applies to cyclists on bridleways and cycle paths as well as public roads.

Insurance

There is no legal requirement for cyclists in the UK to have insurance, but it is a good idea to make sure you are covered, not just against the possible theft of your bike, but also for injury and damage which may result from an accident in which you are involved. If you swerve to avoid a hazard and cause a car which is passing to collide with someone else, or if you hit a pedestrian, you could be sued and be bankrupted if you don't have insurance cover.

Some household contents insurance policies cover such matters as cycle theft and personal liability to third parties, but there may be restrictions as to which members of the family are covered and in what circumstances, so check the fine print. There are also specialist insurance policies for cyclists – see an insurance broker for information.

Safety

Many people are put off cycling because they think it is dangerous in today's traffic conditions. In fact, the chances of having an accident and being injured are really very small. You can reduce the risks still further (and increase your enjoyment of cycling at the same time) by improving your skills in cyclecraft. Books such as *Cyclecraft* by John Franklin (published by Unwin Paperbacks, 1988) contain a great deal of valuable guidance, or you can enrol on a cycle safety course (ask your council or police road safety officer for details). The notes given here are no substitute for either.

The routes in this guide avoid main roads as far as possible, but it is important to remember that few roads in Surrey are completely quiet. Even on country lanes you will come across motorists who do not expect you to be there. Keep to the proper side of the road, and make sure you are fully in control of your bike at all times. Always wear clothing that makes you easily and quickly visible to the motorist. The driver of an approaching car may have only seconds to realise you are there, and bright colours draw attention to your presence. High-visibility jackets also seem to encourage drivers to give you more room when overtaking.

It may seem strange advice, but it is not a good idea to ride too close to the side of the road. It can be more difficult for motorists to see you there, you are more likely to encounter obstacles, and you have no room to manoeuvre in case of emergency. You will also find that motorists will be more inclined to squeeze past you in dangerous circumstances. Some less experienced cyclists ride close to the edge of the road because they feel guilty about getting in the way of the traffic and, sadly, that seems only to reinforce the prejudices of some drivers. The law is quite clear. A cyclist has as much right to be on the road as any other road-user, and if you are in front you have the right of precedence. The fact that you are slower than the rest of the traffic has no bearing on the matter – when did you ever see a tractor driver who worried about going slowly?

Obviously, you must not obstruct the free flow of traffic by negligence or mis-behaviour (as the law puts it), but that doesn't mean you have to keep out of the way of, or constantly give way to, other vehicles. You should allow them to overtake, but only where it is safe and reasonable. However, having said that, you must judge each situation sensibly.

Most drivers are considerate to cyclists and will overtake only when it is safe, but a few can make life unpleasant. It is tempting to insist on your rights, but it isn't worth it. You will only antagonise them – and you're the vulnerable one. Give in with grace. In general, if the traffic is building up behind you, it is often better to stop and let it pass, if only because it's not much fun riding along with a queue of impatient cars on your back wheel.

In a few places our rides have to venture onto busy roads. Don't be put off by this; even on the busiest of roads you will come to no harm if you ride sensibly and take care. In fact busier roads tend to be wider, giving you more room to keep clear of the traffic.

Whatever you read elsewhere (even in the Highway Code), it is not a good idea to ride two abreast, especially on narrow roads. You will constantly have to drop back into single file to let other vehicles pass, and, while riding abreast is very sociable, your attention may be distracted from a possible hazard. If you are riding with children, there must always be an adult behind them and, ideally, one in front as well.

Always carry lights on your bike and use them whenever the light is poor. It's better to waste a set of batteries than risk an accident through not being seen. Don't leave your lights at home because you expect to be back before dusk – you may be delayed.

The Country Code

In the country, whether you're a cyclist, walker or motorist, always abide by the Country Code:

- Guard against fire risks
- Fasten all gates
- Keep dogs under proper control
- Keep to paths across farmland
- Avoid damaging fences, hedges and walls
- Leave no litter
- Safeguard water supplies
- Protect wildlife, wild plants and trees
- Go carefully on country roads
- Respect the life of the countryside

Cycling and Animals

Cycling in the country means you're bound to meet animals of various types. Most of them will be in fields, or otherwise out of harm's way, but some of them will be in your path, occasionally with disconcerting results.

Many horses get worried about bikes. We don't recommend trying to overtake a horse on a track, but if you are keeping your speed down the situation will rarely arise. If you have to overtake a horse on the road, make sure the rider knows you are there and is fully in control. Then pass at a reasonable speed, giving the horse plenty of room. If a horse is coming towards you on a narrow road or track, stop and let it pass. If the horse seems

Cycling and animals – occasionally you might have a close encounter of the herd kind!

particularly agitated it may help if you dismount.

If a herd of cows is heading along the road in the same direction as you, don't try to overtake or push through. Wait for them to turn off. If you meet a herd coming towards you, back off. Whatever you do, never try to push past or let them push past you.

Dogs love cyclists and will often charge at you (usually in fun) the moment they see you. The best advice is usually to stop, especially if the owner is present to bring it under control. The problem is that a dog leaping around can make you swerve or even send you crashing to the ground. Fortunately they seem to lose interest as soon as you stop.

Most other animals, especially wild ones, will scatter as soon as they see or hear you but they may dart across your path, so slow down and be prepared to stop.

Wildfowl will sometimes react in this way, but often they will continue on their way regardless of your presence. Stop and let them get out of the way before you proceed. From time to time, especially on canal or river towpaths you will come across larger birds such as swans who simply refuse to move. They need to be treated with respect, especially if they have young. Dismount and edge round them, keeping the bike between you and the bird.

Geese can be very aggressive and may chase you if they don't like the look of you. This can be quite an unnerving experience, and a hasty withdrawal to a discreet distance seems the best advice!

Find out more about Surrey

If you enjoy these rides you may want to discover more about the many different aspects of the county. There are hundreds of books about Surrey, its towns and villages, but we have listed some of the best to look out for. Most are available from libraries throughout the county and many good booksellers have a local interest section.

Highways & Byways in Surrey by Eric Parker (Macmillan, 2nd edition 1935): this wonderful book is long out of print but it can be borrowed from libraries – well worth reading.

Surrey: a County History by John Janaway (Countryside Books, 1995): an extremely readable account of the story of Surrey from ancient to modern times.

Hidden Surrey by Chris Howkins (Countryside Books, 1987): begins where most guide books leave off. (There is a companion volume *Hidden Surrey – Town & Country* for the towns and larger villages.)

Portrait of Surrey by Basil E Cracknell (Robert Hale, 2nd edition 1974): a picture of the county in words as its title suggests.

All Surrey towns and most of the villages have at least one history or guide book. The Local Studies section in Guildford Library has an impressive collection of them, many of which are available on loan to members of any branch of the Surrey County Libraries.

THE RIDES

Here are hill and dell in endless variety. Here are the chalk and the sand, vieing with each other in making beautiful scenes. Here is a navigable river and fine meadows. Here are woods and downs. Here is something of everything but fat marshes and their skeleton-making agues.

Those that travel on turnpike roads know nothing of England. Against a great road things are made for show. Here we see the people without any disguise or affectation. And here we gain real knowledge as to their situation.

William Cobbett

Key to Maps

▶	Direction of main route	▷	Alternative route (see text)
③ etc	Stage of route (see text)		
═══════	Road	═══════	Dual Carriageway or Motorway
==========	Bridleway or Track	- - - - - - -	Footpath
▬▬▬▬▬▬	River or Canal	⌒⌒	Stream

┼┼┼■┼┼┼ Railway Line
⇌   with Station

Public House

⏚ Shop (for general provisions)

⛽ Petrol station with shop

☕ Light refreshments

🅿 Car park (charge may be payable)

WC Toilets (charge may be payable)

★ Place of Interest

⌂ Notable Building

🎓 School

☀ Viewpoint

⛳ Golf course

✝ Church

☎ Public telephone

🗼 Radio or TV mast

🏰 Castle

🪖 Army camp, training area or range

┼┼┼✳┼┼┼ Level crossing

)(Bridge

🚦 Traffic lights

Ride A:
A Journey through Three Villages

Burntcommon • Send Prison • Holride Farm • Jury Farm • West Horsley •
Ripley • Send Marsh • Send • Fell Hill • Woodhill • Burntcommon

Distance:	12 miles
Landranger Maps:	186 & 187
Pathfinder Maps:	1206

This ride follows lanes and tracks through three Surrey villages and the
countryside which surrounds them. Despite the A3 trunk road, which is never
a great distance away, and even though a commuter railway passes through
the area, the ride travels through surprisingly peaceful countryside. And in
several places you will probably find yourself alone, apart from the pheasants,
rabbits, and even the occasional deer.

All this tranquillity can be found less than five miles from the built-up areas of
Woking and Guildford, showing that you really do not have to travel very far in
Surrey to find unspoilt rural surroundings. Sometimes it can be on your very
doorstep.

The ride takes in a couple of stretches of old green lanes and a track through
open fields linking two farms. Other than that, most of the ride is on quiet
country lanes. The route is fairly easy riding and can be covered in a couple of
hours, but allow yourself plenty of time to have a look around each of the three
villages. There are pubs and shops in several places on or near the route.

Starting Points

The best place to begin this ride is at the
Burntcommon roundabout (grid reference
TQ 037547), south-east of Send, where
the A247 Woking to Dorking road crosses
the B2215. The section of old dual
carriageway leading west from the
roundabout (once part of the old A3
Portsmouth road) is now a minor road
leading to Fell Hill, and provides a handy
place to leave a car. There are some limited
parking facilities at other points along the
route, such as in Ripley.

≥ The nearest station is at Clandon on
the Waterloo–Guildford via Cobham line

(South West Trains). It is on the A247, 1
mile south of Burntcommon. Horsley
Station, on the same line, is in the village
of East Horsley and is about 1½ miles from
the route.

Ride A
A Journey through
Three Villages

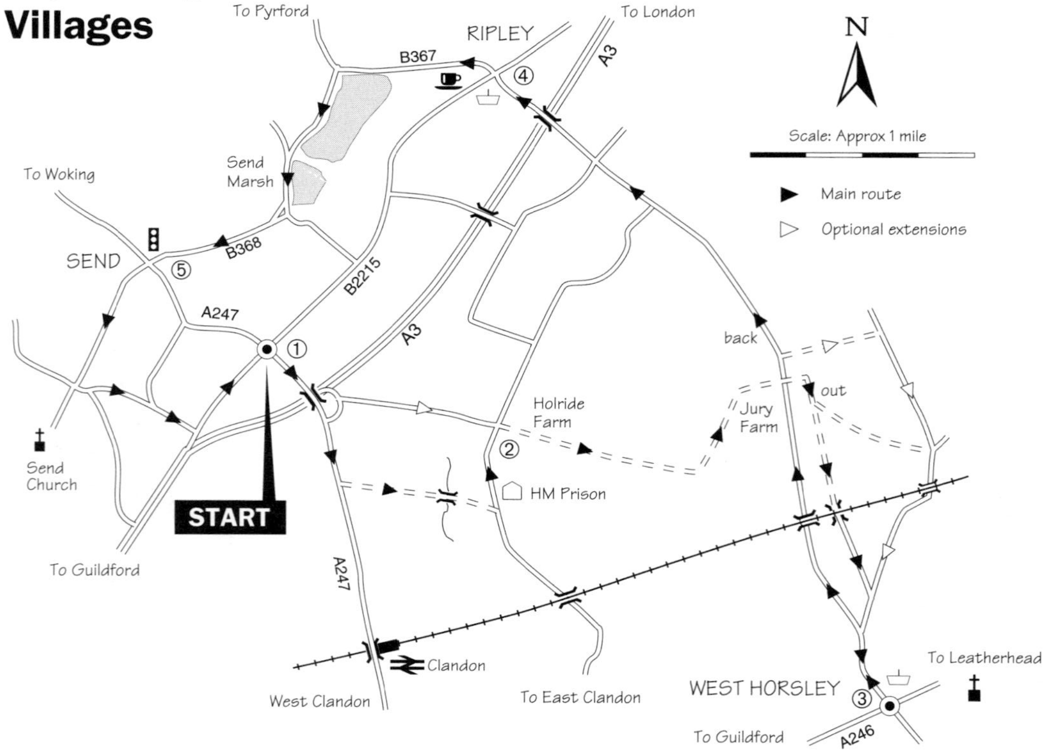

Scale: Approx 1 mile

▲ Main route
△ Optional extensions

N

To London

A3

RIPLEY ④

B367

To Pyrford

Send Marsh

B368

B2215

A3

To Woking

SEND ⑤

A247

①

START

To Guildford

Send Church

Holride Farm

Jury Farm

out

back

② HM Prison

A247

West Clandon

Clandon

To East Clandon

WEST HORSLEY ③

A246

To Guildford

To Leatherhead

The Route in Brief

① From the roundabout at Burntcommon follow the A247 in the direction of Clandon and Dorking. SO over the A3 and past the junction with the slip road leading to it. TL onto rough lane (BW) SP 'Green Lane'. Follow track past houses and on into open country, then through wooded area, crossing stream. At road TL past prison.

② At junction with Tithebarns Lane TR onto BW (concrete track) SP Holride Farm. Follow BW for about 1½ miles to Jury Farm. At junction with road SO onto BW (unmade track). Follow track as it bends to R, then take R fork when track divides. Up slope and cross railway bridge into Silkmore Lane. Keep SO to junction with The Street then TR. Continue to roundabout on A246.

③ Retrace steps along The Street but TL into Ripley Lane. Continue for 3 miles, crossing A3, to Ripley.

√ Leave Ripley by Newark Lane then, just beyond of village, TL into Polesdon Lane. At Send Marsh Green TR into Send Marsh Road.

⑤ At Send traffic lights SO into Send Hill. At junction at Fell Hill TL then fork L into Vicarage Lane, SP Ripley. At end TL onto old A3 dual carriageway (CAUTION) to Burntcommon.

The Anchor, Ripley

" THE ANCHOR," RIPLEY.

The Ride

① Burntcommon to Send Prison

Head south along the A247 in the direction of West Clandon. Cross the modern bridge over the A3 bypass and continue past the junction with the A3 slip road.

☞ *The slip road also leads to Tithebarns Lane, which is part of the alternative route for the next part of the ride.*

About half a mile beyond the slip road, turn left into a lane signed 'Bridleway' and 'Green Lane'. The lane is lined by houses on the right and is reasonably well-surfaced, even if it does have rather a lot of potholes.

When the houses come to an end, the lane continues through the fields, and then, after a final group of three houses, it becomes a narrow trackway leading on into a wooded area. (Be careful not to follow the lane into the driveway of the last house!) The surface of the bridleway is not so good on this length. After rain it can get quite muddy, but the distance involved is fairly short.

☞ *An alternative route via Tithebarns Lane is described on page 30.*

After a couple of hundred yards the track comes to a small stream which you can cross by using the ford or the somewhat basic concrete footbridge next to it. (There are numerous small streams in this area. They come from springs which emerge along the line where the chalk of the North Downs meets the clay of the London basin.)

Across the stream the track widens and after another 300 yards it comes out on Ripley Road. Turn left along the road, past

the high wire fence of Send Prison. Note the boundary stones along the verge marked with the government arrow symbol and PD (for Prison Department).

② Send Prison to West Horsley

Continue along the road for about 700 yards, past the prison entrance, to its junction with Tithebarns Lane. Turn right here onto the bridleway which is signed 'Holride Farm', this being one of the several farms which make up the Ryde Farm Estate. The bridleway is a concrete farm track which passes the farmyard and then climbs a short but abrupt hill into some woodland. Beyond the crest of the hill is a 'crossroads' of bridleways; go straight on.

The concrete surface and lack of traffic might tempt you to bowl along, but resist the temptation. You should certainly take time to enjoy the scenery, but be careful as well, as the concrete is cracked in places and some of the cracks are wide enough to trap a wheel. Although you may be able to hear the distant hum of traffic on the A3, all you can see from this point are fields and trees. If you are lucky, you may even catch sight of some of the deer who live in the woods.

The track heads on down hill and passes through Jury Farm, where there is a dairy, to the road. Cross the road and join the bridleway directly opposite. It is not well surfaced and, as it is used by farm vehicles, it could be rather muddy for a short distance.

☞ *An alternative route is described on page 30 in case this bridleway is too muddy for comfort.*

After about 50 yards the bridleway turns abruptly to the right, and then, after another 50 yards or so, widens out and comes to a junction. The most obvious track forks to the left across the fields in the direction of Round Tree Farm; it is shown

The barn at Charles Cottage, West Horsley

only on recent Ordnance Survey maps and it is not a right of way. Instead, follow the much less obvious grassy lane heading straight ahead into what appears to be an avenue of trees. This is Silkmore Lane. It runs roughly parallel to the public road you have just crossed and less than 200 yards away from it. It is shown on old maps of the area and has probably existed for as long as the other lanes. The only difference is that it has never been surfaced and is still in the condition of a country lane of a hundred years ago. It climbs quite sharply up hill to enter the back of West Horsley village via a brick bridge over the railway.

On the other side of the bridge the lane is bordered by a contrasting mixture of old and recent housing. Once upon a time the houses and cottages were surrounded by open land, but much infilling has taken place in recent times. It is worth walking along this part of the route to take a

glance at some of the interesting older properties, most of which date from the 16th and 17th centuries, but please respect the privacy of the occupants. Charles Cottage, about halfway down on the right-hand side, dates from the 17th century but the unusual barn in its front garden (see photograph) is even older. It is thought that it was re-erected on its present site during the 19th century, when the owner of the cottage ran a carrier service.

Silkmore Lane ends at a junction with The Street; with the Village Hall on the right-hand corner. In the nearby bus shelter you will find the Parish Map. Completed in 1990, it took two years' work by a number of local people and shows the many interesting features of the village. The village has no centre as such but is spread out along its main thoroughfare, The Street. The church, though, is some distance to the east along the A246,

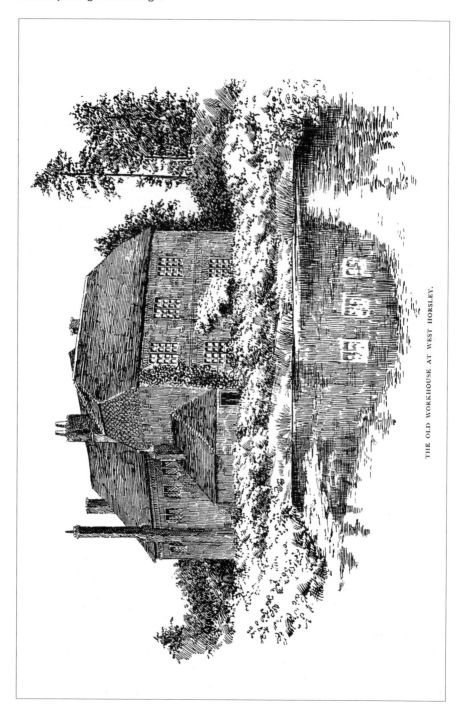

THE OLD WORKHOUSE AT WEST HORSLEY.

across the road from West Horsley Place. A network of footpaths links it to different parts of the village.

Just to your left, on the other side of The Street, is The Old House, the village workhouse for nearly 100 years, until the 1830s. As the old illustration (opposite) shows, there was once a large pond in front of the building, but this has now disappeared.

Turn right into The Street. On the right is the King William IV pub, originally a pair of estate workers' cottages. Another pub, the Barley Mow, is a short distance back along The Street. Originally a farmhouse, parts of it date from around 1500. It has a priest's hole in an old chimney.

King William IV, The Street, West Horsley. Courage. 01483 282318. Food

The Barley Mow, The Street, West Horsley. Ind Coope. 01483 282693. Food

Ripley Lane branches off to the right a short way along The Street. The return leg of the ride will take you that way but, for the time being, continue along The Street to the roundabout on the A246 Guildford to Leatherhead road. This is an old part of the village and some of the buildings, including High Bank House on the right and Sumners on the left, date back about 600 years.

West Horsley: *Some of the stonework of St Mary's Church dates from Saxon times. Its main claim to fame is that the head of the executed Sir Walter Raleigh is said to be buried there. (Carew, one of his sons, owned West Horsley Place and was Lord of the Manor between 1643 and 1664.)*

According to the story, Sir Walter's widow retrieved his severed head and had it embalmed, thereafter carrying it about with her in a red leather bag! When she died Carew is supposed to have had the head decently buried.

The Guildford–Epsom Road has always been an important and busy route, and, indeed,

when it was turnpiked in 1755 new lengths were built to bypass some of the congested village centres along the way. Sounds familiar! The main road at West Horsley has been further improved and levelled out in recent years; short sections of the old road can be seen on either side of the junction, and a milestone just along the road is a relic of those days.

Opposite the roundabout is a water pumping station, built in 1893, which extracts water from the chalk of the Downs. Outside it, at the side of Shere Road, is a water trough provided in 1909 by the Metropolitan Drinking Fountain and Cattle Trough Association. They were once a common sight, but few are left today, with fewer still in working order.

C Pain & Son, Grocers & Wine Merchants, 10 The Street, West Horsley.

Horsley Newsagents & PO, 12 The Street, West Horsley

To link with Ride F, cross the A246 into Shere Road and go up the hill past the Sheepleas. Turn right at the junction with Green Dene, and join Ride F at the North Downs Way in the car park in Staple Lane.

③ West Horsley to Ripley

Retrace your steps down The Street. On the left at the bend you pass a sign marking the site of the village pound in which stray animals were once kept. Fork left into Ripley Lane, and pass Upper Hammonds Farm with its 14th century Tithe Barn (now in the care of the National Trust, but not open to the public).

Shortly after the farm come the ornate gates and lodges marking the former entrance of the Hatchlands Estate. The house and its gardens are now owned by the National Trust, but the rest of the estate remains in private hands. The Dene Place Retirement Home, a short distance

Riding the Ripley Road
'The Mecca of all good cyclists'

Ripley was once an important coaching stop on the road to Portsmouth and many of its buildings date from that era. Some are even older but were 'improved' with new facades in Georgian days – the Talbot, for example, where Lord Nelson and Lady Hamilton are said to have stayed, dates back to 1483. Its tall archway allowed coaches access to the yard at the back.

When the stagecoaches succumbed to the competition of the railways in the 1830s and 40s, Ripley entered a period of decline. However, by the 1870s it had achieved new-found popularity as a destination for cycle trips from London. Not only was the distance about right – a convenient 50-mile round trip – but the 16th century Anchor pub in Ripley, run by the Dibble sisters, Annie and Harriet, was one of the few places which welcomed cyclists. Most people were uneasy about the new-fangled machines and their riders – 'Cads on castors' one prominent Victorian called them.

The Earl of Albemarle saw things differently, commending the Anchor as 'The Mecca of all good cyclists'. Around the turn of the century, the road heading south-west from London became known not as the road to Portsmouth but as the 'Ripley Road'. On Whit Sunday 1894 it is said that 20,000 cyclists rode through Kingston making for the village! It is hard to imagine what they all did once they got there, but apparently it was nothing out of the ordinary to see two or three hundred bicycles stacked in front of the Anchor while their owners enjoyed a refreshing pint.

Such was the affection in which the Dibble sisters (and Ripley itself) were held by members of the cycling fraternity that they subscribed to a memorial window in St Mary's Church.

In the Anchor you can still see a visitors' book containing the signatures of many cyclists who called in, including the writer H G Wells. Sherlock Holmes may also have visited the Anchor, though we cannot be certain because he failed to sign the book. Dr Watson recorded that while he was working on the Case of the Naval Treaty in nearby Woking, Holmes took a break and 'went for a charming walk through some admirable Surrey scenery to a pretty little village called Ripley, where I had my tea at an inn'.

By the 1970s life in Ripley had become unbearable because of the traffic on the A3 streaming along its main street and the construction of the bypass was universally welcomed. Fortunately little lasting harm had been done to the village and it is a lot more peaceful today, though it is regrettable that traffic from the A3 heading for Woking still has to pass through.

further down the road, was once the Hatchlands estate manager's house.

Hatchlands was built in the 1750s by the little-known architect Stiff Leadbetter for Admiral Boscawen, who paid for it with prize money won during the wars with the French. The interior was designed by Robert Adam, the first piece of work commissioned from him in England. The surrounding 400 acre park, laid out in 1800, was designed by Repton, while the gardens – the work of the noted Victorian Surrey gardener Gertrude Jekyll – have recently been restored. Public access to the house is now from the A246 road. There is an entrance fee for those who are not members of the National Trust.
☎ 01483 222787 for details of opening days and times. (Closed in winter.)

Ripley Lane takes you for a pleasant three miles through open countryside punctuated by woodland, crossing the outward route at Jury Farm. As you approach the bridge over the A3 bypass the prominent red-brick buildings of Guileshill Farm can be seen on the right, and between Guileshill and Ripley are the lands of Ockham Park.

Ockham Park was originally a Jacobean house dating from the 1620s but was extensively altered in later centuries. It became the home of the first Earl of Lovelace until he moved to East Horsley in the 1840s. The house itself was burned down in 1948, leaving only the kitchen wing, stables, and orangery. The park was later cut in two by the construction of the A3 Ripley bypass in 1976. One of the former entrances to the park can be seen as you leave Ripley on the London road; after many years of dereliction the gateway was restored when the adjacent lodge was renovated as a private home.

The ride approaches Ripley along Rose Lane, passing Chapel Farm and Ripley Court. On the left is the old fire station – Ripley had its own Fire Brigade until the

1950s. Follow the road through to the main street. The route continues straight across the High Street into the narrow Newark Lane opposite, but it is well worth pausing for a while to take a look around before going on. The village has a good selection of shops, teashops, restaurants and pubs, as well as several antique shops.

🕮 *The Anchor, High Street, Ripley. Free House. 01483 224120. Open all day. Food*
🕮 *The Half Moon, High Street, Ripley. Free House. 01483 224380.*
🕮 *The Ship, High Street, Ripley. Courage.*
🕮 *The Talbot, High Street, Ripley. Ind Coope. 01483 225188. Food C G Rest Acc*

√ Ripley to Send

From Ripley, follow Newark Lane until you are clear of the village and then take the first turning on the left, Polesdon Lane.

🖙 *To connect with Ride B continue along Newark Lane for about half a mile or so, past the Seven Stars pub, until you come to the car park just before Newark Bridge.*

Follow Polesdon Lane past the disused sand pit on the left which is now used for sailing activities. On the right is another sandpit which is coming to the end of its use.

The lane emerges at Send Marsh, where the green is overlooked by the Manor House, and forks to the left and the right. Turn right (into Send Marsh Road), although if you are thirsty you may prefer a short diversion to the left to find the Saddlers Arms pub.

🕮 *The Saddlers Arms, Send Marsh, Send. Friary Meux. 01483 224209. Food G*

Send Marsh Road runs past Aldertons Farm and Boughton Hall, the latter now a nursing home, but previously a hotel, and before that a family home. It also passes, on the right, a curious cottage called Goodgrove which, despite its Victorian-looking gothic windows, is over 400 years old. The road bends to the left, and comes to the traffic lights at Send crossroads.

Send derives its name from the sandy soil of the area. It straggles along the main A247 road for a mile – more if you include the Burntcommon area – and it's difficult to know which part represents the centre of the village. In fact Send began more as a scattered parish than a village, but over the last hundred years or so most of the gaps have been filled. The church is situated a considerable distance from the rest of the village, down beside the River Wey. It has a substantial tower, made of sandstone, which is a landmark from much of the surrounding valley (see ride B). Inside it is quite unusual for having no aisles to the nave.

⑤ Send to Burntcommon via Fell Hill

Go straight ahead at the traffic lights into Send Hill. A short sharp climb past the Sandfields Estate leads to a level stretch of road lined with houses and bungalows. At the far end there is a small cemetery on the left and a disused sand quarry on the right. The road then narrows considerably and an abrupt descent brings you to the junction at Fell Hill.

Turn left here, then, almost immediately afterwards, fork left into Vicarage Lane; it is signposted 'Ripley'. Although the lane is almost entirely lined by residential properties, their large grounds provide a very rural atmosphere.

After about half a mile, the lane comes to a sudden end at a T-junction. The road ahead was once a dual carriageway stretch of the A3 Portsmouth road, but today it is a slip road off the bypass. Take great care and watch for traffic approaching from the right at high speed. Turn left and follow the road through to

the roundabout at Burntcommon and the end of the ride.

Alternative sections of route

① Burntcommon to Send Prison

After crossing the bridge over the A3, turn left onto the slip road and about halfway down, turn right into Tithebarns Lane. Follow this through to its end at the T-junction. The bridleway on to Holride Farm (see stage ②) is straight ahead.

② Send Prison to West Horsley

If the entrance to Silkmore Lane (across the road from Jury Farm) is in very bad condition, turn left along the road for about 150 yards. There is another bridleway on the right and this may be in a better state. Follow it through – it's about 600 yards long – until it comes out onto the road, and then turn right. After about half a mile you will come to a road junction by Round Tree Farm. Turn right again here and go along the road under the railway bridge. Pass the Village Green on your left and the Barley Mow pub on your right. In a few minutes you will arrive at the Village Hall, where you rejoin the main route.

Ride B:
Wey Valley Wanderings

Newark • Pyrford • Wisley • Wisley Common • Byfleet • Pyrford Lock •
Walsham Gates • Newark Lock • Papercourt Lock • Send Cartbridge • Send •
Papercourt • Newark

Extension 1: Wisley Common • Elm Corner • Hatchford End • Martyr's Green
• Chatley Heath • Ockham Common • Wisley Common (extra 5 miles)

Extension 2: Send Cartbridge • Triggs Lock • Bowers Lock • Jacobs Well •
Sutton Green • Triggs Lock • Send Cartbridge (extra 6½ miles)

Distance:	10 or 14 miles (main ride)
Landranger Maps:	186 & 187
Pathfinder Maps:	1206 & 1190

This ride explores the valley of the River Wey between Byfleet and the outskirts
of Guildford and the surrounding heath-covered commons which divide it from
the neighbouring River Mole. Although the local roads tend to be extremely
busy, most of the ride is along quiet country lanes and bridleways, as well as
the towpath of the Wey Navigation, so avoiding the traffic almost completely.
The ride beside the river is especially delightful on a warm summer's afternoon.

There is a main section and two optional extensions, so you can choose
exactly how far you want to travel. Most of the route is level and is fairly easy
going, although the bridleway and towpath sections are a little more strenuous
than those on the road. Some of the paths can become very muddy after wet
weather but, because of the busy roads in the surrounding area, there are no
acceptable alternative routes. If you prefer not to get muddy don't try the ride
during the two or three days after heavy rain.

Starting Points

Begin at the small car park near Newark
Bridge on the B367 Ripley–Pyrford road
(grid reference TQ 040573). From Ripley,
the car park is on the left, just before the
traffic lights for the single lane bridge.
Byfleet village also has parking facilities,
but these are well-used on shopping days.

There are some small parking areas on
Wisley Lane, but at peak times these may
be full of visitors to the RHS Gardens.

On extension 1 there is a large car park
just off the slip road from the M25 to the
southbound A3. Follow the 'Semaphore
Tower' direction signs to reach it.

⇌ The closest station is Byfleet & New
Haw on the Waterloo–Woking line, about
a mile from the ride. From the station head
south along Oyster Lane. Cross the
roundabout at Parvis Road (A245), then
take High Road to reach the Clock House.

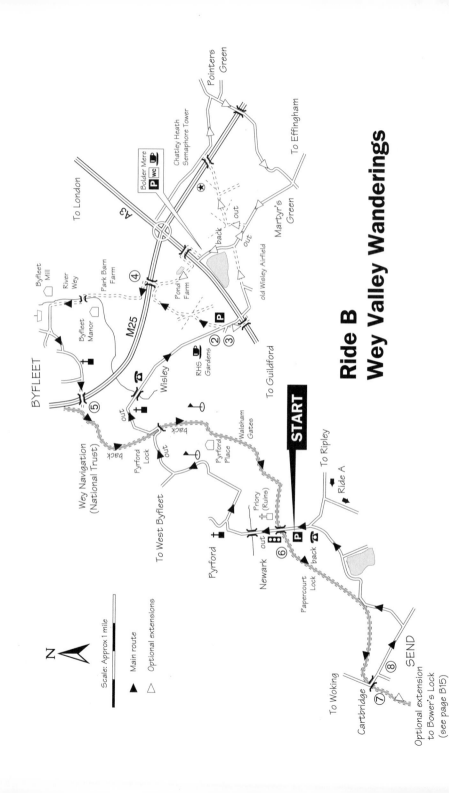

Ride B
Wey Valley Wanderings

N

Scale: Approx 1 mile

▲ Main route
△ Optional extensions

START

To London

To Guildford

To Ripley

Ride A

To West Byfleet

To Woking

SEND

Cartbridge

Optional extension
to Bower's Lock
(see page B15)

Pyrford

Newark

Priory
(Ruins)

Walsham
Gates

Papercourt
Lock

Wey Navigation
(National Trust)

Pyrford
Lock

Pyrford
Place

out
back

out
back

out
back

BYFLEET

Byfleet
Mill

River
Wey

Byfleet
Manor

Park Barn
Farm

Pond
Farm

M25

Wisley

RHS
Gardens

P

Bolder Mere

P wc

A3

Chatley Heath
Semaphore Tower

Pointers
Green

To Effingham

Martyr's
Green

old Wisley Airfield

out
back

out
back

① ② ③ ④ ⑤ ⑥ ⑦ ⑧

The Route in Brief

① TL from CP at Newark and cross light-controlled bridge. Midway up hill TR into Warren Lane. TR into Lock Lane, SP RHS Gardens. Over bridge at Pyrford Lock and SO to Wisley. Stop at small CP before entrance to Wisley Gardens.

② *Direct route to Wisley Common*
TL into CP and follow blue waymark arrow on post. SO at junction of paths and SO over Permissive Horse Ride. At M25 fence follow track round to R. TL onto concrete track to bridge over M25 (see √).

③ *Extension via Chatley Heath*
At RHS Gardens entrance follow SP for footbridge to Guildford-bound bus stop. Over A3 then TR into Elm Lane. Follow lane L at entrance to old airfield. After 400 yds SO onto unmade track when lane bends sharp R .

At end TR onto road for 400 yds, then TL onto BW after Hatchford End. After 300 yds THR at small clearing, then R fork. (CARE not to miss turning - see post with blue waymark arrow. If lost follow signs to Semaphore Tower.) L at next fork then SO at BW junction, SP Pointers Road. Fork R (almost SO) when track splits then continue to tarred drive (Semaphore Tower to L).

Follow drive to bottom of slope then cross M25 and TR at road. At TJ TR into Ockham Lane then TR into Old Lane at Black Swan XR. SO to main Bolder Mere CP entrance. Through CP and along path

beside A3 layby to reach footbridge.TL at bottom of slope at far end of bridge. After 50 yds follow track to R at bend. TR after Pond Farm onto concrete track to bridge over M25.

√ TL at far side of M25 then follow track to R at bottom of slope. When track divides take narrow, sandy BW to left of gateway. SO alongside river and over bridge. Join drive from Byfleet Manor; follow it to L when it joins Mill Lane. At end TL into Church Road, then L again at Brewery Rd XR. At sharp R bend beyond church SO onto unmade track. Cross M25 then TL onto towpath.

⑤ Follow towpath to Pyrford Lock. Cross road and continue on towpath past Walsham Gates. TR at far end of weir for towpath to Newark lock and bridge.

≈ Cross bridge and TR onto towpath (through field) to Papercourt Lock. SO along towpath to Send Cartbridge.

∆ *Optional extension to Bower's Lock*
Over bridge and TR onto towpath. Pass Trigg's Lock, Sutton Park and Bower's Lock. Under modern road bridge then TL at old bridge, L again up slope and L again onto Clay Lane. At Jacob's Well TR into Blanchards Hill to Sutton Green.

TR off main road after pub then SO at junction with Robin Hood Lane. TR onto track (FP) to Trigg's Lock before Runtley Wood Farm. TL onto towpath to Send.

⑧ At Cartbridge TR onto road. TL after garage into Tannery Lane to Newark. TL by Seven Stars pub for CP.

The Ride

① Newark to Wisley Gardens

From the car park at Newark cross the traffic-light-controlled bridge and head north along the B367 towards Pyrford. On the right, as you cross the meadows, are the remains of Newark Priory.

Newark is situated in the broad valley of the Wey, which is here divided into seven separate streams. The wide floodplain has ensured that, in an area where the pressures for development are high, this is still a strangely remote spot.

Newark Priory was founded for the Augustinian Canons (the Black Canons) during the 12th century, although there may have been an even older foundation on the site. It was suppressed in the 1530s during Henry VIII's Dissolution of the Monasteries. Most of its buildings were pulled down in the 18th century as a source of stone for building and road mending. The ruins stand on private land and there is no access to them.

Close to the narrow bridge over the Navigation is the site of Newark Mill, mentioned in the Domesday Book. The final structure, a huge weatherboarded 19th century building, was destroyed by fire in 1966 and only foundations remain.

The road crosses the Bourne Stream bridge and then bends to the right to climb the steep hill, on top of which sits Pyrford's Church of St Nicholas. Rather than make the dangerous right turn into Warren Lane (about half way up the hill) continue all the way to the top. While you're there, take a look at the small Norman church, one of the few in Surrey to have escaped 'restoration' in Victorian times. Spot the wall paintings – two layers of them. The top layer, dated around 1200, covers a fresco painted in 1140 when the church was built.

On leaving the church, return down the hill and turn left into Warren Lane. Keep an eye out for the old threshing machine in the field on the right just before Wheelers Farm. After a short climb the road bends sharply to the left, becoming Lower Pyrford Road (1 mile), and passes Pyrford Golf Club, one of many new courses which have sprung up in this area in recent years. Take the next turning on the right (Lock Lane), indicated by the 'RHS Garden' signpost.

Continue past Pyrford Marina (2 miles) to Pyrford Lock. The road crosses the river by another steep, narrow bridge and then turns back on itself along the far bank. The pub is a popular venue on fine summer days, when customers can sit outside and watch the boats as they pass.

🍴 *The Anchor, Pyrford Lock. Scottish & Newcastle. 01932 342507. Open all day in summer. Food available summer lunchtimes only G C*

Beyond the pub the lane parts company with the river and winds through the fields. To the right, over the fields, you can see Wisley's parish church, smaller even than that at Pyrford. It is of a similar mid-12th century date, although in 1903 foundations of an older Saxon chapel were found beneath the present building.

The lane bends around towards the church and its adjacent farm, passing the sewage works where the remains of an Iron Age village were discovered. Another historic relic, a dugout canoe of uncertain age, was found in the riverbed nearby and is now in Weybridge Museum.

Wisley Bridge crosses the main channel of the Wey and leads to the tiny village. On the left, just after the bridge, are the 'RHS Cottages', occupied by some of the staff from the nearby Wisley Gardens. As you might expect, their gardens look an absolute picture (3 miles).

Newark Priory ruins

Wisley has amazingly managed to survive almost untouched when neighbouring villages such as Pyrford and Byfleet have been unable to resist the developer. It is even more surprising when you consider the popularity of the Royal Horticultural Society's gardens just down the road and the volume of traffic that passes through.

The original 60 acres of the gardens were established in the 1870s when the skilled amateur gardener G F Wilson of Weybridge bought the site and developed part of it with an incredible variety of plants. On his death in 1902 it was bought by Sir Thomas Hanbury and presented to the RHS. The massive Rockery and the wooded Wild Garden are among its many and varied features. As well as the formal and informal gardens, there are trials areas where new varieties of plants, fruits and vegetables are tested.

The gardens open at 10am every day. From February to October they close at 7pm or sunset if earlier. From November to January closing time is at 4.30pm. Sunday entry is restricted to RHS members.

There is a charge for entry to the gardens themselves (except for members), but the souvenir shop, the well-stocked plant centre and refreshment facilities are accessible without going into the gardens. ☎ 01483 224234 for details.

As you leave the village itself, slow down for a sneak glimpse through the fence on the right into the grounds of the RHS Gardens. These are the Heather Gardens, which produce such a marvellous display in the late summer and autumn.

On the left are the less-tamed surroundings of Wisley Common; this particular area is known as Wren's Nest. The lane is very narrow, so be careful of traffic leaving the Gardens or coming up behind you. And don't get too close to the edge of the road – it has quite a camber to it! Immediately before the entrance into the RHS Gardens there is a small parking area on the left and a bridleway sign.

☞ *From here you have a choice of routes. The direct route is across Wisley Common (see stage ② below) or you can explore the heaths and commons on the far side of the A3, adding five miles to the ride (stage ③).*

② Wisley Gardens to Wisley Common *direct*

☞ *After wet weather this part of the route may have some very muddy patches. Unfortunately there is no handy alternative route, but the County Council hopes to make some improvements as soon as funds allow.*

Turn left into the parking area and look for the post with the blue waymark arrow which marks the start of the bridleway; it heads back at a very sharp angle to the road. (The surface of the car park has been raised and is supported by a 'kerb' of old tree trunks so there is quite a step as you join the path.)

The path is quite obvious, although it winds a bit. The surface of grass and pine needles makes for good cycling, but watch out for tree roots. After a short while you'll come to a clearing where several tracks meet (4 miles). Go straight on, as indicated by another blue waymark arrow on a post.

The track now becomes quite narrow and runs through tall bracken, but it is still easily passable and, now that some of the scrub has been cleared to restore the more open heathland habitat, there are good views over the Common on the left. Shortly after this, the bridleway crosses a track marked as a 'Permissive Horse Ride'. From there it continues straight ahead, but just beyond the crossing is a patch which can be extremely muddy after wet

weather, and you may need to divert around the spot.

The path now runs along the edge of the woods with open fields to the right. The scene is pleasantly rural, but if the wind is blowing from the north you'll soon hear the drone of the traffic on the motorway ahead. In a short while you'll come to a junction where a footpath joins the bridleway. A sturdy waymark post by the junction says you have been riding along a Permissive Horse Path, not a bridleway, but it is wrong! Keep straight on, heading ever-closer to the motorway.

The path bends to the right as it reaches the motorway fence and joins a track coming out of a field. The track has a solid gravel base, but if tractors have been using it and the weather has been wet, it will probably be covered in mud. Despite appearances, you can cycle in the tyre tracks without getting stuck.

From here you should be able to see the bridge over the motorway ahead of you. A rough path climbs up the slope towards it, but it's easier to stay on the farm track for a short while longer and then turn left onto a concrete track leading to the bridge. See stage √ for the onward route to Byfleet.

③ Wisley Gardens to Wisley Common *via Elm Corner, Ockham Common, Chatley Heath, and Bolder Mere*

For this optional extension continue along Wisley Lane as far as the entrance to the RHS Gardens and then follow the path indicated by the sign for the pedestrian route to the Guildford-bound bus stop. It leads to a footbridge over the A3 – dismount to cross it. At the far end of the bridge, follow the sign for 'Elm Corner' into Elm Lane, ignoring the 'No Through

Road' signs. Just before the gate leading onto the disused Wisley airfield, take the turning off to the left. Follow this lane for about 400 yards and then, when it bends sharply to the right, continue straight ahead onto the unmade track directly in front of you.

Follow the track for about 600 yards across Ockham Common until it comes out on Old Lane. Turn right onto the road, but take care because drivers often take this corner too fast.

About 400 yards along the road, just after the house called Hatchford End, turn left onto the bridleway. Go around the end of the gate which keeps motor traffic out. Pass a small pond and then, about 300 yards from the road, you'll come to a small clearing. Ignore the broad track which continues straight ahead and, instead, turn sharp right to continue along the bridleway. The blue arrows on a nearby waymark post show the route.

(It is easy to miss this junction so keep a close watch out. If you do go too far, follow the signs to the Semaphore Tower and pick the route up again there.)

Keep going roughly straight ahead on this path. It narrows after a hundred yards or so (just after another track turns off to the left), and it becomes rather sandy, so you may find it necessary to walk. The woods here are thick with rhododendrons and will reward a visit in the late spring when they are in flower. At the fork a little further on take the left-hand branch.

At the following junction continue straight ahead, as indicated by the sign for Pointers Road. When the track divides again, take the right-hand of the two paths – it actually continues almost straight on. Shortly afterwards you will come out onto a tarred drive and if you look up to your left you'll see the tower of the Semaphore Station.

Chatley Heath Semaphore Station *was one of a series of 13 which linked the Admiralty in London with the Naval Dockyard at Portsmouth. Chatley Heath was also the point at which a never-completed branch to Plymouth diverged from the Portsmouth line. Messages were passed from station to station by the use of signal arms mounted on masts. Built in 1822, the tower saw service until 1847, when the system was replaced by the railway's electric telegraph line.*

Although several semaphore stations still exist, Chatley is the only one of the tower design remaining and is the only one to be restored and opened to the public. After a long period of use as a home, the tower stood empty for a time until vandals set fire to it in 1984. It was then restored and opened to the public in 1989 to commemorate the centenary of Surrey County Council.

The Tower is usually open to the public from April to September (inclusive) on Saturdays,

Chatley Heath Semaphore Tower

Sundays and Bank Holidays, and on Wednesdays during Surrey school holidays. (Santa events are held on selected dates in December.)

For a modest entrance fee you can visit the exhibition which demonstrates how the system worked, and you can also climb to the roof, from which some magnificent views can be had on a clear day. On the ground floor there is a souvenir shop and Countryside Information Room and, although the former garden is no longer cultivated, it is used as a picnic area.

☎ *01932 862762 or 01483 517595 for details of opening times and charges, or see the excellent 'Environment News' newspaper published by Surrey County Council (available from public libraries).*

From the Semaphore Tower, continue along the tarred drive and down the hill. The bridleway diverges to the left (note the blue waymark arrow on a post), but it's in a poor state for cycling. You may as well stay on the drive as they both come out at the same place, although you may have to lift your bike to get past the padlocked gate at the bottom of the drive. From the gate, cross the bridge over the motorway and come out in Pointers Road.

(The stretch of Pointers Road to the left once continued right through to the A3 but the final few yards were closed when the M25 interchange was built across its path. As a result, the lane is now virtually traffic-free and very peaceful. The round trip of a mile and a half to the dead-end and back is well worthwhile both for the solitude and the views it offers over farmland beside the River Mole below.

On the way you'll pass Chatley Farm where a Roman bath house was found in 1942; this may have been part of a much larger villa which has been destroyed by changes in the river's course over time.)

From the motorway bridge turn right into Pointers Road. The ornate gateway just down the road is the old entrance to Hatchford Park, once the home of the Earls of Ellesmere but more recently a school. The M25 was built across the old drive and the gates lead only into a yard.

At the end of Pointers Road turn right into Ockham Lane. The road climbs quite steeply as it leaves the Mole valley, crossing the motorway as it does so.

The top of the climb is reached at the appropriately-named 'Wisley View', then a few hundred yards of downhill riding will bring you to the crossroads at the Black Swan pub. Fans of old British comedies may recognise this pub as it featured in several films, but usually under another name.

▤ *The Black Swan, Old Lane, Martyr's Green. 01932 862364. Free House. Open all day. Food (from 12 for all day; eve meals 6.30 to 9.30) C G Rest (book in advance).*

At the Black Swan turn right into Old Lane and continue for more than a mile as far as the entrance to the main Bolder Mere car park. Interrupt your ride for a moment and take a short walk along the tarred path on the left which takes you to the water's edge.

Bolder Mere: *The expanse of water alongside the A3 has now reverted to its old name of Bolder Mere, having been known in recent times as Wisley Pond or the Hut Pond. No-one knows for certain how it came to be created, but it is probably man-made. Not so long ago, on the far side of the Portsmouth Road overlooking the pond was the Hut Hotel. It stood on the site of an even older inn, which must have been a welcome sight for travellers in the days when the road between Cobham and Ripley crossed lonely open heath! All that now remains is a bit of rubble beside the A3.*

⚑ *Gales Diner, Bolder Mere car park, off Old Lane. Open 8–4.30 every day. Also toilets and information centre.*

Bolder Mere

Go through the Bolder Mere car park and leave it by the path at the left-hand end of the refreshments building. This leads to a lay-by beside A3, from where you can see, to the right, a bridge carrying a bridleway over the busy dual carriageway. Follow the path beside the lay-by, but just before you reach the bridge follow the track through the bushes on your right. It will take you to the ramp leading to the bridge.

On the far side of the road continue down the long ramp from the bridge until you come to the tarred road at the bottom. (In front of you is a now-disused car park.) Turn left onto the road and go through the gate (normally left open) beside which is a 'Private Road' sign.

The road is officially a footpath but, as it is regularly used by vehicles, there are unlikely to be any objections to your riding along it. About 50 yards or so beyond the gate follow the main track as it bends

sharply to the right. You'll soon pass a large marshy pond on the right, and then Pond Farm, on the left.

Continue along the track for another 150 yards and then turn right onto a concrete road which leads to the bridge over the M25. Rejoin the main ride there. Add 5 miles to the mileages shown in the rest of the ride (6½ miles if you went on to the dead-end of Pointers Road).

√ M25 to Byfleet Village

Cross the motorway bridge and turn left down the slope on the other side. At the bottom follow the track as it curves round to the right (5 miles). Within a short distance the track divides; the main branch goes straight on through a gate into private land, so keep to the bridleway, which runs to the left of the hedge. The path is narrow and rather sandy, so you may need to walk along parts of it. The

Byfleet Manor

II in the early 14th century. Its last royal owner was Anne of Denmark, wife of King James I. She decided to have it rebuilt, but died in 1619 before the work was finished and it was left to the subsequent owner, Sir James Fullerton, to complete it. The massive front walls, the unusual gate piers (designed by the celebrated German architect Wendel Dietterlin), and the forecourt are believed to date from that time.

In 1675 the house was leased to the Earl of St Albans, and about 10 years later he sub-leased it to William Sutton. Although it was only 65 years since it was last rebuilt, Sutton petitioned King Charles II for permission to rebuild it again on the grounds that it was in ruinous condition! The authorisation for the work was signed on behalf of the King by Sir Christopher Wren, but it is not known if he played any part in the design. Old material from the house was used for some of the work, which resulted in a much smaller building. One chimney at the west end of the house remains from the previous building.

The house was restored in 1905, when asymmetrical wings were added, and it has now been divided into three. Neither house nor grounds are open to the public.

It is said that Anne of Denmark's ghost has occasionally been seen in the lower rooms of the house, and there is a tradition that a dwarf dressed in purple velvet wanders about the forecourt.

stretch beside Park Barn Farm can also be muddy after rain.

Immediately beyond the farm – now a modern house – is the River Wey. This is the natural river rather than the man-made Wey Navigation; the two make their separate ways through Byfleet and do not meet again until Weybridge, shortly before the river joins the Thames. The bridleway runs along the riverbank for about 300 yards before crossing it by a modern steel bridge. From the far side of the bridge you can see Byfleet Manor House on your left.

Follow the path round the curve away from the river (another sandy bit) and you will come out on the drive leading up to the Manor. (Turn to the left if you want to make a short diversion to see it at closer quarters, but remember it is private property.)

Byfleet Manor, *a one-time royal hunting lodge, was given to Piers Gaveston by Edward*

Turn right along the drive and continue past a pretty river backwater until you come to Mill Lane (6 miles). The bridge to the right leads to Byfleet Mill, which dates from 1647 but was restored after a fire in 1991. Like the Georgian Mill House next door, it is private property and not open to the public.

Turn left into Mill Lane, then, at the far end, turn right into the section of road which is blocked by a row of bollards.

Byfleet's *parish church dates from 1280 but its extensive later additions include the*

Victorian south transept. There is a wall-painting in red ochre over the north door, but the figure depicted is not now thought to be Edward II, as was once claimed. The white stuccoed building next to the end of Mill Lane is known as the Clock House, now converted to flats for the elderly by the Fellowship Houses Trust.

There are many shops and several pubs in the village, but most are further along High Road. Those near the Clock House include a newsagent, and both Chinese and Indian take-away restaurants.

In 1924 the Blue Anchor pub was the scene of an infamous murder. The landlord, Alfred Jones, was poisoned by his wife's Swiss lover, Jean-Pierre Vaquier. He put strychnine in the Bromo-Seltzer which Jones was in the habit of taking after a night's heavy drinking. After being found guilty at Guildford Assizes, Vaquier was hanged for the crime.

The Blue Anchor, High Road. 01932 346301. Food G

Kelly's of Byfleet, High Road. Newsagent. Open all weekend.

Turn left out of Mill Lane into Church Road. At the crossroads with Brewery Lane turn left again to stay on the continuation of Church Road. The church itself is quite a distance further on – you may even think you're out of the village before you come to it.

Keep going until the road bends sharply to the right and becomes Rectory Lane. At the bend go straight ahead onto a gravelled track which will take you over the motorway and onto the towpath of the Wey Navigation at Murray's Bridge (7 miles). The track is incorrectly signed as a footpath; it is actually a bridleway.

⑤ Byfleet Village to Newark

To connect with Ride J, turn right along the towpath. It is about 3 miles to Weybridge Town Lock.

Turn left onto the towpath of the Navigation. The field on the left often contains a herd of Highland cattle, not a breed usually associated with the water meadows of southern England! The surface of the towpath is in fairly good condition (if a touch sandy in places) and makes for pleasant riding. This stretch is heavily used by walkers, and you must give way to them.

About 600 yards along the towpath is Dodd's Bridge, which carries a path to West Byfleet across the canal. Half a mile after that is the entrance to Pyrford Marina, with the Anchor pub, which you first passed some miles back, just beyond (8 miles). Follow the towpath beside the pub, up to the road, but watch for ducks wandering about! Cross the road to the lock, staying on the same side of the river.

Moored boats occupy much of the canal bank on this stretch. Half a mile further on another footbridge crosses the Navigation, taking a path from Wisley to Pyrford. On the left is the recently developed and exclusive Wisley Golf Club. The ornate white-painted wooden bridge crosses one of the river channels which run through the golf course – the bridge just beyond it, carrying a footpath to Ockham Mill, is much more utilitarian. It is obvious along this stretch how the man-made Navigation has been built up on an embankment above the level of the natural river on the left.

To the right are the grounds of Pyrford Place, where the bend in the river has been landscaped into the gardens.

Pyrford Place: *The original house was built in the 16th century, when the manor of Pyrford was owned by Sir John Wolley, Secretary to Elizabeth I, who visited the house on at least one occasion. Sir John's wife Elizabeth was the eldest daughter of Sir William More, who built Loseley House, south*

The Wey Navigation
Weston's wonder

In 1613, at the age of just 22, Sir Richard Weston inherited the estate of Sutton Place and began to apply the agricultural methods he had learned while studying in Flanders. One of his ideas was to build an artificial channel from the River Wey at Stoke, near Guildford, to irrigate 120 acres of otherwise dry land. Traces of this pioneering development can still be seen in the fields of the old estate. He is also credited with having introduced the growing of clover to this country.

Having seen how locks had been used in Flanders to make rivers navigable, Sir Richard decided to promote a scheme for the Wey between Guildford and the Thames. In 1635 he obtained a commission from King Charles I to carry out the work, but the situation became complicated because of the Civil War, in which Sir Richard's sympathies were with the losing side.

An Act of Parliament to authorise the work was passed in 1651, but Sir Richard died the following year, just before it was completed. Much of the Weston fortune disappeared into the scheme, and part of the estate had to be sold. (It was bought by the Onslow family and became Clandon Park.)

However, the Navigation was an enormous success and in 1763 the five-mile stretch of river between Guildford and Godalming was also made navigable. In 1794 the Basingstoke Canal opened, joining the Wey near Byfleet. Then, in 1816, the river became part of a through route between London and the English Channel with the opening of the Wey & Arun Canal, linking the Wey at Shalford with the River Arun at Newbridge, near Billingshurst.

The next two decades were the heyday of inland waterways before the railways took their traffic. First to go was the Wey & Arun Canal, closed in 1871 after only 55 years of use. The Basingstoke Canal managed to hang on, despite the bankruptcy of its owners in 1866, until the last cargoes – timber to Woking – ended in 1949.

Use of the Wey above Guildford all but ceased with the closure of the Chilworth gunpowder works in 1920, although a couple of barges continued to work until after the Second World War. Traffic to Stoke Flour Mill ended in 1957 and to Moon's timber wharf the following year, but by this time the use of rivers and canals for recreational boating and other leisure pursuits was becoming well established. In 1964, Harry Stevens, owner of the Wey Navigation, presented it to the National Trust. In 1969 the Godalming Navigation was also given to the Trust by its owners, Guildford Corporation. The Basingstoke Canal has now been reopened as far west as Greywell Tunnel, and an ambitious scheme to reopen the Wey and Arun is making steady, if slow progress.

The Summerhouse, Pyrford Place

of Guildford. She, too, served the Queen, as a lady-in-waiting.

Three weeks before Christmas in 1600, Elizabeth's 16-year old niece, Anne, ran away with and married the poet John Donne. Anne's father, Sir George More, was outraged – Donne was just a commoner (a mere secretary to Sir Thomas Egerton) and very much below the Mores in social standing.

Donne broke the news to his father-in-law in a letter dated 2nd February 1601 from 'my lodginge by ye Savoy'. Sir George's reaction was to have him locked up in the Fleet Prison for more than a year. However, the marriage was found to be legal, and friends negotiated his release.

Sir George's anger took a considerable time to subside though, and from 1602 to 1604 the couple took refuge at Pyrford Place.

Donne later achieved fame and became Dean of St Paul's. Local tradition insists that the summerhouse, which still stands beside the Navigation, was there in Donne's time and was used by him as a place for quiet study, if not to live in. However, architectural historians reckon it wasn't built until late in the 17th century – but they're not infallible!

In 1677 the manor was bought by Mr Denzil Onslow. The diarist John Evelyn recounts a visit there in 1681 when he partook of an 'extraordinary feast' provided entirely from the estate, including 'venison, rabbits, hares, pheasants, partridges, pigeons, quails, poultry, all sorts of fowl in season from his own decoy near his house, and all sorts of fresh fish.'

The subsequent story of the house is confused. Some say that the original timber-framed house either burned down or was demolished in 1776 by Robert, Lord Onslow. Others believe that much of it survived beneath a mass of later additions, only to be demolished as recently as 1990. A new building has now been erected with the same ground plan as the demolished house and is divided into 15 apartments.

A quarter of a mile beyond the summerhouse is the lock known as Walsham Gates (9 miles). It is unusual in that both sets of gates are normally left open, so that the water level is the same above and below the lock and boats pass straight through. The lock is used only during flood conditions, and therefore survives largely in its original form, with sloping turf banks.

Go past the lock house and follow the towpath as it turns to the left and crosses the weir. The substantial flow of water which cascades over the weir even in dry spells shows just how powerful a river this is. In years gone by there was enough water to power an immense number of mills along its course. At the far side of the weir turn right to continue on the towpath – ignore the footpath going straight ahead which leads to Ripley.

After a few hundred yards the towpath, which can be a little muddy after wet weather, ends at a gate which leads into Walsham Meadow. Go through the gate and follow the worn path across the open fields, running roughly parallel with the river. It can be a bit bumpy, but as long as you keep your speed down and stay in low gear it shouldn't be too uncomfortable. After about 350 yards go through another gate onto a footbridge over the stream from Newark Mill.

On the right the ruins of Newark Priory can be seen very clearly in the middle of the field beyond the far bank of the river. The towpath changes side at Newark Lock, so cross by the small bridge (10 miles). Beyond the lock the foundations of Newark Mill are visible on the other bank of the river. The towpath slopes steeply up to the road bridge and it is advisable to dismount here. Road traffic is controlled by traffic lights and, faced with a green light, drivers may not expect anyone to emerge from the side of the road.

☞ *You can end your ride at this point by crossing the bridge and returning to the car park.*

≈ Newark to Send Cartbridge

The towpath continues on the left-hand side of the river, so you must cross the narrow bridge to reach it. Once again, the towpath runs through the open fields; keep to the rough path alongside the river across the field. There may be cows and horses around but (apart from the obvious hazard) they don't seem to cause any bother to towpath users, although they may take an inquisitive but friendly interest in your progress.

After half a mile you will come to Papercourt Lock. As you approach the lock, go through the gate into the fenced area around the lockside. Cross the first bridge and then turn left along the other side of the lock, following the small sign indicating the towpath.

On a sunny day this is a truly delightful spot, remote from everywhere and extremely tranquil. The towpath runs beside the cascaded weir, and above the lock the weir channel is used for boat moorings. A few hundred yards over to your right are the remains of Woking Palace, the birthplace of Mary Tudor and a favourite home of Henry VIII. The site has been derelict for many years but Woking Borough Council plans to restore it over the next few years. (In the meantime it is not open to the public.)

The towpath is in good condition for the half-mile beyond the lock leading up to the Tanyard Bridge (just over 11 miles). There was a tannery on this site for many years, but the present buildings date from the 1970s and are supreme examples of the worst that the architectural profession had to offer in that period. The quality of

Send Cartbridge and the New Inn

the road frontage is bad enough, but the river side is even worse. It is incredible to think that the planning authorities actually approved such an appalling development in an otherwise pleasant rural setting.

The risk of flooding has generally deterred housing development along most of the river but, as the risk is minimal along this stretch of the Navigation channel, some housing has sprung up on its banks in recent years. There are one or two developments on the approach to Send, notably at Wharf Lane (where the steep footbridge over the river is known as High Bridge) and along the half-mile beyond.

The Navigation follows a broad curve to the left as it approaches Send Cartbridge (12 miles). Take care as you come out onto the road at the bridge. Despite the speed limit, traffic on the A247 tends to hurtle along here.

Send Cartbridge *presumably owes its name to the fact that this is the only bridge over the Wey Navigation between Newark and Burpham (near Guildford) capable of taking anything more than foot traffic. The present steel and concrete deck was built in 1915 to replace a timber structure, but the date 1759 appears on one of the wingwalls.*

The present bridge is in poor condition, and Surrey County Council plans to replace and realign the entire bridge, although there are many local objections. If the work does go ahead, the towpath will be extended under the bridge to provide a pedestrian underpass.

The New Inn, Send. 01483 762736. Friary Meux. Opens at 5.30pm Mon–Sat (open all day Sat in summer). Food G. The single storey extension to the building once served as a mortuary!

☞ *From Send Cartbridge you can, if you wish, continue along the Wey Navigation towpath past Triggs and Bowers Locks to*

Burpham, returning via Jacobs Well and Sutton Green, a distance of an extra 6½ miles. If you prefer not to follow this extension, skip to stage ⑧ for directions for the route back to Newark.

Δ Optional extension to Bowers Lock

At the Cartbridge the towpath reverts to the left-hand side of the river, so cross the bridge to the opposite corner beside the New Inn.

A gravelled track leads down from the bridge to the river bank. Pass the footbridge a short distance along the track; it leads to a network of footpaths which cross the flood meadows between Sutton Green, Westfield and Old Woking.

Immediately after the bridge join the towpath proper. The lock which follows is known as Worsfold Gates. Like the lock at Walsham, it is used only in flood conditions and is normally left open to boats. Some of the workshops in the small yard beside the lock date back to the early days of the Navigation.

The towpath crosses a narrow bridge over a weed-choked backwater as it heads out into the open and peaceful countryside. The length after the bridge is rather bumpy, but if you keep in low gear and ride slowly you should have no problem. However, this is a delightful stretch of river along which to walk if you find your saddle too punishing. A bridge over another backwater leads to the neatly-kept surrounds of Triggs Lock with its

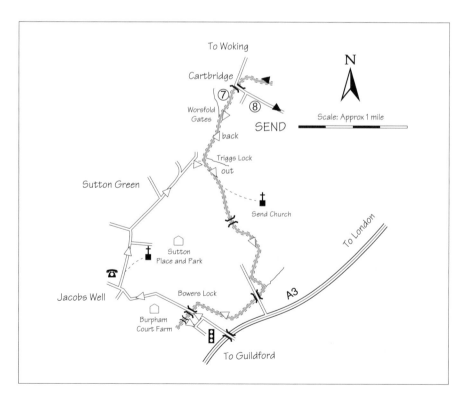

lonely lock-keeper's cottage. Note the insurance company firemark on its front wall. About 250 yards beyond the lock a bridge over the river carries a footpath from Sutton Green to Send Church. Standing here, looking across the broad and virtually deserted valley, it can be hard to believe that you are only a couple of miles from the outskirts of Woking and Guildford.

The towpath has been repaired along the next stretch but the surface is quite soft and sandy, so take care. At the next bridge the towpath crosses to the opposite bank. You will find it easier to get through the two gates which lead onto the bridge if you dismount. On the far bank turn left to continue along the towpath..

The land on this side of the Navigation is part of the Sutton Place estate, but the house itself is too well hidden by the trees to be easily seen. Across the fields to the left is the small cluster of houses at Three Fords, and ahead, though partially obscured by the tall poplars lining the road, you will probably be able to see the traffic moving on the A3.

The river itself becomes more tree-lined just before it turns sharply left to run beside the driveway of Sutton Place. This section has also been repaired and, although the towpath is now wider (previously it was little more than the minimum 18 inches demanded by the Navigation's original Act of 1651), it is extremely sandy, so be careful.

After about 250 yards the river bends sharply to the right, and the driveway climbs up and over it onto Broadoak Bridge. This was a tight turn for horse-drawn boats, and you can still see the rollers which guided the towrope round the corner.

The bridge abutment carries a plaque commemorating Sir Richard Weston, founder of the Wey Navigation and one-time owner of Sutton Place. Just after the bridge the towpath passes through a gate and into an open field, but before long it reverts to the edge of the river beside a fenced copse of fairly young trees. This part of the towpath is rather bumpy, and you may prefer to walk. You cannot help hearing the traffic now since the A3 is right beside the river here, though masked by a high bank. Fortunately they soon part company.

Just beyond this point the natural river makes a large loop, but the navigation takes a short cut through Bowers Lock,

SIR
RICHARD
WESTON
FOUNDER OF THE
WEY NAVIGATION
1591 – 1652
WOKING BOROUGH COUNCIL

which is on the opposite bank and is reached by a footbridge. Cross the bridge over the lock itself and then turn right, crossing another but broader bridge over a side channel. On the left is Bowers Mill, now converted into a home. Continue along the towpath under the modern road bridge, passing the hollow, but still living, oak tree.

The old lattice steel bridge ahead carried the road from Burpham to Jacobs Well until it was moved to its present course. Turn left into Bower's Lane at the bridge and left again, almost immediately, up the slope. At the top turn left into Clay Lane.

☞ *If you want shops and other local facilities, turn right instead and cross over the A3 to reach Burpham village.*

Although Clay Lane is only a C-class road, it carries a lot of traffic and you may prefer to stay on the footpath alongside. In fact, it is not a bad idea to walk along this stretch of road, because Burpham Court Farm on the left is now a conservation centre for old and rare breeds of farm animals, and there are always interesting sights to be seen. Sometimes there is even a llama in a field near the entrance!

Burpham Court Farm Park *has many rare breeds of sheep, cattle, goats, pigs, poultry and pets. There is a farm walk and nature trail, as well as a children's play area, a picnic area and an indoor pets' corner. The tea room is open at weekends and holidays. Souvenirs, honey, eggs, and refreshments are available at the shop. The farm is open every day from March to October and during winter school holidays, otherwise at weekends only; 10am–6pm or dusk if earlier. £2.50 adults, £1.95 benefit holders, £1.50 children (2–16 years). ☎ 01483 576089.*

The road narrows and bends as it approaches Jacobs Well crossroads, where you turn right into Blanchards Hill. At the top of the fairly abrupt climb there is a

view on the right of the Roman Catholic church of St Edward the Confessor, King of England. Further on, at the bottom of the hill, are the lodges marking the entrance into Sutton Place.

Sutton Place: *Henry VIII granted the manor of Sutton Green to Sir Richard Weston in 1521, with permission to impark six hundred acres of land and pasture, fifty of wood, and four hundred of heath and furze.*

The house that Sir Richard built was one of the first large houses in the country not to be fortified. Its style has been described as Tudor Perpendicular Gothic; vast amounts of terracotta complement and decorate the red brickwork, giving it a strong but early Renaissance look, which Sir Richard may have admired during his previous travels on the continent. The house originally formed a quadrangle but the North side, with its gatehouse, was demolished in 1786. The East side was rebuilt in 1878; it had been gutted by fire in the previous century.

Sir Richard was a close friend of the King, but their friendship must have been tested hard when his only son, Sir Francis, was accused of adultery with Anne Boleyn and beheaded on Tower Hill in 1536, two days before Anne suffered the same fate. Sir Richard was succeeded by his grandson, Sir Henry, who entertained Elizabeth I at Sutton Place in 1591. Sir Henry was succeeded by his son and then his grandson, both called Sir Richard; it was the grandson who built the Wey Navigation.

The fascinating history of the estate is fully described in the book 'Annals of an Old Manor House' by Frederick Harrison, who lived there in the late 19th century. Over the years it passed to increasingly distant branches of the Weston family, and became rather neglected. In the early years of the present century it was leased to Alfred Harmsworth, better known as Lord Northcliffe, the newspaper baron, who spent over £70,000 restoring it.

Subsequent owners included the Duke of Sutherland, Paul Getty, and Stanley J Seeger,

SUTTON PLACE.

another American oil tycoon, and it has now been placed in the ownership of a Trust. Further vast sums have been spent on restoration work, but neither the house nor the grounds are open to visitors at present.

Continue along Blanchards Hill past the junction with Whitmoor Lane, after which the road becomes Sutton Green Road. Just after the Fox and Hounds pub, where the main road bends sharp left, you must turn off to the right – going straight ahead, in effect – into the continuation of Sutton Green Road.

Fox and Hounds, Sutton Green. 01483 772289. Friary Meux. Food C G Rest.

Go straight ahead at the junction with Robin Hood Lane, then turn right onto the track, signed as a footpath, just before Runtley Wood Farm. A barrier blocks the way to vehicles but you should be able to get your bike under it without a problem. Follow the track the short distance to the lock, cross the lock bypass channel and the lock itself by the small footbridges, and then turn left onto the towpath to return to Send Cartbridge.

⑧ Send Cartbridge to Newark

From Send Cartbridge pass the New Inn and head along the main road. Pass the shops at Send Parade and then turn left into Tannery Lane, just beyond the petrol station. Until recently this area was dominated by sand quarrying and the area beyond Heath Farm was an industrialised landscape. Now all that has gone and a superb restoration job has returned the countryside to almost its original state. One of the few reminders of the old works is the reinforced section of road where heavy quarry trucks once crossed. However, industrial use of the area has not ceased completely, for another couple of hundred yards will

bring you to the front of the factory and offices on the site of the old tannery (13 miles).

Follow the lane on past Brook Lane and Prews Farm. Further along on the left the impressive and historic farmhouse of Papercourt Farm is thought to have been the manor house of the one-time Manor of Papercourt. It has some similarities in design to the Manor House in nearby Ripley. Notice how the flint-built chimney is on the outside of the building.

From Papercourt Farm continue straight ahead along Papercourt Lane. The narrow lane winds its way through the fields and then past the collection of cottages, bungalows, and houses which forms the closest thing there is to a village of Newark. At the end of the lane there is a phone box on the left and the Seven Stars pub on the right (14 miles). Turn left into Newark Lane to reach the car park and the end of the ride, or turn right to link with Ride A at Polesdon Lane.

Seven Stars, Newark Lane, Ripley. Free house. 01483 225128. Food G C.

Ride C:
Basingstoke Canal & Congo Stream

St Johns • Brookwood • Pirbright Bridge • Deepcut • Frimley Green • Mytchett • Tunnel Hill • Furze Hill • Pirbright • Fox Corner • Crastock • Hook Heath • St Johns

Distance: 19 miles
Landranger Maps: 186
Pathfinder Maps: 1205

If neither Basingstoke nor the Congo are situated in Surrey, why should a cycle ride in this book be named after those two places? Of course, as most readers will already know, much of the canal which once linked Basingstoke to the River Wey runs through the county of Surrey, but the link with the Congo may be less obvious. Intriguingly, though, there is a stream running through the Surrey countryside which bears its name. If you want to find out why, you'll either have to read on or, better still, come on the ride.

Your journey starts at St Johns, on the western outskirts of Woking, and heads along the towpath of the Basingstoke Canal almost to the western boundary of Surrey, and then returns by tracks and roads, mostly across military and common land. The ride along the canal appears to be virtually flat, although it actually climbs about 100 feet in the course of passing 17 locks. The towpath is mostly in very good condition and makes for easy riding. The return leg is a little more demanding, but not excessively so. The canal is well known for its immense variety of wildlife, while the military areas and commons include large areas of unspoiled heathland.

If you are to enjoy the ride to the full you will want to travel at a fairly easy pace, so allow yourself the best part of the day for the trip.

Starting Points

Start at St Johns, near Woking (grid ref SU 979579). There is a free public car park on the edge of the Lye, right in the village centre, adjacent to the canal. St Johns has a full range of facilities, including shops and toilets. There is also a small car park on the Green at Pirbright.

If you want to start at the western end of the ride, try Frimley Lodge Park, off the A321 Frimley–Ash road just south of Frimley Green. The canal runs along the back of the park, in which there are free car parks, toilets and refreshments.

≥ The only station on the ride itself is at Brookwood; from the station cross Connaught Road into Sheet's Heath Road to reach the canal towpath. North Camp (on the Thames Trains Reading–Guildford line) and Ash Vale (served by South West Trains Woking–Alton and Guildford–Aldershot–Ascot routes) are both about half a mile from Mytchett Lake.

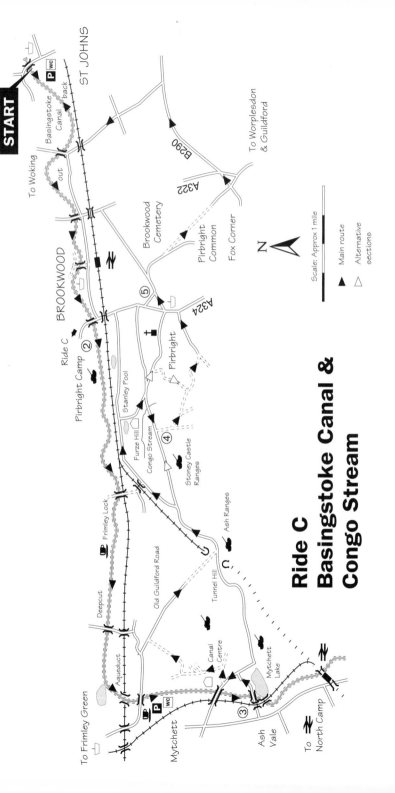

Ride C
Basingstoke Canal & Congo Stream

START

ST JOHNS

To Woking

Basingstoke Canal back

P WC

out

BROOKWOOD

Ride C

Pirbright Camp

②

Brookwood Cemetery

B290

A322

To Worplesdon & Guildford

Pirbright Common

Fox Corner

A324

⑤

Pirbright

Stanley Pool

Furze Hill

Congo Stream

④

Stoney Castle Ranges

Ash Ranges

Frimley Lock

Deepcut

Old Guildford Road

Tunnel Hill

Aqueduct

To Frimley Green

Canal Centre

Mytchett Lake

Mytchett

P WC

③

Ash Vale

To North Camp

N

Scale: Approx 1 mile

▲ Main route

△ Alternative sections

If you wish, you can begin the ride in Woking. There is a canalside car park at Brewery Road (charges may be payable) or you can travel to Woking by train. From Woking, ride west along the canal towpath to St Johns. This will add just over 3 miles to the return distance.

The Route in Brief

① Join canal towpath at Kiln Bridge, heading west, away from lock. At Brookwood Bridge towpath changes to other side of canal. Continue to Pirbright Bridge.

② The towpath changes sides again at Pirbright Bridge and passes the first of 14 locks in the Deepcut Flight. Continue along towpath to Guildford Road Bridge, just beyond Frimley Aqueduct. The towpath again changes side: TR over bridge then TL onto towpath. Continue to Mytchett Lake Bridge.

③ Immediately after bridge TR off towpath and TR onto road to cross canal bridge. TL at next TJ, then TR opposite Potters restaurant onto BW. (NB: BW forks right at gate after 50 yds.) After 250 yds turn sharp left at junction of tracks, the keep to leftmost track as others branch off to right. Pass through fence at edge of military area then FR when track divides. Climb short, steep hill then join drive to reach Old Guildford Road. TR onto road, which becomes unmade BY.

TL when BY meets road and continue to junction beside railway bridge. SO onto main road for just over ½ mile then TR into Stanley Hill. TR at TJ at far end and continue to Stoney Castle Ranges.

√ TL onto road leading into ranges then FL onto track along side of range fence. At end of straight stretch, by corner of danger area, TL away from fence then FL

when path divides after 10 yds. SO at junc of paths after 400 yards then TR at driveway to Vines and Bramble Cottage. At open area where FPs converge follow main track as it curves to L, becoming Mill Lane. Continue to TJ with A324. TL through village then TR at corner of green.

⑤ Pass pond and pubs then TR into Chapel Lane. Continue past most of the houses and into woodland then bear L onto track across Pirbright Common (watch for hidden red BY arrow) then keep on main track over heath. After yellow hydrant sign FR when track divides around tree. Track approaches houses and becomes Malthouse Lane. Continue to road at Fox Corner.

TL into Berry Lane. At far end cross busy main road and continue SO to junction with Blackhorse Lane. TL and continue for more than 1 mile. Just after railway bridge TR onto canal towpath to return to St Johns.

The Ride

① St Johns to Pirbright Bridge

Join the towpath by the Kiln Bridge at St Johns, but make sure you set off in the right direction. You want to head west, away from the lock. The towpath is on the south side of the canal, nearest to the Lye, and is approached by a ramp leading down from the corner of the bridge.

Between St Johns and Brookwood the canal curves in the shape of an inverted 'S', bending round the Hermitage Woods housing estate. A modern steel footbridge joins the estate to the towpath. Beyond this the main line railway borders the canal and is supported by retaining walls along the back of the towpath.

After the Hermitage Road Bridge the canal widens into Hermitage Flash, where houseboats have been moored along the towpath since the 1960s. Beyond the houseboats the towpath briefly merges with the track, giving access to some canalside houses. At the end of the track a gate bars vehicles from the towpath beyond. Ride around the side of the gate, ignoring the incorrect 'No Cycling' sign on the adjacent tree.

On the hill behind the far bank of the canal is the site of Brookwood Hospital, much of which is being redeveloped as a superstore complex and for housing.

The next bridge, known as Brookwood or Stumps Bridge, carries the A322 Guildford–Bagshot road over the canal (1¾ miles). Lock 12 is immediately beyond the bridge, and the towpath switches to the other side of the canal here. Go up the ramp onto the bridge itself and cross to the towpath entrance in the far corner by the petrol station. If you are with young children it

might be safest to dismount until you are past the lock.

🍺 *The Hunter's Lodge, Bagshot Road, Brookwood (past petrol station, about 200 yards north of canal). Free house. 01483 797240. Food G*

As the towpath continues past the next two locks the countryside on the right-hand side opens up and the noise of traffic fades away. On the other bank are the gardens of houses along Brookwood's Connaught Road. Shortly after lock 14 the canal and towpath are crossed by Sheet's Heath Road bridge, which gives access to the centre of Brookwood with its station, pub and shops.

🍺 *The Brookwood Hotel, Station Approach, Connaught Road, Brookwood. Open all day. 01483 472109. Food*

Another half-mile brings you to Pirbright Bridge, which was rebuilt in 1993; a plaque on the bridge commemorates its previous rebuilding in 1915 by the former Guildford Rural District Council (2¾ miles).

☞ *At Pirbright Bridge you can link directly with Ride D.*

② Pirbright Bridge to Mytchett Lake

At Pirbright Bridge the towpath changes sides again, so go up the slope onto the bridge and cross to the far left corner. On the other side of the bridge the towpath passes lock 15 and the adjacent lock cottage. Just after the cottage but before the gate across the towpath, you will see an unusual structure on the left consisting of a brick wall and iron columns. If you look across the canal you will see something similar on the other bank, but slightly offset. These are the supports of a bridge which once carried the Bisley branch railway line. Squeeze between the

The Basingstoke Canal

The canal was built to link Basingstoke with the River Wey Navigation near Byfleet, and thus to the Thames. Construction was authorised in 1778, but the economic crisis caused by the War of American Independence meant that work did not start until 1788 and the canal was not finally opened until 1794. It had 29 locks, which raised it by 195 feet in its 37-mile length. A tunnel over 1,200 yards long took the canal under Greywell Hill in Hampshire.

With no major industries along its route, the canal's purpose was to help local agriculture, bringing in goods such as fertiliser and coal and taking out the produce of the area. Schemes to build extensions to Southampton and Salisbury came to nothing and it was never a financial success. Canal traffic declined with the opening of the London & Southampton Railway through Basingstoke in 1839. Thereafter it survived on purely local traffic, conveying materials for building the vast army camps at Aldershot, timber to a wharf in Woking, and, around the turn of the century, serving a brickworks at Up Nately in Hampshire. The last barge left Basingstoke in 1910; an attempt to reach the town in 1913 had to be abandoned at Basing.

The canal was eventually bought in 1923 by Mr A J Harmsworth for just £5,000. He ran it in conjunction with his transport business until he died in 1947, increasing traffic from 1,300 tons in 1907 to 31,000 tons in 1935. However, the western end was lost in 1932 when Greywell Tunnel collapsed.

In 1949 the canal was bought by the New Basingstoke Canal Company, but by the 1960s it was in very bad condition, with most of the locks unnavigable, the channel silted up and overgrown, and only isolated stretches used for boating. In 1966 the Surrey & Hampshire Canal Society was formed to press for its restoration with volunteer help, but in 1967 the canal's owners announced plans to culvert the urban lengths and redevelop the land. A campaign resulted in the compulsory purchase of the canal by Surrey and Hampshire County Councils, and restoration work began. The massive task was completed in 1991, when the Duke of Kent officially re-opened the complete length of the canal from Byfleet to Greywell.

In 1994–95 the local authorities prepared plans to renovate the final stretch of the canal through to Basingstoke, but objections from local residents along the line of the route appear to have put paid to this imaginative scheme. However, much of the towpath of the abandoned length of canal is now being turned into a public footpath. This will create a towpath and riverside link for long distance walkers all the way from Basingstoke to the centre of London.

Ride B in Volume 3 of this series (East Hampshire) follows the towpath of the canal from Odiham right up to the tunnel mouth at Greywell.

column and the gate to continue along the towpath.

The Bisley Bullet *was the affectionate nickname given to the train which ran from Brookwood along the short branch line to Bisley Camp. The mile-long private line was built in 1890, when the National Rifle Association moved its ranges to Bisley from Wimbledon. Trains usually ran only during its July event.*

During World War I the War Department extended the line for about three miles to serve the army camps at Pirbright, Deepcut and Blackdown. The extension was removed in the 1920s although the section to Pirbright was reinstated during World War II. The service to Bisley continued until 1952. Although the track was later removed, the bridge girders over the canal remained until 1980.

The canal banks all along this section are edged with yellow loosestrife, an extremely overgrown member of the primrose family which flowers in July and August. Also to be seen along here is the purple loosestrife, a tall plant which produces spikes of purple flowers in June and July. Many of the broader parts of the canal provide a home for water lilies. The canal is also renowned as a habitat for dragonflies with 25 of the 39 British varieties having been found here. Dragonflies can be distinguished from the rather similar-looking damselflies by the fact that they rest with their wings outstretched, as damselflies rest with them folded back. The most readily-spotted variety is the Common Blue which is coloured vivid blue and black (male) or green and black (female).

Lock 15 at Pirbright marks the start of the Deepcut flight of 14 locks which, between them, raise the canal by 100 feet in about 2 miles. The way in which the canal climbs can seen by comparing it with the (near) level railway which runs alongside throughout this stretch. At Pirbright the railway runs on an embankment high above the canal but before long the positions are reversed. The locks come thick and fast on this section and it is easy to lose track of where you are, particularly as some lock numbers are hard to see. Cowshott Manor Bridge (3¼ miles), a little beyond lock 16, has been completely rebuilt in the style of the original 1792 hump-backed bridge, which had become entirely derelict. The work was carried out by Manpower Services Commission trainees and completed in 1982. The bridge is now barred to vehicles since the land to which it gave access is now Army property.

Security precautions are also visible in the form of barbed wire fences protecting the Pirbright Guards Depot on the opposite bank of the canal after lock 18. Young saplings have been planted between the canal and the fences which will eventually reduce the visual intrusion. The Army helped in many ways during the restoration of the canal, including work by a detachment of Royal Engineers from Chatham on and around locks 17 and 18.

Just above lock 22 a concrete wall forms the opposite bank of the canal. Steps lead down the wall into the canal and there are handrails along the side. Look carefully and you will see an inscription on the wall noting that the construction was carried out by the Brigade of Guards in 1942. It was built to provide a cheap and cheerful 'swimming pool' in the near-derelict canal. It provided a useful facility for at least 10 years – until a group of soldiers on a night exercise managed to blow up the gates of lock 22 and drain that length of the canal!

At the Curzon Bridges by lock 25 the canal has climbed so much that it has reached the level of the adjacent railway. Go under the modern bridge which crosses the canal at the far end of the lock.

Frimley Lock Cottage

Just before lock 27 there appears to be a short branch leading off from the canal on the far side. In fact it is there to increase the water capacity of the very short length of canal between the locks. Without it, boats going down through the next lock would drain this stretch of canal dry.

Beyond lock 27 you can see the half-sunken remains of an old canal narrow-boat on the far bank.

Lock 28 is the last one in the flight. It is called Frimley Lock, as the nameboard on the lock cottage proclaims (5 miles). Just after the lock on the other side of the canal is a dry dock, part of the canal's main maintenance yard until 1900. It was restored in 1983, having been filled in since 1930.

🍵 *Frimley Lock Cottage. Tea, coffee, soft drinks or traditional home-made cream teas on summer Sundays and Bank Hols, 2–6.*

Above Frimley Lock the canal enters Deepcut. From here it is level (with the exception of one more lock at Ash) for the rest of its route.

Deepcut: *When the canal was built, the cutting taking it through the ridge which crosses its path was regarded as an immense triumph of civil engineering, and rightly so. It is half a mile long and 70 feet deep in places, and the whole thing would have been dug with shovels and wheelbarrows. The surrounding area took its name from the 'Deep Cut'.*

Deepcut also gave its name to an event which will live long in the history of inland waterways restoration. In October 1977, 600 volunteer navvies from the Waterway Recovery Group and canal societies all over the country headed for Surrey to take part in the 'Deepcut Dig'. In two days of massive effort, they completed what would have taken the normal weekend working parties a year to carry out, clearing derelict locks, rebuilding decayed brickwork, and building new bypass weirs to prepare the way for full restoration. They used up 400 bags of cement, 90 tons of ballast, 10 tons of sand, half a ton of reinforcing, and 3,500 bricks.

The cutting's depth and its tree-lined sides mean it is usually cool along this stretch, and the water clear. Watch for the flash of brilliant blue and the splash which is almost all you will see of a kingfisher hunting for its food. Another uncommon bird seen at Deepcut is the Grey Wagtail.

The cutting is crossed by Deepcut road bridge, a modern but quite stylish bridge in white concrete. Beyond the bridge, as the canal bends to the left to run due south towards Ash, an opening in the far bank leads into Wharfenden Lake (6 miles). A short distance further on, note the stop gates in the canal. These are used to block the canal should there be a need to work on the aqueduct ahead, or to prevent it draining if there is a breach.

For anyone who has ever 'floated in the air' across Telford's slender, magnificent Pontcysyllte Aqueduct on the Llangollen Canal in North Wales, 126 feet above the River Dee, the solid brick-built Frimley Aqueduct may come as a disappointment. It is even possible to cross it without realising you have done so. The width of the canal hardly changes and the railway is hidden by a brick wall, athough you may hear a train passing through the arches beneath the bed of the canal.

Just after the aqueduct the towpath leads onto the road at the King's Head or Guildford Road Bridge. The towpath changes to the opposite bank here, so cross the narrow bridge, which is controlled by traffic lights. The easiest access to the towpath is on the left at the bottom of the slope down from the bridge. As the name of the bridge suggests, there's a pub nearby – you'll find it on the right just after the bridge. A 1960s guide to

Surrey pubs said this about the Kings Head: 'You could imagine you were living a century ago when motor-cars were unknown – although there is room for cars between the trees at the front. It used to be a country cottage and still gives that impression'. Things have changed since then, and not necessarily for the better!

The King's Head, Guildford Road, Frimley Green. 01252 835431. Free House (Harvester). Rest G

Back on the towpath, Frimley Lodge Park is on the right-hand side shortly after the bridge. This 60-acre open space includes sports fields, a nine-hole pitch and putt course, informal areas, and even a miniature railway run by the local model engineering society.

Frimley Lodge Park pavilion. Turn off the towpath into the park at the first entrance (by the sports fields). Also toilets.

On the towpath by the park is a commemorative stone marking the reopening of the canal by the Duke of Kent on May 10th, 1991. Take care on this stretch because some parts of the towpath edge have crumbled.

The miniature railway runs alongside the towpath for some distance but when it comes to an end its place is taken by another railway line – only this time it's a full-sized one! On the opposite bank is the entrance to Potter's Pool (7 miles), and shortly after that is the Basingstoke Canal Visitor Centre.

If you are in a hurry, you can reach the Canal Centre by leaving the towpath at the next bridge (the newly-rebuilt Mytchett Place Road Bridge). However, you'll pass close to the entrance of the Centre on the return leg of the ride, so we suggest you continue along the towpath now.

On the other bank beyond Mytchett Place Bridge is the water entrance to Potter's steak restaurant, and on the right of the canal as it approaches the next bridge (Mytchett Lake Bridge), is a small, modern housing estate. Mytchett Lake is on the other side of the bridge (7¾ miles). It acts as a reservoir for the canal and is up to 12 feet deep in places. The canal channel is fenced to keep boats out of the lake, which is a haven for water birds.

③ Mytchett Lake to Stoney Castle Range

Immediately after you pass under Mytchett Lake Bridge, take the path on the right which leads to the road. Turn right onto the road and cross the canal bridge. The road passes open fields on the left, while to your right is woodland with the lake beyond it. Turn left at the junction opposite Mytchett Place, about 500 yards from the canal. Follow the road down the hill until just before the entrance to

Potter's restaurant. The ride turns off here along a bridleway on the right, but if you want to visit the Canal Centre continue along the road for a few yards, and come back here afterwards.

Basingstoke Canal Visitor Centre includes an exhibition, shop, and limited refreshment facilities. The canalside grounds provide picnic and barbecue facilities. Rowing boats can be hired and there are boat trips at certain times. There is a small charge for entry to the exhibition, and rowing boats can be hired for about £5 an hour. Boat trips are from £1 per person. The Canal Centre is open Tues–Sun and BH Mons Easter–31 October from 10.30–5.00. In winter it is open 10.30–4.30 Tues–Fri only. ☎ 01252 370073.

Gourmet Cruises (☎ 01374 649540) run wine and dine trips on the 40-seat restaurant boat 'The Lady of Camelot'.

Turn right onto the track virtually opposite the entrance to Potter's. There is

Mytchett Place Bridge

no bridleway sign by the road, but there is one about 50 yards along the track where it forks to the right. (Ignore the route which continues straight ahead through the tubular metal gate.) Go around the end of the bar across the track.

The surface is quite sandy but if you keep to the edge it's not too bad. After about 250 yards you'll come to a junction; take the track which turns off sharp left – the bridleway sign by the concrete blocks shows the correct way to go. It leads through pine-covered heathland and eventually comes to a spot where a number of routes diverge to the right.

Don't get confused here. The first time we visited this spot there was a bridleway sign but, as it had become detached, a helpful passer-by had placed it in the crook of a tree – but pointing in entirely the wrong direction! You want to go straight ahead, which means taking the leftmost of the three paths. You'll soon know if you're going the right way because you should quickly come to a fence which marks the edge of the military land (8¾ miles).

The land on the other side of the fence, which is signed 'Out of Bounds to Troops', is more heavily wooded. Continue to a fork in the path where there is another bridleway sign, albeit partly broken, and take the fork to the right. After an initial curve through the trees, the path follows a straight course for nearly half a mile. It is in fairly good condition but watch for tree roots sticking up above the surface. Cross the cleared path, through which some power lines run (9 miles). Not long after this there is a short but steep hill and then the path joins the drive to some houses. Follow this to the road and turn right.

Before the army took over the surrounding heathland in the mid-19th century this road was, as its name of Old Guildford Road suggests, the direct route from

Canal life

Frimley to Guildford. The tarred surface ends after about a quarter of a mile; the track that continues is potholed but generally in reasonable condition. You are re-entering army land but the public is allowed access, so don't be deterred by what appears to be a bullet hole in the military by-laws sign!

On either side of the road you can see the boundary banks marking the edge of the highway. In times past many property boundaries were marked in this way. They took more effort to construct, but they were more permanent and needed less maintenance than fences or hedges.

As you proceed along the track there are one or two patches which may be very muddy in winter or after rain, but it should be possible to avoid them. Keep going until you come out on the public road at Tunnel Hill (10¼ miles) opposite the entrance to Ash Ranges and turn left. It is very tempting to head down the winding hill at speed, but make sure you don't miss the splendid views over the virtually unspoiled heathland by doing so. The other thing to watch is the traffic; it's sometimes heavier than the road's C-classification might suggest, especially during rush hours, so take care.

☞ *If the traffic on this road bothers you, there is a short cut which avoids most of it, but you'll miss a worthwhile part of the route. Turn off to the right about half a mile on down the road – keep an eye out for the turn because it is not signposted. Continue along that road (Grange Road) until you come to the entrance to Stoney Castle Range, where you rejoin the main route.*

If you don't want to take the short cut, continue along the road until it meets the B3012, which emerges on the left from under a railway bridge. Go straight on up the short hill, after which the road runs beside the railway fence for some distance. At the end of this straight length, a T-junction sign gives advance warning of the junction with Stanley Hill. Turn right here, but be extremely careful of the traffic.

Stop immediately after turning into Stanley Hill (12 miles) and listen for the sound of the small stream which passes under the road. When you've found it, peer through the hedge on the right-hand side of the road. You should just be able to make out Stanley Pool, its surface usually covered with water lilies during the summer.

The land on both sides of the road is part of the estate bought by Stanley around the turn of the century. Furze Hill, the somewhat forbidding Victorian house in which he spent the last years of his life, is just along the road. On the woodwork above one of the gateways are the initials 'HMS' and the date 1900. The house is still owned by the Stanley family.

Sir Henry Morton Stanley *is best remembered for his immortal words "Dr Livingstone, I presume"*, with which he concluded his African expedition to rescue the Scottish missionary and explorer in 1871. (Livingstone had set out five years earlier to trace the source of the Nile, and Stanley was sent by the New York Times to find him.) A journalist and explorer by profession, Stanley is closely associated with the Congo Free State (now Zaire), which he helped to secure for Belgium. Parts of his estate in Pirbright are named after places in Africa, hence Mazamboni Farm, Ruwenzori Hill, Manyuema, and the Congo Stream.

Even the name 'Stanley Pool' is of African origin. This was the former name of Pool Malebo, a lake between Zaire and the Congo formed by a widening of the Congo River. It was somewhat larger than the Pirbright version though, as it covered an area of over 300 square miles!

Stanley had wanted to be buried in Westminster Abbey beside Livingstone, but this was not allowed, and his grave is to be found in Pirbright churchyard.

Continue past Furze Hill to the junction at the end of the road and turn right. After a short distance there is a small bridge which carries the road over the Congo Stream. A quarter of a mile further along the road, turn left into the entrance of Stoney Castle ranges.

√ Stoney Castle Range to Pirbright

☞ *The next part of the ride follows a bridleway beside the army ranges and across the heath. This bridleway was legally diverted in 1994, so follow the signs and the instructions below; don't rely on an out of date map. However, on one visit we found the bridleway signs missing and it's not clear who removed the signs or why. We are assured by Surrey County Council that the bridleway still exists, and the MOD says it sees no need to close it even if the red flags are flying. In case you*

Pirbright Church

do have any problems, there is an
alternative route on page 66 to enable you
to bypass this section. (The alternative is
quite an attractive option in its own right).

Follow the road leading into the range for
about 60 yards then fork left onto a track
which runs along the outside of the range
fence – go around the end of the tubular
metal gate at the start of the track. The
track curves left and then runs straight,
parallel to the fence, for about 300 yards.
At the end of this straight stretch, at the
corner of the danger area, turn sharp left
away from the fence, then take the left fork
when the path divides about 10 yards
further on.

From here the bridleway runs along the
edge of some woods and there are
extensive rabbit warrens in the banked
edge of the field on your left. At the
junction of paths about 400 yards further
on continue straight on.

☞ *The alternative route via West Hall
Farm rejoins at this junction.*

About 200 yards after this junction the
path curves to the left and comes to the
driveway leading to Vines Farm and
Brambles. Turn right onto the driveway.
(The official bridleway actually follows a
slightly different route, but its course has
disappeared.)

Go along the drive until you come to a
wide, open area where a number of
footpaths diverge. Follow the track round
the curve to the left, passing the entrance
to Pirbright Lodge (once home to Admiral
John Byron, the poet's grandfather) where
the track becomes a tarred road, Mill Lane.

Continue past Manor Farm and the Old
Mill House, where you can hear the fall of
the mill stream and see it as it crosses
under the road, but the mill and its pond
are hardly visible from the road. Just along
the road is the Manor House itself, a 16th
century house built on the moated site of
an older medieval house.

Keep going until you come to the main
A324 Aldershot–Woking road (14 miles)

and then turn left. The road is busy but you won't be on it for long. Pass the shops and then, at the corner of the Green opposite the White Hart, turn left off the main road and left again into Church Lane. Leave your bike by the churchyard gate and go inside to find the granite monolith marking Stanley's grave. The name *Bula Matari* is Stanley's African name. Stanley died in 1904 but his wife Dorothy survived him by another 22 years. A plaque commemorates other family members. From the grave you can continue through the churchyard to look at the church if you wish.

Pirbright Church is dedicated to St Michael and All Angels. It was rebuilt in the late 18th century, having apparently fallen into considerable disrepair. One source even suggests that the previous church had burnt down about a hundred years before. The village could not afford to finance the rebuilding itself, so George III granted them a charter in 1783 which allowed the parishioners to collect from house to house all over England the £2024 and five old pence they needed. (A copy of the charter is on display inside the church, where there is also another memorial to Stanley.)

The rebuilding gave us one of the very few Georgian churches to be found in Surrey. It is somewhat unusual in that the nave is built of brick, while the tower and the rest of the building is of grey stone. If you look closely at the mortar of the stonework, you will see that small pieces of ironstone have been inserted in it. This is known as galleting, a technique which may simply be decorative or which may have some superstitious origin.

Return to the Green and follow the one-way system to get back to the junction by the White Hart, then turn left. Pass 'The Shop' – its identity made plain by a plaque above its doorway, although it is known today as 'The Shop on the Green'. To the left of the road is the attractive village pond.

☞ *It has been proposed that the road along this side of the Green should become the A324 road instead of the route through Brookwood. The road layout in Pirbright will change if this is implemented.*

Pirbright: You'll not be in the village long before you become aware of the paternalistic influence of Lord Pirbright. Born Henry de Worms, he was educated at Kings College, London, becoming a Fellow in 1863. In the same year he was called to the Bar at the Inner Temple. Entering politics, he was MP for Greenwich 1880–85 and Liverpool (East Toxteth) 1885–95. He served as a minister in Lord Salisbury's governments, as Parliamentary Secretary at the Board of Trade (1885–88) and Under Secretary of State for the Colonies (1888–92). He was made a Privy Councillor in 1889 and a peer in 1895. His home was at nearby Henley Park, which

Stanley's grave in Pirbright churchyard

Lord Pirbright's Hall and the Diamond Jubilee Drinking Fountain

is why he was buried not in Pirbright but at Wyke.

The village hall, called Lord Pirbright's Hall, is his most prominent benefaction. It was built in 1899 and given to the village two years later to commemorate the accession of King Edward VII. A marble obelisk in the grounds stands as a reminder of the gift. (The hall was later extended and the children's playground provided as a memorial to those villagers who lost their lives in World War II.) Just a few years earlier, to mark Queen Victoria's Diamond Jubilee in 1897, Lord Pirbright and his wife had presented the village with the drinking fountain which stands outside the hall. It is surmounted by a bronze statue of a young girl reading a book. The posts which surround it bear Lord Pirbright's emblem – the letter P with a coronet – as do many buildings in the village.

🍺 *The White Hart, Pirbright. Friary Meux. Open all day. 01483 472366. Food C G*
🍺 *The Cricketers, Pirbright. Courage. 01483 473198*

🛒 *Bentley's Stores, Guildford Road, Pirbright*
🛒 *Netherton's, Newsagents, Guildford Road, Pirbright*
🛒 *The Post Office, The Green, Pirbright*
🛒 *The Shop, The Green, Pirbright*

⑤ Pirbright to St Johns

Pass the Cricketers pub and then, just after the end of the Green and, as the road becomes Cemetery Pales, turn right into Chapel Lane, ignoring the 'No Through Road' signs (15 miles). Follow the lane for quite some distance until you are past most of the houses and into the woodland. After you pass a sign listing the names of houses served by the continuation of the road, keep a careful watch for a track heading off to the left onto Pirbright Common. There is no sign, only a discreetly placed red byway arrow. (If you get as far as some more houses you've missed the turning.) The first part of the track (around the locked barrier) can be muddy, but matters improve as it crosses an open area where the heather is being encouraged to regenerate.

Keep on the main track (the most obvious one) as other lesser paths turn off or join it. Just after a yellow hydrant sign take the right fork when the track divides around a tree. Pass a Pirbright Common signboard and follow the track towards some modern houses where it acquires a tarred surface and becomes Malthouse Lane, leading to the road at Fox Corner (16 miles).

The Fox, Fox Corner, near Worplesdon. Courage. 01483 232520. Food G

At the junction with the main road turn hard left into Berry Lane. The far end is blocked at its junction with Bagshot Road and you will have to dismount to cross over the main road into the continuation of Berry Lane on the far side. The main road is extremely busy so be very careful.

Continue along Berry Lane, passing the entrance to Bridley Manor. The house itself can best be seen through the tradesman's entrance, which is just after the main gates. There is something of a climb along this part of the route. On the left shortly before the crest of the hill is an old granary building, now converted into homes (17 miles).

Good views over the surrounding country can be had from the top of the ridge before a welcome downhill stretch brings you to the junction with Blackhorse Road, by the entrance to Crastock Manor. Turn left here. Blackhorse Road is over a mile long; take care at the busy crossroads about half way along where the road meets Saunders Lane and Heath House Road.

Further along, the road passes under the main railway line by one of the narrow tunnel-like bridges which date back to its opening in the 1830s. Just after the bridge on the right-hand side is the towpath of the Basingstoke Canal. Turn right onto the towpath and follow it for a mile back to St Johns and the end of the ride.

Pirbright Green and village pond

Alternative section of route

√ Stoney Castle Range to Pirbright

☞ *This alternative route has been included in case you should have any problems on the bridleway past the Stoney Castle Range.*

From the entrance to the ranges, return along the road past the junction with Stanley Hill and take the turning on the right shortly afterwards. There is no signpost but the road can be recognised by the No Through Road warning signs. After about 300 yards, turn right into the entrance of West Hall Farm, which is signed as a bridleway. Follow the winding, tarred drive leading to the farm, but when it forks, keep to the right-hand branch which takes you between some barns. From here the track is unmade. Follow it around to the left past the out-buildings and beside a pond. Cross a small bridge and go through a tubular metal gate onto a very pleasant grassy track between the fields. Pass some gates leading into the fields on either side, and then, at the junction just a few yards further on, turn left to rejoin the main route.

Ride D:
Highways, Byways, and a Wayward Stream

Bisley • Lucas Green • Donkey Town • West End • Windlesham • Westcroft Park
• Pennypot • Beldam Bridge • Bisley Church • Stafford Lake • Cowshot
Common • (Bisley Range • Pirbright Bridge) • Coldingley • Bisley

Distance:	11, 14 or 16 miles
Landranger Maps:	186
Pathfinder Maps:	1189 and 1205

The north-west corner of Surrey today is a maze of busy roads heading in all directions and, at first sight, it might seem far from ideal territory for a rural bike ride. But in the midst of these crowded roads there is a network of peaceful rural byways – narrow country lanes, almost-forgotten green roads, and bridlepaths – winding their way through pleasant countryside. It is those byways which this ride explores and exploits. Contact with the teeming highways of the district cannot be wholly avoided, but in most cases the ride simply crosses them and disappears back into the country on the other side. And as for the 'wayward stream' – if you want to discover the meaning of that you'll just have to come on the ride. We wouldn't want to spoil the surprise awaiting you!

One potential blot on the landscape of this ride has fortunately now been removed. Plans to build a dual carriageway bypass around West End, Bisley, and Knaphill would have cut right through the countryside surrounding the ride, and would even have obliterated part of the route itself around Kiln Lane. It would have been one highway too many. Thankfully, Government cutbacks in road-building meant that the plans were abandoned in 1997 because of the lack of funds, which will come as a great relief to anyone who has been on and enjoyed this ride.

Starting Points

The ride starts at Bisley, at the small free car park by the junction of Guildford Road (A322) and Shaftesbury Road (grid reference SU 948595). There are shops and a pub on the main road. Alternatively, start in Windlesham where there is a free car park at the Field of Remembrance at the top of Updown Hill.

≋ This ride is poorly served by railways – perhaps that is why the local roads are so busy. The only nearby station is Brookwood on the Waterloo–Woking–Basingstoke line. Turn left out of the station approach and ride along Connaught Road for about half a mile to the traffic lights at Pirbright Bridge. Turn right, cross the canal bridge, and follow the signs for Bisley NRA Camp to pick up

Ride D
Highways, Byways and a
Wayward Stream

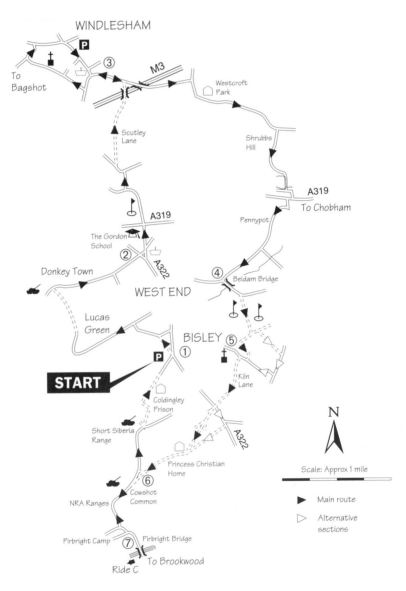

WINDLESHAM

To
Bagshot

③

M3

Westcroft
Park

Scutley
Lane

Shrubbs
Hill

A319
To Chobham

The Gordon
School

A319

Pennypot

②

A322

Donkey Town

④

Beldam Bridge

WEST END

Lucas
Green

BISLEY

⑤

START

①

Kiln
Lane

Coldingley
Prison

N

Short Siberia
Range

A322

Princess Christian
Home

Scale: Approx 1 mile

⑥

Cowshot
Common

NRA Ranges

▶ Main route

▷ Alternative
    sections

Pirbright Camp

⑦

Pirbright Bridge

To Brookwood

Ride C

the route at stage ≈ . The only other station anywhere near the route is at Bagshot, about 1½ miles from Windlesham.

The Route in Brief

① Follow BW which starts by CP entrance. Follow it SO along edge of sports field and past pond, then TL into Ford Road. TL at next TJ into Lucas Green Road (unsigned) which finally becomes unsurfaced BW. At end TR into Brentmoor Road. Cross A322 to Streets Heath.

② TL into Windlesham Road then FL at war memorial. Pass school grounds then SO at A319. After 700 yds (just after power lines) TR into unsigned lane. At far end TL, then after 200 yds TR past wooden gate into Scutley Lane (BW). At end, TL onto driveway and cross M3 bridge. At Woodlands Lane TL for Windlesham.

SO past end of Updown Hill then TR into Church Lane. Continue past church and junc with New Road. TR at TJ with Kennel Lane. At Sun Inn, TR into Updown Hill, SP Lightwater & Chobham.

③ TL at end of Updown Hill and return along Woodlands Road. Pass end of Scutley Lane and cross M3 bridge. At TJ at bottom of hill TR into Windlesham Road. After 1 mile TR into Ford Road. Continue for ½ mile, then see main text for guidance. At end of Ford Road TL into Clappers Lane. TR at TJ with A319 (care!) then L into Pennypot Lane. SO to TJ at Beldam Bridge.

√ At Beldam Bridge TL and over bridge into Scotts Grove Road. After North Hill Nurseries TR at SP 'Public Bridleway no 176'. After 150 yds bend R and cross pathway linking golf course, marked '7th tee'. Just after similar crossing at '6th tee' TR onto narrow BW. At end TR into Church Lane.

⑤ After 150 yds TL at gate onto BW (Kiln Lane). At A322 go SO onto BW 147. After few yards BW forks L off driveway and runs close to factory fence (rightmost of several paths). Keep L of blue BW marker post, then SO to Stafford Lake and join tarred drive to Princess Christian Homes. Beyond Homes SO onto BW 144. At far end (Water Lane) TR to return to Bisley (see Δ) or TL for out and back ride to Pirbright.

≈ *Optional extension Pirbright*
Pass barrier and cross site of old army camp. At Queens Road TL and pass entrance to Bisley Ranges. TL at Billesden Road then L again at Brunswick Road to reach Pirbright Bridge. Return by same route, continuing along Queens Road past end of Water Lane.

Δ [If coming out of Water Lane (see ⑤) TR onto Queens Road.] Pass corner of rifle range, then at sign for 'Short Siberia Range' turn into entrance on R of sign. After 50 yds FR and follow path along side of range boundary. At eventual corner of fence follow path to L then after 120 yds TR. Continue SO along grass track past prison, then SO along Shaftesbury Road to car park.

Stafford Lake Bridge

The Ride

① Bisley to West End

Take the signposted bridleway which starts immediately beside the car park entrance and runs along the side of the car park – don't worry about the 'Access Only' signs, they don't apply to cyclists.

Pass the sports pavilion and then bend to the right by the house called 'Cornerways', following the path along the edge of the sports field and past the pond. This will bring you to Ford Road opposite Bramble Cottage, with a sundial on its front wall.

Turn left into Ford Road and cross the small bridge which replaced the ford after which the road was named. About 150 yards after the entrance to Lucas Green Farm you will come to a T-junction. Turn left, ignoring the 'No Through Road' signs.

A long straight stretch of country lane (Lucas Green Road) follows until, shortly after a timber yard, the road bends sharply to the right and becomes Priest Lane. Once again, ignore the 'No Through Road' signs.

The open heath on the left was taken over by the War Department during the second half of the 19th century and has remained in military use ever since, although some public access is now allowed. On the right are the premises of an enterprise called 'The Compost Centre'. The farmland in most of this part of Surrey is of poor quality, and its two main uses are as pasture for horses and for nurseries. The Compost Centre appears to be the link between these two activities!

After passing some modern houses the lane crosses a small brick bridge. The tarred surface ends and the lane, now signed as a bridleway, becomes a gravelled track running through the woods. Looking through the trees on the left, you can see the heights of Chobham Ridges in the distance, but between you and them is an area of boggy heath. Several streams rise from springs here, and the track crosses them on small brick bridges.

The woods soon give way to open fields and the track ends at a T-junction with Brentmoor Road. Turn to the right. The pretty cottage on the left just after the junction is called, most appropriately, 'Range End'.

This locality is known as Donkey Town. The origins of this curious name are lost in the mists of time, but the surroundings are more rural than it might suggest. Indeed, to the left, almost opposite Brentmoor Cottage, is the Brentmoor Heath Nature Reserve (2 miles).

Further along the road, as you get nearer to West End, modern housing estates border the road. There is a phone box on the left just before the junction with Fenns Lane. The Hare and Hounds pub, on the right shortly before you reach the main road, has re-opened its skittle alley.

Hare & Hounds, Brentmoor Road. Hall & Woodhouse. 01276 858161. Food G C

Take care as you cross the busy A322 road to reach Streets Heath opposite. There are shops and a phone box on the far side, but if you want to go to the Wheatsheaf pub, do so before you cross.

Wheatsheaf, Guildford Road. Courage. Food G

West End Post Office, High Street.
West End Newsagents, High Street.

② West End to Windlesham

After just a few yards turn left off Streets Heath into Windlesham Road, then fork to the left of the War Memorial. Continue past the school grounds on the left.

The Gordon School, founded in 1885, is named after General Charles Gordon who was killed in that year while trying to relieve the 10-month siege of Khartoum. He gained the nickname 'Chinese Gordon' as a result of his part in crushing the Taiping rebellion in 1863-64, and was later Governor of the Sudan. The statue which shows him mounted on a camel and overlooks the school playing fields once stood in Khartoum. The extensive red-brick buildings of the school cost £24,000 when they built. They were designed by William Butterfield.

Cross the A319 Bagshot Road into the continuation of Windlesham Road. Just after the crossroads is another link with General Gordon in the form of Khartoum Cottages, and on the left, just around the corner, is the entrance to the Windlemere Golf Club (3 miles).

As you pass the end of Hookstone Lane, the road's name changes to Blackstroud Lane East. A short distance beyond this are pylons which carry power lines across the road. They are the sign for you to be ready to turn right just ahead. The junction is unsigned, but can be identified by a small triangular island of grass.

This short lane – only some 200 yards long – is called Burnt Pollard Lane. It crosses a small bridge over the Hale Bourne about halfway along and ends at a T-junction opposite Manor Farm. (The present farmhouse was built in 1757, but its origins date back to the 13th century.)

Turn left at the junction into Hook Mill Lane and follow it for about 200 yards. Then, on the right, you'll see a wooden gate which marks the start of an old green lane called Scutley Lane, now a bridleway. Go through the gap beside the gate.

For much of its length the surface of the unmade lane has been improved with roadworks scrapings, which can be soft in places but at least they provide reasonable

General Gordon's statue

drainage. The lane is narrow to begin with but soon widens out between boundary banks, although the surfaced path occupies only part of the width and winds about.

After a while you will come to a stony driveway which, as the sign on the nearby gateway indicates, leads to a house called Twelve Oaks. Turn left and climb up to the bridge over the M3 motorway (4 miles). On the far side of the bridge, follow the driveway round a double bend to its end at Woodlands Lane, then turn left. (From here the ride loops round Windlesham before returning to this point.)

As you approach the village along Woodlands Lane go straight on past the end of Updown Hill into Thorndown Lane, then turn right into Church Road about 400 yards further on. The church is quite a distance along the road; you must climb the hill and pass the end of Pound Lane before you come to it.

Beyond the church (just over 5 miles) the road continues downhill past the Half Moon pub and bends to the right by the junction with New Road. Follow it round and you'll come to a T-junction at Kennel Lane. A right turn here brings you past the Field of Remembrance at the top of Updown Hill (6 miles). Continue down the hill to the shops and the Sun Inn.

Windlesham: *The village's main claim to fame is its nurseries, and the country's first garden centre is said to have been started here. The then-marshy area towards Lightwater was famed in the 17th century for growing bog myrtle or sweet gale, as it is more properly called. The aromatic leaves of this shrub, which grows to about 18 inches in height, were put in linen chests.*

The Church of St John the Baptist was largely rebuilt in the 1870s. It overlooks a large graveyard which is carefully tended by the parish council. Victorian headstones often carried moral messages for those still living. One which stands close to the churchyard wall marks the grave of Mary, the wife of Thomas King, who died on January 11th 1864 at the age of 55, and warns of the hazards of an unexpected demise:

> *"All you that pass this way along*
> *See how sudden I was gone*
> *Death do not always warning give*
> *Therefore be careful how you live."*

Just along from the church, Cedars, an attractive 18th century mansion, has now been divided in two to make Cedar House and Cedar Court, while next door a contrast in styles is provided by the red brick and tiles of Cedar Lodge.

The village centre in Updown Hill includes a surprisingly wide range of shops.

The Half Moon, Church Road. Free house.
The Sun Inn, 1 Chertsey Road. Free house.
01276 472234. Open all day. Food G

③ Windlesham to Beldam Bridge

From the Sun Inn turn right into the continuation of Updown Hill, signposted 'Lightwater and Chobham', then turn left to return along Woodlands Lane. Pass the end of Scutley Lane and cross the motorway. The hill on the far side of the bridge may not look very steep, but you will soon find yourself gathering speed as you descend (7 miles).

At the T-junction at the bottom of the hill turn right into Windlesham Road. On the left, just after the junction with Halebourne Lane, is Westcroft Park; the road passes its 'Western Lodge' and then the gates of the house. Although it is difficult to see very much of the early 19th century house itself, look through the gates to see the unusual half-timbered bell tower within the grounds. It was built around 1910 for an owner who wanted his own peal and contains a carillon of twenty-five bells!

After the junction with Woodcock Lane, and about 100 yards beyond the Dingley Dell nurseries, keep a look out for Steep Acre Farm, with its lovely old half-timbered house (8 miles). About a quarter of a mile after that turn right into Ford Road. The entrance is surrounded by broad grass verges and a faded signpost states 'Leading to Shrubb's Hill'. Once again, you can ignore the signs warning of a 'No Through Road'. Go straight ahead, passing Shrubb's Hill (a private road on the right) and Shrubb's Farm. About a quarter of a mile beyond the farm the road suddenly becomes just a narrow, muddy lane with water visible ahead.

The warning signs which once stood here have now been removed – they always were something of an understatement! Practical experience suggests it is *not* a good idea to continue along the road, even in summer, although the urge to attempt it will no doubt be strong! Instead, dismount and go through the gate on the left of the road, then take the narrow footpath which runs behind the roadside hedge, pushing your bike.

Cross the narrow wooden footbridge near the far end of the path and go up the slope to Clappers Lane. Once back on the road, turn left past Bournebrook Cottage and continue to the junction at the busy A319 Chobham–Bagshot road (9 miles).

Turn right onto the main road – be very careful because the traffic really does speed along this stretch – and then just a few yards along the road turn left into Pennypot Lane. Ahead of you, on the left, is the half-timbered Pennypot Cottage and next to it the appropriately-named 'Cottage on the Bend'. Notice the diamond pattern on its roof, created with lighter-coloured tiles.

Pennypot Lane continues for very nearly a mile, passing the end of Lovelands Lane. (A quarter of a mile down this lane there is a small but delightful ford across the Bourne stream. Divert to see it if you wish, but then make your way back to Pennypot Lane.) On your right, as you come to the junction at the end of Pennypot Lane, is Hatchgate Farm; the 18th century brick farmhouse (another building with a patterned roof) and other beautifully-maintained buildings help to make this a charming spot.

√ Beldam Bridge to Bisley Church

At the junction turn left into Scotts Grove Road and cross Beldam Bridge. Pass North Hill Nurseries and then turn right at the signpost 'Public Bridleway no 176'. The bridleway, which is known as Sandpit Lane, goes between a chain link gate

Lovelands Lane ford

Hatchgate Farm, Beldam Bridge

leading into Chobham Golf Course on the right and a five-bar gate on the left. There may be a muddy patch at the very start (although the last time we were there someone had dumped a load of sand into this wet spot) but the rest is in generally good condition.

A short slope leads up to a junction of paths about 150 yards from the start of the bridleway. Turn (or rather bend) to the right and go straight over the pathway linking the two sides of the golf course (marked '7th tee'). Cross the similar pathway about a quarter of a mile further on at the 6th tee.

Immediately after a similar oathway at the 6th tee, about a quarter of a mile further on, turn right off the main track between some wooden posts. This bridleway, which is known as 'Romany Road', has been resurfaced and should give you no

problems but, just in case, an alternative route is given on page 77. The bridleway ends a quarter of a mile further on at Hill Place Farm (11 miles). Turn right into Church Lane and continue for about 150 yards until you come to a metal gate on the left, marked by a bridleway sign. (It is just before the Bisley village sign.)

The gate leads to Kiln Lane, yet another of the area's old green lanes, but before you turn into it, you may want to continue along the road for a short distance to take a look at Bisley Church. To be able to see it you will have to go through the churchyard gate and up the path, as it is hidden from view by the trees.

The Church of St John the Baptist, Bisley *is situated some distance away from what most people today would regard as the centre of the village. Its 14th century porch is made of massive pieces of timber and is overlooked by* *an old yew tree. The belfry tower is clad with wooden planks and tiled with wooden shingles. The beautifully tended churchyard is entirely rural and peaceful, but whether this peace will survive the building of the bypass only a short distance off remains to be seen.*

Nearby, reached by walking along a footpath which leads from the back of the churchyard, is St John's Well, the water from which was used for christenings in the church. It is now capped, but water still trickles from it, staining the stones over which it flows bright orange.

⑤ Bisley Church to Cowshot Common

Return to the gate at the end of Kiln Lane. Access for cyclists is provided at the side of both this gate and the next one a short distance beyond it. Kiln Lane has a good surface throughout, and it is easy to see the banks marking the edges of this ancient highway. The lane is extremely peaceful but this is quickly shattered as you emerge onto the A322 Guildford Road by the Fox public house.

🍽 *The Fox, Guildford Road, Bisley. 01483 473175. Courage.*

Wait for a gap in the incessant traffic and then cross the road to reach the sanctuary of bridleway no. 147 directly opposite. The first part of this bridleway runs across the open common and is rather bumpy; there are a few muddy patches too. (If you want to avoid this section see the alternative on page 78.)

The bridleway begins on a driveway but forks left after only a few yards. There are several other paths around here, so be careful not to get confused. The bridleway is the rightmost path, which runs close to the fence of a factory on your right.

Before you reach the far end of the fence you will see a marker post bearing the blue bridleway arrow. Take the path to the left

of this post, as indicated. From this point the route of the bridleway is fairly straight and obvious. Barring one or two muddy spots, its condition improves after it crosses a drive leading to some houses (12 miles).

Continue broadly straight ahead along the bridleway until you come to the pretty bridge at Stafford Lake, and then turn right onto the tarred drive leading past the Princess Christian Homes.

The Princess Christian Homes were established in 1900 as a convalescent home for servicemen returning from the Boer War. They are named after HRH Princess Christian of Schleswig-Holstein, the sixth child of Queen Victoria. Her son, Prince Christian Victor, was killed in the Boer War, as was the son of Field Marshal Lord Roberts, C-in-C of the Forces in South Africa. Together, realising that something had to be done for men returning disabled from the war, they set up the Soldiers and Sailors Help Society (now the Forces Help Society) in 1899.

The land for the Homes was donated to the Society by Lord Pirbright and the buildings constructed as a gift from the Building Trades Federation of England. The Homes were furnished by public subscription.

Originally there were four separate Homes and a service block. They were joined by pathways which were later enclosed to make long corridor walkways. These have now been modernised and look out onto the courtyards and surrounding grounds.

The use of the Homes has been adapted over the years in line with the changing needs of ex-servicemen and women. Today, the emphasis is on the provision of sheltered accommodation and residential care. In 1988 a new East Wing added 15 single rooms and a central dining room with an adjacent kitchen, and in 1992 the new Lord Roberts Wing was opened to provide a 17-bed care unit with all specialist facilities. The Homes are now registered for a total of 35 residents.

The Princess Christian Homes, Stafford Lake

At the end of the buildings the driveway becomes a gravelled track and is signed 'Bridleway no 144'. Keep going straight ahead, past some houses on the right, and through a slightly overgrown stretch. At the end of this you will pass some cottages and arrive at a road called Water Lane, which loops off Queens Road.

From here you can either turn right, then right again into Queens Road, to head straight back to Bisley (see stage Δ) or you can continue along the optional extension to Pirbright Bridge, a distance of about a mile each way.

☞ *If you want to connect with Ride C, continue to Pirbright Bridge.*

≈ Cowshot to Pirbright Bridge and back

To continue to Pirbright Bridge, turn left at Water Lane, passing around the end of

the barrier which blocks the road to vehicles. You are now crossing the site of a wartime army camp, and if you look in the grass on the side of the road you will see the old foundations of huts.

After a couple of hundred yards go around another barrier and come out on Queens Road as it crosses the heather-clad Cowshot Common (13 miles). Turn left and follow the road past the entrance to the National Rifle Association's Bisley Camp ranges to the junction with Billesden Road. Just before the junction, on the right, is Cowshot Manor House, set in lovely gardens, a civilian oasis among the surrounding military establishments. In the trees on the opposite side of the road you may be able to see the remains of a cutting which was once part of the Bisley Camp railway.

Turn left at Billesden Road and again at the next junction (Brunswick Road), and, after winding through some woods, you will arrive at Pirbright Bridge and the Basingstoke Canal. Here you can either link with Ride C (which runs west along the towpath of the Basingstoke Canal) or return to Cowshot Common by the same route, continuing along Queens Road past its junction with Water Lane.

△ Cowshot Common to Bisley

From its junction with Water Lane follow Queens Road round the bend by the corner of the huge rifle range – it has no fewer than 108 targets – which is now clearly visible on your left (15 miles via Pirbright Bridge).

If you come on this ride during the fortnight in July when the National Rifle Association's annual championships are taking place, they will also be clearly audible. Indeed, you can almost look over the shoulders of the competitors closest to the road!

About 300 yards beyond the corner of the range you must make a choice of onward route. You can continue along Queens Road to the busy A322 Guildford Road and then turn left for almost half a mile to get back to the Bisley car park.

Alternatively, you can turn off the road and cross the common. Turn left off Queens Road by the sign for the 'Short Siberia Range' just opposite a builder's depot. Turn into the track to the *right* of the sign and, after 50 yards or so, fork to the right. The path runs parallel to the range fence, although to begin with this is hidden behind some prolific brambles. Watch out for the sawn-off remains of small tree stumps on this stretch.

Eventually you will come to the far corner of the fence; follow the path to the left around the corner. Continue beside the

fence for 120 yards and then turn right. The route onwards is fairly clear.

The path is in reasonable condition; there are one or two patches which may be muddy but they should be relatively easy to bypass. After 200 yards you will come to the corner of Coldingley Prison; continue straight ahead along the grass track. This will bring you out onto Shaftesbury Road; keep going on and you will arrive at the entrance to the car park.

If you completed both the ride around Windlesham and the diversion to Pirbright Bridge, you have now cycled just over 16 miles.

🍺 *The Hen & Chickens, Guildford Road. 01483 473184.*

Alternative sections of route

🖝 *These alternative sections of route bypass some lengths of bridleway which may be in bad condition.*

√ Beldam Bridge to Bisley Church

After passing the '6th tee' golf course crossing, continue on the Sandpit Lane bridleway as it bends to the left, as indicated by the line of wooden posts. The path now becomes a much wider track and, after a short distance, at a junction with another track, turn right.

The track climbs slightly up to the crest of a hill, and there are views through the trees on the left over the golf course and far beyond. Unfortunately some people have found this a handy place to dump rubbish. Go down the hill until the bridleway ends at Chobham Road. Turn right onto the main road (which can be busy at certain times of day, especially weekday rush hours) and continue for about 300 yards. Pass the junction with Barrs Lane and then turn right into Warbury Lane. This takes you to Hill Place Farm, where you rejoin the main route. Continue straight ahead into Church Lane.

⑤ Bisley Church to Cowshot Common

When you come out on the A322 Guildford Road by the Fox, turn left onto the road and continue for about 300 yards to the traffic lights. Be careful because this road is very busy. Go straight ahead at the lights; if you have children or inexperienced cyclists with you it is a good idea to dismount at this junction. A few yards further on there is a lane on the right called 'Stafford Lake'. This will take you to the Princess Christian Homes, where you can resume the main route.

Ride E:
Forest, Wood and Heath

Peaslake • Lawbrook Lane • Parklands • Shere Heath • Little London • Brook • Farley Green • Farley Heath • Woodhill • Shamley Green • Stroud Common • Willinghurst • Winterfold • Ewhurst Windmill • Hurtwood • Peaslake

Distance:	9 miles (shorter route) up to 13 miles
Landranger Maps:	187 (and 186 for Shamley Green route)
Pathfinder Maps:	1226

The Surrey Hills offer some truly magnificent scenery and some parts are very well known, of course. Box Hill on the chalk downs and Leith Hill in the Greensand hills are very popular and can even be too crowded at times. However, there are plenty of other beautiful spots close by which you could well have almost all to yourself. This is despite the efforts of the County Council's Surrey Hills Visitor Project, which is trying to persuade people to discover these less familiar areas and their marvellous forests, woods and heathland – many of which are freely open to the public.

We want this ride to appeal to as many as possible, so, because it inevitably involves some hill-climbing, we have deliberately kept the main part short to make up for it. However, if you do find the hills a little tough, there's no reason why you shouldn't get off and enjoy a walk. And remember, you can look forward to the magnificent views from the heights and the bonus of some delightful downhill dashes.

For those who want a longer and more demanding ride, there is an alternative route between Farley Green and Winterfold which involves a descent into the valley at Shamley Green and a climb back up the steep scarp face of the hills. With the choice of shorter and longer routes, plus the various alternatives to sections of the route, you can enjoy so many different permutations of the ride they will seem totally different each time you try it.

Starting Points

Begin at the Pond Lane car park in Peaslake (grid reference TQ 086 448), which can be reached from the A25 at Gomshall or from the south through Ewhurst.

There are a number of other car parks along the route, many of them being provided by the Hurtwood Control, but they may be locked from time to time to prevent trespass. Besides, we hope you would prefer not to spoil the peace and quiet of the area by driving through it unnecessarily.

≥ The nearest station is at Gomshall on Thames Trains' Guildford–Dorking line, but be careful not to miss your train back – there is only one every two hours or so; for information ☎ 0345 484950.

Ride E
Forest, Wood and Heath

N

Scale: Approx 1 mile

▶ Main route

▷ Alternative sections

To Shere

Ride F

To Gomshall

Little London

② Parklands

Brook ☎

Lawbrook

Farley Green

Ride F

④ ③

PEASLAKE

Ride B
(Vol 2)

START

Roman Temple ✪

P Farley Heath

To Shalford & Guildford

SHAMLEY GREEN

Woodhill

Hurtwood

Winterfold Forest

Lawbrook Lane

Duke of Kent School

B2128

Stroud Common

Willinghurst

Winterfold Heath

⑤ P

P

Course of Roman Road

Ewhurst Windmill

Pitch Hill

Gaston Gate

Smithwood Common

To Ewhurst

To Cranleigh

The Route in Brief

① TL out of CP into Pond Lane. At TJ at end TR into Lawbrook Lane. Just before bottom of hill TL onto BW. Follow BW along edge of field then through gap in corner of hedge onto fenced-in section of path. At road TR. Part way up steep climb TL into drive to Parklands Farm (BW). At farm itself bear R. After 250 yds cross railway at level crossing. *Caution:* make absolutely sure no trains are coming before crossing and close gates after use.

On far side of crossing keep SO along BW to road and TL into Little London, SP Farley Green & Shamley Green.

② Continue down hill and under railway. At TJ at Brook TL, SP Farley Green & Shamley Green. Keep SO to Farley Green

③ *Shorter route to Winterfold Heath*
TL into Shophouse Lane, SP Smithwood Common & Cranleigh. Follow lane for about 2 miles through forest to junc with Winterfold Heath Road, SP Ewhurst & Shere. TL and follow directions at ⑤.

√ *Longer route to Winterfold Heath*
From Farley Green continue SO into August Lane, SP Farley Heath & Shamley Green. Follow lane over heath and down through Woodhill, then continue SO to Shamley Green. TL onto B2128, SP Cranleigh.

About 250 yds after junc with Stroud Lane at Stroud Common, TL into driveway of Willinghurst Estate (BW). Keep R at entrance to farmhouse and follow drive past modern farm buildings and bungalows. When drive bends to R, TL onto very sandy track which climbs steeply up hillside. At junc of paths after 100 yds, TR onto track along hillside. Continue to top of hill. Keep SO when tracks merge at top. At road TL past car park 6 to junc with Winterfold Heath Road, SP Ewhurst & Shere, and TR.

⑤ Follow lane through to TJ at far end then TL. At TJ at bottom of hill TR, SP Ewhurst & Cranleigh. Climb hill to junc of Lawbrook Lane.

TL for direct route back to Peaslake (FR at junc with Walking Bottom, SP Peaslake).

Otherwise, keep SO down hill past Windmill Inn, then take next on L, Moon Hall Road. At end TL into Peaslake Road. Follow this past Duke of Kent School and Gasson Farm to reach Peaslake.

Hazel Hall, Peaslake

The Ride

① Peaslake to Little London

Turn left out of the car park into Pond Lane and almost immediately you begin climbing a short hill out of the village. The climb is well worthwhile, because there are splendid views from the top over the surrounding countryside and the North Downs. The red brick Hazel Hall, on the left, was built in about 1720 and is said to have been a smugglers' safe house, with tunnels linking it to the village.

Continue past the junctions with Burchetts Hollow and Jesses Lane, then, at the T-junction at the end of the lane, turn right into Lawbrook Lane. This runs downhill, gently at first but then more steeply through a tree-lined cutting. About 100 yards after you come out of the cutting, and just before you reach the bottom of the hill, turn left onto the signed bridleway (just under 1 mile).

☞ *If you would rather stay on the roads, there's an alternative route on page 92.*

The bridleway is a fairly obvious path along the edge of a field. It's mildly bumpy, with one or two sandy spots which need some care. To make up for this there are some excellent views to the south across the fields.

At the end of the field, go through the gap in the corner of the hedge onto a narrower fenced-in section of the path. This stretch is a little more overgrown but there are even better views. A stretch through a tree-lined cutting follows, before the path comes out on the road opposite Cotterell's Farm – turn right. A short downhill stretch is followed by quite a steep climb. Turn left at the tarred drive to Parklands

Farm; it isn't marked as a right of way but it is, in fact, a 'road used as a public path'. At Parklands Farm itself, bear round to the right – if you go straight ahead you'll end up in the farm – but beware of chickens on the road! After about 250 yards you'll come to the railway (2 miles).

Cross the railway by the level crossing. You have to open the gates yourself, so make absolutely sure no trains are coming before you start to cross. *If you are in any doubt, or if you have any problems, call the signalman* **immediately** *on the telephone provided.*

After using the crossing make sure the gates are firmly closed and latched to prevent children and animals getting onto the railway. On the far side of the crossing keep straight on along the bridleway until you come to the road.

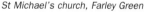 *For a real challenge you can connect here with Ride F.*

Turn left into Little London (signposted 'Farley Green & Shamley Green') and freewheel down the gentle slope through the hamlet, passing the William IV pub.

William IV, Dark Lane, Little London. Free house. 01483 202685. Open eves from 5.30 excl Sun. Food C G

② Little London to Farley Green

Continue down the hill from Little London and under the railway. After a further stretch of downhill riding you'll come to the T-junction at Brook. Turn left into Brook Hill, still following the signposts for 'Farley Green & Shamley Green'. There is a phone box on the left shortly after the

St Michael's church, Farley Green

junction. From Brook the road climbs and bends towards Farley Green, passing Middle Farm (just over 3 miles) on the way.

Farley Green: *This small hamlet features in few books about Surrey. Granted it has none of the noteworthy features of some other villages, but it is nonetheless a very pleasant spot. Shophouse Lane, on the eastern edge of the green, is a tarred road, but crossing the green is the unmade Ride Lane, known locally as Smugglers' Way. In the hills to the south it exists as a deep, narrow cutting through the sandstone, reminding us of what roads in this area used to be like before they were surfaced. If St Michael's Church looks like a 19th century wooden barn, that's because it used to be one. It was converted to its present use in 1929. You can find it along a short track off Shophouse Lane.*

☞ *The shorter and longer routes divide at Farley Green. The longer one – see stage √ – crosses Farley Heath to Shamley Green, returning to Winterfold up the scarp slope of the hills. This adds another 3 miles and a substantial climb to the ride but it goes through very attractive scenery, and has the benefit of passing the pubs and shops at Shamley Green.*

③ Farley Green to Winterfold *short route*

Turn left at Farley Green into Shophouse Lane in the direction of 'Smithwood Common & Cranleigh'. Ahead of you are the considerable buildings of Farley Green Hall Farm, beyond which Shophouse Lane takes on the character of a typical narrow country byway, lined by high hedges which mask the fact that there are quite a few houses along this stretch.

At the next junction, take the road to the right, which is signposted 'Winterfold'. Shophouse Farm, on the right, is about 4 miles from the start of the ride. A short distance further on the road turns to the left and then to the right as it joins Row Lane.

The outlying houses of Farley Green are soon left behind and the lane then enters the woods – Winterfold Forest on the left and Helmet Copse on the right. Both are commercial woodlands, and access is limited to public footpaths and bridleways. The lane passes an entrance into the forest, then it narrows and begins to climb in earnest.

At the bend just beyond the second 'SLOW' warning the lane crosses the course of an old Roman road, but there are no traces of it to be seen here (see panel 'The Roman Temple on Farley Heath'). Shortly after this bend the road levels out and passes the driveway leading to Winterfold Cottage (just under 5 miles). A stretch of wooded heathland brings you to the junction with Winterfold Heath Road, signposted 'Ewhurst & Shere'. Turn left and follow the directions in stage ⑤.

√ Farley Green to Winterfold *longer route*

From Farley Green continue along August Lane (signposted 'Farley Heath & Shamley Green') which soon begins to climb towards the open heath. There are two Hurtwood Control car parks on the right of the road, the first a small one, the second (no 8) larger. On the right of the road immediately before the entrance to the second car park (just under 4 miles) is the site of the Roman temple of Farley Heath. You can reach it by going through the car park gate and turning right.

The heathland continues for another half mile beyond the temple and then the lane descends into the valley of the Bramley Stream. Upper Woodhill Farm, on the left, has a truly delightful cottage garden, offering a blaze of colour during the summer. After that the lane passes the

The Roman Temple on Farley Heath

On Farley Heath are the remains of a Romano-British temple which is thought to date from the 1st century AD. It was one of the few temples in Britain to remain in use throughout the period of the Roman occupation – more than 300 years. The building consisted of a square tower about two storeys in height – the shrine itself – surrounded by a portico or verandah, all of which stood in an enclosure called a temenos. The shrine was not like a modern church, but was looked upon as the dwelling place of the gods.

The Romans were happy to adopt and adapt local religions, provided they weren't political in nature (a problem they had with both the Druids and the Christians). They took the pragmatic view that there was no point in upsetting local gods, just in case there might be something to them! This resulted in a blend of religions and gods, which is why most temples in Britain are referred to as Romano-British. The Farley Heath temple was dedicated to the Celtic gods Sucellus, Nantosvelta, and Taranis (the Celtic equivalent of the Roman Vulcan) and may have been associated with the iron industry.

Farley Heath was first excavated by the antiquarian Martin Tupper of Albury in the mid-19th century; sadly, due to the lack of archaeological skills at that time, much valuable evidence was destroyed during this excavation, but a priest's crown, a unique sceptre binding, and many coins were discovered. Most of these items are now in the British Museum. The site was re-excavated in the 1930s, and again in 1995.

It was once thought there was a complete Roman town on Farley Heath (many old local history books describe the site as such) but this is not the case. However, Roman temples were not simply religious sites. They also acted as markets and were often placed near the borders of tribal areas – neutral zones, as it were, where trade could be carried on.

The temple on Farley Heath was reached by a road which branched off Stane Street, the Romans' London–Chichester road, diverging at Rowhook, just over the Sussex border. Apart from one minor deviation where it climbed Winterfold Hill, the road followed a perfectly straight alignment throughout its course. Signs of the branch road have been found along much of its course across the Weald Clay but there are few indications of it once it reaches the Greensand Hills. It is not clear if it came to a dead end at Farley Heath or if it continued north-westwards, either through Guildford or over the North Downs near Newlands Corner, and then on towards Bracknell or Staines.

junction with Madgehole Lane, with Woodhill Farm opposite on the right, followed by Woodhill Manor. They occupy an idyllic situation, tucked away in a small side valley.

Shortly after Woodhill Manor are a couple of small, well-kept ponds, formed by damming the little stream which flows down the valley (5 miles). The final run downhill passes Reel Hall Farm and Reel Hall itself. A short distance further on is Tanyard Farm, where there used to be a tannery, an industry which relied on the plentiful local supplies of water.

Even if you know Shamley Green from the main Cranleigh road, the approach from Farley Heath gives a totally different view of the village. The sign 'Slow! Ducks Crossing' warns you that around the corner is the green with its small pond. Take the right-hand branch when the road forks just before the pond, as this takes you into the centre of the village for the shop, post office, telephone box and pubs.

Shamley Green: *There's nothing really spectacular here, but when the different elements are put together they make up what, for many people, is the typical English village – a large green with its cricket pitch, houses and a couple of pubs scattered around its edge. The houses are a mixture, some ancient, some not so old, and others quite modern, but they all seem to fit well together. The only obvious feature missing from the village scene is the church. That's to be found on top of a slight rise beside the road to the south.*

🍺 *The Red Lion, The Green. Free house. 01483 892202. Open all day. Food G Rest Acc*

🍺 *The Bricklayer's Arms, The Green. Courage. 01483 898377. Open all day. Food (lunchtime only) G*

🥤 *Village Stores, The Green. Open 8–1, 2– 5.30 (Sat 2–4), Sun 9–12.30 only*

Turn left onto the B2128 in the direction of Cranleigh. The road is fairly busy, especially at commuting times, so take care. Pass the Bricklayer's Arms pub and make the short but sharp climb past the delightfully-named Plonks Farm up the rise on which Christ Church is situated (6 miles). From there the road runs gently downhill towards Stroud Common, where the lane from Woodhill joins.

About 250 yards beyond the junction turn left into the entrance of the Willinghurst Estate (not quite 7 miles).

☞ *The next part of the ride is along the tarred driveway of Willinghurst House and then along a rather rough sandy track which climbs across the steep face of the hillside. If you would prefer to avoid this route, follow the very pleasant alternative via Smithwood Common on page 92.*

The driveway, a public bridleway, climbs quite steeply, although this may not be immediately obvious, except for the effort it demands. But look back from the top of the slope, shortly before the farmhouse, and the difference in height is obvious. You can also see Hascombe Hill away in the distance at the end of the range of hills behind you. When the drive forks at the entrance to Willinghurst Farm keep to the right-hand branch which bypasses the old farmhouse and the cluster of buildings around it.

Willinghurst: *The farm is old and was built at the point where the Greensand hills meet the Weald clay in the valley. Water percolates through the sandy soil of the hills until it meets the impermeable clay barrier beneath, with the result that springs emerge from the ground all along the line of the join between the geological strata. Clearly, this springline was an ideal place to build a farmstead, and there are several hereabouts. There is a pond in the garden of the farmhouse, which was formed by blocking one of the spring-fed streams with a* *substantial dam; you cannot see it from the driveway but a public footpath runs through the garden past it. The pond may be the remains of an old ironworks.*

Willinghurst House is a late Victorian building, originally called Lapscombe after a nearby farm. It was built on the site of an intriguingly-named farmstead called 'Sparelands', which was situated in the centre of a small detached part of the Parish of Ewhurst. Willinghurst Lake, now used as a coarse fishery, was created as an adjunct to the house. The estate is now used mainly for forestry and sporting pursuits.

Continue past the modern farm buildings and the bungalows immediately after them. The next stretch of the drive passes through what almost looks to be parkland with the towering hills as a backdrop. To the right, Willinghurst Lake can be seen down among the trees. As the drive bends to the right, turn left onto a very sandy

track which leads into an area of coppiced woodland and immediately begins to climb steeply straight up the hillside.

Coppicing *is a method of woodland management which has been practised since ancient times, though few woods are now worked in this way. It involves cutting back a tree to its 'stool' (or stump). The outer, living, ring of the tree then puts out new shoots which grow into poles, producing a crop every 7 to 15 years. The wood is used for a variety of purposes including fencing, pulp, hop and bean poles, charcoal, and even firewood. Far from being a destructive process, coppicing seems to encourage long life in a tree and also provides the perfect habitat for many birds and plants.*

The coppice being grown at Willinghurst is sweet chestnut. After harvesting, the poles of this wood are normally split and used to make roll-up fencing. In times past it was favoured for producing the long straight poles needed for hop-growing.

Shamley Green

The Hurtwood

The Hurtwood gets its name from the local word for bilberries – hurts – which grow profusely on the light, sandy soils of the Greensand hills. (There's another Hurtwood between Hascombe and Hambledon, a village not far from Godalming called Hurtmore, and a Hurt Hill near Hindhead.)

The Hurtwood centred around Peaslake is part of the Manor of Shere, which has been in the ownership of the Bray family ever since it was granted to Sir Reginald Bray by King Henry VII in 1497. Sir Reginald was one of the King's ministers and was rewarded with the manor when its previous holder was executed for high treason.

Another noteworthy lord of the manor was William Bray, who died in 1832 at the age of 97. When the Rev Owen Manning, the vicar of Godalming, began to go blind he had to abandon his life's work of writing a History of Surrey. William Bray took on the task and completed the first volume in 1804. By the time the third volume was published Bray was 78! 'Manning & Bray' is still regarded as one of the key sources for anyone interested in the county's history.

William Bray also edited the 'Memoirs' of John Evelyn, the diarist who lived at Wotton House, and he is credited with having planted the first Scots Pines in the Hurtwood, back in 1778.

In 1926 another Reginald Bray granted a right of public access to much of his land for 'air and exercise' under the 1925 Law of Property Act. He was joined by other local landowners, including the Albury Estate, so that the area involved is about 4,000 acres. It includes much of the Hurtwood, Winterfold Heath, Shere Heath, Farley Heath, and parts of Smithwood and Blackheath Commons, and is now cared for by the Hurtwood Control Committee, a registered charity.

As a result, the people of Surrey and its surrounding counties have been given a truly magnificent facility for recreation. Rambling and horse riding are the most common activities, along with bird-watching and other nature studies, but one of the most fascinating and unlikely sports which takes place there nowadays is husky racing!

NOTE: Although the public is allowed onto most of the Hurtwood, access for cyclists is rightly restricted to public roads and bridleways throughout the area. On the soft, sandy soil bike tyres – especially those of mountain bikes – can do tremendous damage and harm fragile plants and wildlife, so please do respect this limitation. If you want to go elsewhere in the Hurtwood, please park your bike and do so on foot.

View from Winterfold Hill

The prospect of the climb in front of you may look daunting from your vantage point at the bottom of the track, but don't be too concerned. Within a hundred yards you'll come to a junction where you turn right onto a track which has a much easier gradient. Even so, you may well find you have to walk all or part of the way as it winds round the hillside.

The track is rough, not helped by recent forestry work which has churned-up the surface. However, the views to the right over the Weald are superb, although they will eventually be blocked out as the young trees grow. Willinghurst House is below the track to the right.

Continue the long climb to the top of the hill. There the track merges with another (8 miles). Join this, and keep going roughly in the same direction. Pass an old sandpit which has been used as a dumping ground in recent years, but thankfully is now becoming overgrown, hiding the rubbish.

In about 200 yards the track comes out onto the road. Turn left and climb the last short stretch of the hill. Pass the entrance to car park 6, and then turn right at the junction with Winterfold Heath Road to rejoin the shorter route. (Add 3 miles to the distances given from this point on.)

⑤ **Winterfold to Peaslake**

Winterfold Heath Road starts with a short climb, but then the road becomes more undulating. Some electricity power lines cross it after which it levels out. Watch out for the gateway on the right which leads into Hurtwood Control car park 5 at Winterfold Hill. Turn into the car park and pause to enjoy the superb views.

Winterfold Hill *may not be the highest spot in the Surrey Hills (although it is nearly 700 feet above sea level), but it is the least-known and therefore probably the most peaceful viewpoint around.*

The view from the car park looks almost due south. The expanse of water in the middle distance is Vachery Pond, a natural pool which was enlarged to act as a reservoir for the Wey and Arun Junction Canal (see Ride I). It is over 3 miles away.

Between you and the Pond is the village – the inhabitants insist it is a village, supposedly the largest in England, and not a town – of Cranleigh. It is well-masked by the trees, though, and you may find it hard to accept that it is really there! In the distance are the South Downs, blocking your view of the sea. The gap in the Downs to the left marks the course of the River Arun, flowing down through Arundel to the sea at Littlehampton.

The best time to come here is on a clear spring day. In summer, haze and pollution tends to spoil the more distant view.

Continue along Winterfold Heath Road from the car park, but don't be in too much of a hurry. This area is rich in wildlife and if you are observant and quiet you might catch sight of a deer for an instant before it bounds away into the undergrowth.

Just beyond the driveway to Hurtwood House is a deep gulley on the right which leads down into Jelley's Hollow (almost 6 miles). The private drive to the left of the gulley is part of the old Roman road to Farley Heath. Keep going past another two Hurtwood Control car parks until you come to a T-junction. (Lock up your bike in car park 4 if you want to walk up to the Ewhurst Windmill. The best route is via the footpath opposite the junction.)

Turn left at the junction and enjoy the half-mile downhill run to the junction with Hound House Road. Turn right there, in the direction of Ewhurst and Cranleigh,

for a thankfully short uphill stretch to the junction with Lawbrook Lane, signposted 'Peaslake' (7 miles).

☞ *At this point you have a choice. You can either turn into Lawbrook Lane to return directly to Peaslake, or you can continue on down the hill past the Windmill pub, and return to Peaslake along the road from Ewhurst.*

Via Lawbrook Lane

Turn left into Lawbrook Lane and enjoy a two-mile downhill run back to Peaslake.

At the junction between Lawbrook Lane and the charmingly-named Walking Bottom (a short way beyond the 8 mile point) take the right-hand fork – it is marked as the main road and signed 'Peaslake'. From there continue down the hill, past the church.

Keep an eye out for the house called 'Copper Beech', which has a magnificent example of the species in its garden. The Hurtwood Inn is just ahead and you are back in Peaslake. Turn left into Pond Lane immediately after the inn to return to the car park.

Via the Windmill Inn

From the junction with Lawbrook Lane go straight on down the hill. Shortly after the junction you'll pass the entrance to Hurtwood Control car park 3, which is the best place to leave your bike if you want to walk to the top of Pitch Hill, 843 feet high. The footpath from here is a good deal less steep than that which starts opposite the Windmill Inn.

A little further down the hill you will come to the Windmill Inn. The present building replaced a 17th century inn which burned down in 1906. It is reputed to have been yet another well-known smugglers' haunt.

The Windmill Inn. Free house. 01483 277566. Opens at 11.30. Food Rest

If you want to link with Ride A in Volume 2 of this series, keep going down the hill from The Windmill Inn until you come to Ewhurst village.

Beyond the Windmill you can take either of the next two turnings on the left, since they both bring you to the same place, but if you choose the second you will go so far down the hill you'll have to climb back up again. If you choose the first turning, Moon Hall Road, go left into Peaslake Road when you get to the junction at its end (8 miles).

Woolpit Wood, on the south-facing hillside to your right, was devastated when it took the full force of the 100mph winds sweeping up from the Channel coast during the Great Storm in the early hours of October 16th, 1987. As the road undulates along you can see the impressive buildings of the Duke of Kent School on the left, and shortly afterwards you will pass its entrance.

The Duke of Kent School *originated as a school run by the RAF Benevolent Fund, moving to Ewhurst in 1976 when it merged with Woolpits (previously St Thomas' of Canterbury) School. It is named in honour of George, Duke of Kent, who was killed on active service in 1942.*

The school was built in 1885 as a house for Sir Henry Doulton, of pottery and sanitaryware fame, and was occupied by his descendants until World War II when, like many other large houses in Surrey, it was taken over by the army. It became a school after the war.

A downhill run follows, and the road begins to enter the narrower wooded valley which leads to Peaslake. On the right is a small pond at the 9 mile mark, shortly before an S-bend in the road. A

Peaslake

pleasant ride through the pine woods takes you past Gasson Farm and on down the hill and into Peaslake. In the centre of the village take Pond Lane to get back to the car park (fractionally under 10 miles).

Peaslake: The odd thing about Peaslake is the way it is left out of most Surrey books and guides. Even Eric Parker, in his 'Highways and Byways in Surrey', totally ignored the village, to the extent of leaving it off his map of the county. Maybe that's because the village is fairly recently developed, as villages go. When the Ordnance Survey produced their first detailed map of the area in about 1871, the only houses were a few clustered around the road junction and beside the Ewhurst road. The place didn't even warrant a church! Its only religious connection was the Quaker Burying Place on Lawbrook Lane.

The village grew during the late Victorian, Edwardian and subsequent periods and is now a thriving community. The famous conductor Sir Adrian Boult lived there for a time.

At one time there was actually a pond in Pond Lane. The noted rambler and writer of the inter-war period, S P B Mais, described its surface as being 'the colour of pea soup'. Perhaps that's how the village came to be named! However, you'll hunt in vain to find the pond now; it's filled in and your car is probably parked on its site.

📖 *At Peaslake you can link with Ride B in Volume 2, East Surrey.*

🍺 *The Hurtwood Inn, Walking Bottom. Free house. 01306 730851. Open all day. Food C G Rest Acc, also morning coffee and afternoon teas.*

🛒 *Peaslake Village Stores and PO. Open 8–8 (Sun 9–8)*

Alternative sections of route

① Peaslake to Little London

Continue along Lawbrook Lane past the entrance to the bridleway. After Lawbrook House (just under 1 mile) the lane climbs considerably for just over a quarter of a mile through a deep sandstone cutting. At the end of the lane turn left along Hook Lane in the direction signposted 'Shere'. Follow the road past Burrows Lea Farm and on to the junction with Hound House Road by the railway bridge. Turn right, cross the railway, then turn left immediately afterwards as signed for 'Farley Green & Albury' (2 miles).

Continue to the next junction where you bear left into Little London, signposted 'Farley Green & Shamley Green'. The main route joins from the left at this point. The alternative is about a quarter of a mile longer than the main route.

√ Farley Green to Winterfold *longer route*

📖 *This diversion avoids the steep and very sandy track up the hillside at Willinghurst.*

Continue along the B2128 past the entrance to the Willinghurst Estate and to the Lake and Fishery (7 miles). At the roundabout turn left, passing the Gaston Gate Garage, which has a handy shop. After little more than 100 yards, turn left again into Smithwood Common Road. It is signposted 'Cranleigh School & Smithwood Common'.

The road passes Smithwood House on the right and Smithwood Farm on the left, both of which are well worth a pause to give you a chance to appreciate them. A short distance after the farm turn left into Alderbrook Road, which is signposted 'Winterfold'. Soon after the junction you will pass another entrance into the Willinghurst Estate. At one time the land on both sides of the road was open common and there was a fairly large pond on the left, but only a marshy area now remains. There was also a smithy on the edge of the common to the left.

From this point the climb to Winterfold Heath begins. The lane passes Pittance Farm (just over 8 miles), the name of which surely does not reflect its present value! Perhaps in years gone by it was difficult for the farmer to make a living on these lands, or was a pittance the landowner's assessment of the rent he received for the farm?

Just after the driveway to Lapscombe Farm the climbs steepens to 1 in 7, so don't be embarrassed about getting off and walking if you haven't already done so!

The road passes the entrance to the Alderbrook estate – unlike Willinghurst on the other side of the road, the house itself has been demolished. Now it climbs through a cutting and soon passes the exit of the bridleway which is on the route through Willinghurst. Continue up the hill past car park 6 and turn right at the junction with Winterfold Heath Road. (Add 3¾ miles to the distances given for the rest of the ride, which are based on those for the shorter ride.)

Smithwood Common

Ride F:
Ups and Downs

Newlands Corner • Pewley Down • Guildford • Hogs Back • Compton •
Hurtmore • Eashing • Godalming • Catteshall • Chinthurst • Great Tangley •
Blackheath • Farley Green • Little London • Shere • Newlands Corner

Distance: 24 miles approx
Landranger Maps: 186 & 187
Pathfinder Maps: 1225 & 1226

This is a ride of startling contrasts. It includes the scenic North Downs ridge, the main streets of Guildford and Godalming, the Greensand hills, heathland, and the charming countryside of the valleys of the River Wey and its tributary, the Tillingbourne.

The ride is designed for a full day. Not only is it strenuous – it includes two ascents of the North Downs and climbs some lesser ridges as well – but also there is much to see on the way. Sunday might be the best day for it, as the towns of Guildford and Godalming are quiet then, and you will have a better chance to observe their rich architectural heritage. Don't be put off by the fact that the ride passes through these town centres; the route has been carefully chosen to involve as little built-up area as possible.

Roads in this corner of Surrey are busy, and so – for safety as well as pleasure – the ride makes extensive use of bridleways. While many of these are in reasonable condition, mountain bikes will have a definite advantage, especially on those that are very sandy. In some cases you may have to get off and walk.

Starting Points

Start at the Newlands Corner car park on the A25 Guildford–Dorking road (grid reference TQ 043492). It has toilet and refreshment facilities, and an information point, but it can get crowded on fine days so arrive early.

If you would rather climb the Downs at the start of the ride instead of the end, there is a car park at the Silent Pool, about a mile further down the A25 near Albury. From here you join stage ⑩ of the route by cycling east along the A25 for just over half a mile to the junction with Combe

Lane. There are public car parks in Guildford and Godalming, at Chinthurst (off the B2128 north of Wonersh, but the entrance is well hidden) and at Blackheath. The latter two are free.

≢ The route passes stations at Guildford and Godalming, both on the London Waterloo–Portsmouth line of South West Trains. Guildford is also served by the South West Trains' Ascot–Aldershot–Guildford services and Thames Trains' Reading–Gatwick line.

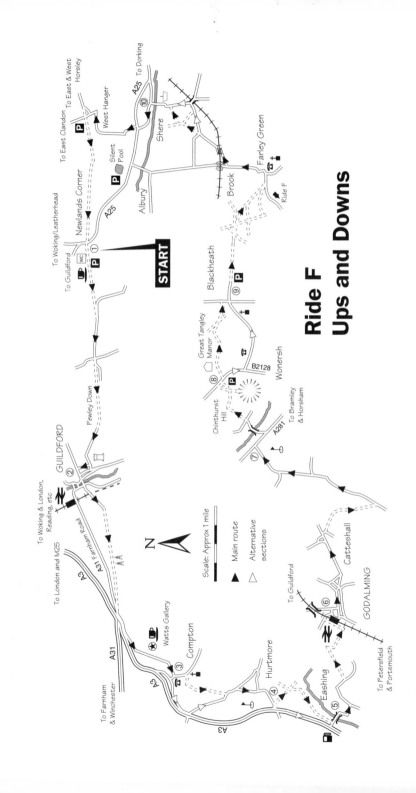

Ride F
Ups and Downs

Scale: Approx 1 mile

▲ Main route
△ Alternative sections

N

START

To Woking/Leatherhead
To Guildford
Newlands Corner
A25
Silent Pool
Albury
West Hanger
Shere
A25 To Dorking
To East & West Horsley
To East Clandon
To Dorking

⑩
Farley Green
Brook
Ride F

Pewley Down

GUILDFORD
②

To Woking & London,
Reading, etc

A31 Farnham Road

A3
To London and M25

A31
To Farnham
& Winchester

Watts Gallery
Compton
③

Hurtmore
④

A3

Eashing
⑤

To Petersfield
& Portsmouth

GODALMING

Catteshall
To Guildford
⑥

⑦
A281
To Bramley
& Horsham

Chinthurst
Hill

B2128
Wonersh

⑧
Great Tangley
Manor

Blackheath
⑨

The Route in Brief

① Leave CP at west end and pass barrier onto track. Track eventually merges into road (White Lane). Follow it for half mile, then at next junc keep SO into Longdown Road, but take narrow path on R as road curves to L. Path leads to Pewley Down – follow track parallel to hedge on R, curving slightly R towards houses. Leave down by Pewley Hill. Dismount at Castle Square and TR into Tunsgate. Go through arch and TL into High St, still walking.

② At bottom of High St use subway to cross road to Town Bridge. On far side of river cross road into The Mount. Climb hill and keep SO past cemetery to end of tarred road (Henley Fort). Pass gate onto trackway. At end TL onto Farnham Road then L into Down Lane, SP Compton. TL again just before lane joins A3. Continue to junc with The Street, the B3000.

③ TL onto The Street for 200 yds, then TR into unmade Eastbury Lane (opp Old Post Office). Keep going until lane divides, then take BW to L across fields and up climb through wood into open field. Keep to L edge of field, then through trees to road, opposite school, and TL. After 300 yds TR into Summers Lane then TR into Hurtmore Road. Continue through Hurtmore then TR, SP A3 Portsmouth.

√ TR immediately into Pub CP then R again through underpass to reach start of BW. At sandy junc after 400 yds TR onto another BW and up short slope. Continue to Lower Eashing Farm, then TL.

⑤ Cross bridge and follow road to R past pub and up hill to TJ. TL and follow road round bend to R past Eashing Farm. After 300 yds TL onto farm track (BW). Pass Halfway House Farm and round sharp bend to R. Follow BW down hill and beside railway to TJ with Westbrook Road and TR

under railway. At Stn Approach TL, then TR into Church Street. Dismount at 'Pepperpot' and TL along High St.

≈ At far end of High St TR into Wharf Lane (still walking) then cross relief road at lights into Catteshall Lane. Remount and follow Catteshall Lane to end, turning R at mini-roundabout on way. Walk along short 'No Entry' stretch on R to reach Ram cider house.

TR at Ram into lane to Catteshall Manor gates, then TL onto BW past Catteshall Farm. Follow track for 1 mile to Munstead Heath Road, then TL for another mile. At next junc keep SO, SP Shalford & Guildford, to junc with A281.

Δ TR onto main road for 400 yds then L into Tannery Lane (Gosden Common). Cross bridges to TJ, then take BW opposite past Chinthurst Farm. Follow BW for about half mile to TJ of paths. TL to reach road (B2128) then TR.

⑧ After 75 yds TL onto BW, SP Gt Tangley Manor Farm. Pass the manor, then SO at next junc of paths onto a narrower uphill section. Continue through woods, keeping to main track past 'Tangley Way' to road. TR, then L at XR past Villagers pub.

⑨ From pub keep SO, through CP onto BW 302. After half a mile FR onto BW 232. Down short hill then merge into track from houses which leads to road. TL through Farley Green, then follow SP for Albury. At bottom of dip TR into Brook Lane. At TJ at far end SO onto BW. When BW divides FR. At end join short road then TL into Shere.

⑩ Through village then TL at TJ. Keep on to A25 then TR and immediately L into Combe Lane. Climb steep hill then at next junc TL (SO) into Staple Lane. After 100 yds TL onto North Downs Way (BW) and follow it back to Newlands Corner.

The Ride

① Newlands Corner to Guildford

Head west through the Newlands Corner car park (away from the road entrance), and pass the barrier that keeps cars off the track beyond. Now a section of the North Downs Way, this track was probably once a drove road. After a while it narrows and winds through the trees.

After a mile a road (White Lane) appears on the left and the track eventually merges into it. Follow the road for half a mile and then, at the next junction, continue straight ahead into Longdown Road but only for a few yards. As the road curves to the left, take the narrow path, signed as a bridleway, on the right. At first it is hemmed in by garden fences and walls, but then it opens out giving views over the downs and finally emerges onto the open space of Pewley Down.

Keep to the main track across the Down – it runs parallel to, but about 10 yards out from the hedge, curving slightly to the right as it heads towards some houses. Leave the down by Pewley Hill which heads down past the reservoir and Semaphore House.

Semaphore House *is one of a chain of semaphore towers which linked the Admiralty in London with Portsmouth in the days before the electric telegraph. Most have long been demolished but this one survives, as does that at Chatley Heath (near the M25/A3 junction) which has been preserved and is open to the public (see Ride B).*

The stations enabled the time signal to be sent from Greenwich to Portsmouth and acknowledged in about half a minute. Longer messages took about 15 minutes. The roof-top cupola was added in 1851 after its closure.

At the foot of Pewley Hill is Castle Square – the ruined keep of Guildford Castle can be seen on the left. Cross over into Tunsgate, then dismount and walk through the arch into the High Street.

From there the next stage of the route can be seen by looking down the hill – over the river bridge at the bottom and up the road directly opposite on the far bank. This is the original road through Guildford, once the main London–Winchester highway.

Guildford *is situated where the River Wey cuts a gap through the chalk hills of the North Downs. Its name probably means the Golden Ford, referring either to the colour of the summer buttercups and celandine on the slopes of Guildown on the west side of the valley or to the sandy silt washed down from the higher reaches of the river.*

The basic layout of the town originated in Saxon times, and its buildings include survivals from every century from the 11th onwards. A passing visit on a bike is hardly the best way to explore the town, but have a look at some of the notable buildings as you go by.

At the eastern (top) end of the High Street are the 16th century Royal Grammar School, the 17th century Abbot's Hospital, and the 18th century Holy Trinity Church. In the centre of the High Street, the Tunsgate Arch was once the facade of the corn exchange and became an archway only in the 1930s.

The Guildhall, with its projecting clock, (see illustration) is probably the building most readily identified with the town. At the lower end of the High Street, Quarry Street has many wonderful buildings including St Mary's Church, (the tower of which is Saxon), the Guildford Museum, and the Castle Arch. The Castle keep is 12th century and is surrounded by the remains of the royal palace, which was a favourite during the reign of Henry III (1216–72). The council has ambitious plans for the future of the keep and grounds.

Guildford was an important coaching stop on the Portsmouth road in the 18th and 19th centuries. Of the 19 inns in the High Street which once served the trade only the Angel remains. The Crown, the White Hart, the Red Lion (at which Samuel Pepys was a regular visitor), and the others have now gone, but there are numerous shops, pubs and other refreshment facilities in the town for today's travellers.

② Guildford to Compton

Walk your bike down the High Street to the very bottom. The modern dual carriageway of Millbrook cuts across the line of the old thoroughfare, and you will have to use the underpass to reach the pedestrianised Town Bridge.

On the far side of the river, cross the road into The Mount, the original route out of Guildford to the Hog's Back above. The road is so steep that in coaching days an extra pair of horses was kept at the bottom to provide assistance, until the present Farnham Road was built around 1800 to ease the gradient. So don't feel ashamed if you have to walk up the hill; it will give you a chance to look at the houses of the medieval suburbs of Guildford on its lower slopes.

Further up the hill on the left is Guildford cemetery, in which is the grave of Lewis Carroll, author of *Alice in Wonderland.*

The formal road soon comes to an end (about 3½ miles from the start) but a broad tarred track continues. It is bordered by hedges but gaps give access to the neighbouring open fields from where there are superb views to be had. To the north is the cathedral on Stag Hill, with Woking (its BAT building standing out) in the middle distance. On a clear day some of the taller buildings in the centre of London can be seen on the horizon.

Guildford from Guildown

The Hog's Back trackway

After a further half-mile the tarred track turns into a school camp on the site of Henley Fort. Continue straight ahead, passing around a gate onto a narrower gravelled trackway. Half a mile further on bollards mark the start of a tarred (if rather potholed!) section of the trackway which provides access to the TV and radio station on the left. After another half-mile (5 miles from the start) the trackway ends and you emerge onto the A31.

Turn left off the A31 immediately, into Down Lane, following the sign for Compton. This may look like a quiet country lane but be wary because this short stretch is a well-used link between Guildford town centre and the A3. Just a few yards before the A3's dual carriageway, turn left onto the lane which runs downhill beside, but at a lower level than, the main road, which soon curves away.

On the left as the lane enters the village of Compton is the Watts Gallery, by the entrance to which are signs indicating the North Downs Way long-distance path, here following the course of the Pilgrims' Way. Further on, beyond Coneycroft Farm, is the Watts Memorial Chapel. Continue along Down Lane to its junction with The Street. This road is the B3000 linking Godalming with the A3 and A31 roads and is very busy, so take great care.

Compton: *The small village has two main claims to fame. The first is its church, dedicated to St Nicholas. Its many fascinating architectural features are described in a short guide book which is excellent value at 50p. The tower and parts of the walls are Saxon, while much of the rest is Norman, including its rare and beautiful double-storey sanctuary. The wooden balustrade of the upper storey, carved from a single large plank, is reputed to* be the oldest piece of Norman woodwork in England.

Inside the church the white stone of the walls and the simple Norman arches give the building a tremendous air of lightness and peace. Many would call this Surrey's most beautiful church and it is hard to disagree; do not miss it.

The village's other claim to fame is as the home of George Frederick Watts, a prolific Victorian artist and sculptor and one of the first members of the Order of Merit. Shortly before he died in 1904 he and his wife Mary built the Watts Gallery to display many examples of his work – a wide variety of paintings of all types, sketches, and full-size models for statues, including that of Tennyson and the immense work called 'Physical Energy', the finished version of which is in Kensington Gardens. Also on display are some of his many portraits of eminent Victorians.

A long single-storey building set in pleasant gardens, the gallery resembles a cross between a Surrey cottage and what has been described as a 'Spanish hacienda'. Mary also designed the Watts Chapel in the local cemetery, an unusual building of red brick and terracotta, now Grade I listed.

The Watts Gallery is open from 2pm to 6pm (4pm in winter) every day except Thursday; on Wednesdays and Saturdays it is also open from 11am to 1pm. Entrance is free, but the charitable trust which runs the gallery will appreciate a contribution. The Teashop next door to the gallery is open from 10.30am to 5.30pm seven days a week and serves home-cooked lunches and teas.

🍴 The Harrow Inn, The Street (about 400 yards beyond the church). Friary Meux. 01483 810379. Open 8am Mon–Fri (for breakfast), 9am Sat, 10am Sun. Food (mornings – as opening – and eves) C G Acc.

③ Compton to Hurtmore

☞ An alternative route for this section using public roads instead of the bridleway is given on page 112.

Double sanctuary in Compton church

Turn left out of Down Lane and go down The Street for about 200 yards. At the Old Post Office (now an antiques shop) turn right into the unmade Eastbury Lane, ignoring the fact that it is marked as a cul-de-sac.

Go along this lane as far as it will take you, passing the entrances to various properties, until you come to a sign indicating a bridleway to the left and a footpath straight ahead. Take the bridleway, which is in a good state but can sometimes be overgrown with nettles. From the slope up the hill towards the wood there is an excellent view back towards the village and its church. Within the wood there are one or two short, steep climbs and maybe a few muddy patches. A final steep climb leads to an open field.

Follow the bridleway along the left-hand edge of the field and into the trees at the far end. After a few yards it emerges onto the road at Prior's Field School (7 miles).

Turn left down the road for about 300 yards, then fork right into the very narrow Summers Lane. At the far end turn right into Hurtmore Road, and follow this down the hill all the way through Hurtmore village to the A3 turn-off, just before the underpass.

√ Hurtmore to Eashing

☞ *This stage includes a stretch of bridleway which may not be in ideal condition. An alternative route is described on page 112, but it means using the A3.*

Turn right in the direction signed 'A3 Portsmouth', then right again into the car park of The Squirrels restaurant. The cottages by the car park date back to about 1500. Bear round to the right to find the start of the bridleway, which heads back under the road through an under-pass. For 400 yards it is tarred but then there is a sudden change.

The bridleway passes the garden of a large cottage on the left, then, immediately before a sandy junction of paths, turn right onto a very narrow bridleway which soon climbs a short slope. This takes you into the valley of the Wey, although you can hardly see the river as it is hidden by the trees and the marshy reed beds through which it meanders. The scenery is pleasant, although some overhead power cables don't enhance it. The bridleway is fairly narrow and fenced on both sides, and parts can be very muddy in wet conditions.

Continuing up the valley, pass the World War II 'pillbox'. Did someone really expect the Germans to invade through the marshy river valley instead of along the main road just a short distance away? Just beyond the pillbox the bridleway passes through a gate onto a concrete farm track which leads towards the buildings of Lower Eashing Farm, where it emerges onto the road (8½ miles). To the right, beside the A3, is a garage with a shop and toilets. Unless you need these facilities, turn left towards the river.

Eashing is only a small hamlet but one which is full of history. Originally called 'Escingum', it was established by King Alfred (of burnt cakes fame) as a Saxon burh (from which word today's 'borough' is derived) late in the 9th century. The burh itself was on top of the cliffs above the east bank of the river and was probably a defensive fort rather than a commercial centre. It was soon replaced by the burh at Guildford.

The most obvious historical feature in Eashing today is the bridge over the River Wey, or more properly bridges, since there are two of them separated by an island in the river. They probably date from the 13th century. Several similar bridges cross the Wey in this area and it is thought they were built by the monks of Waverley Abbey when great floods destroyed the existing bridges. In 1901 the Old Guildford Society gave Eashing Bridges to the newly-formed National Trust, and in 1922 the local architect Hugh Thackeray Turner donated the nearby cottages as well.

There was a mill at Eashing for hundreds of years. The last one had been disused for some time and was finally demolished in 1997 to make way for a scheme to redevelop the site for offices. It was hardly the most scenic of buildings, and one hopes that the development will produce something more in keeping with the beauty of the area.

🍺 *The Stag Inn. Friary Meux. 01483 421568.*

⑤ Eashing to Godalming

Cross the bridges, then follow the road round to the right past the pub and up the hill. At the T-junction turn left into

Eashing Bridges

Cottages at Eashing

Eashing Lane and follow the road round the bend past Eashing Farm. The buildings of Charterhouse School, which moved here from London in 1872, can be seen across the fields to the left. About 300 yards beyond the bend turn into the farm track which branches off to the left; it is a public bridleway, although the sign may not be obvious.

The bridleway heads north-east for about half a mile, passing Halfway House farm, but then turns sharp right at a field gate. (Ignore the footpath which continues straight ahead through the gate and across the field.) The bridleway continues past some more farm buildings and then becomes a shady, narrow track, rough in places, descending a hill.

At the bottom of the hill the track comes out beside the railway line and becomes a tarred lane called New Way. As you pass the station you can see, through the hedge on the left, the Meath Home.

In the days before the coming of the railway this was an unspoilt area called 'The Valley of the Nightingale'. The lane ends at a junction with Westbrook Road.

Westbrook: *The Meath Home in Westbrook Road, now a home for asthma sufferers, was formerly called Westbrook House. In the 1790s it was owned by Nathaniel Godbold, an inventor of patent medicines, including his vegetable balsam. Clearly his was a profitable business. He also acquired the mills, the site of which is through the fence opposite the end of New Way. The old mill buildings have gone and the site on which they stood has been redeveloped into offices, but just inside the gate leading off Westbrook Road can be seen the remains of some mill machinery.*

An earlier occupant of Westbrook House was General James Oglethorpe who founded the American colony of Georgia. He brought the

Godalming

first American Indians to Britain, including the chief Tomochichi, and displayed them to the public in a Godalming inn.

Turn right out of New Way into Westbrook Road. Follow it under the railway and over the River Ock, passing the splendidly-restored vicarage on the left. At Station Approach turn left, but almost immediately afterwards turn right into the semi-pedestrianised Church Street. As its name implies, this leads past the fine medieval church, and brings you out in the High Street by the 'Pepperpot' – the Town Hall of 1814.

Here you will have to dismount in order to turn left into the High Street against the direction of the one-way system. However, don't be in too much of a hurry to pass through the town, for there is much to see and enjoy here.

Godalming: *The town's fortunes were based on wool and cloth-making thanks to the presence of rivers to power the mills and the suitability of the farmland for keeping sheep. Its best known feature is probably the Pepperpot, the nickname bestowed on the Town Hall built in 1814 to replace an earlier market or hundred house on the same site. The new building did not meet with universal approval however, for in the late 19th century there were several campaigns to have it demolished.*

For a brief tour of the town, turn right out of Church Street at the Pepperpot and proceed up the High Street. At the far end on the left is a shop with a facade of blue tiles in art deco style added to the original building. As the projecting bull's heads on either side suggest, this was once a butcher's shop. It subsequently became Stovold's dairy shop, but is now in use as a charity shop.

Turn right at the end of the High Street into Station Road and immediately left into Mill Lane. This and the surrounding streets form the historic centre of Godalming, and it is still full of interesting buildings. The Rose & Crown pub is thought to be one of the oldest in the

town, and was converted from three shops, including a baker's and a butcher's. Hatch Mill, now converted into offices, had its waterwheel replaced in 1940 by the turbine which can be seen on the outside of the building. Work your way back to the Pepperpot by way of Station Road, Mint Street, and Church Street (again).

A short distance further down the High Street is the last survivor of the town's coaching inns; several others still exist as buildings but have long been converted into shops. The King's Arms is appropriately named. Its guests have included Emperor Alexander I of Russia and King Frederick William of Prussia, who dined there a year before Waterloo.

Peter the Great also stayed there. He and his party of 20 managed to consume half a sheep, a quarter of lamb, ten pullets, 12 chickens, three quarts of brandy, six quarts of mulled wine, and seven dozen eggs, with salad in proportion. And that was breakfast! Dinner was five ribs of beef weighing three stone, one sheep, 56lbs of lamb, one shoulder and one loin of veal, both boiled, eight rabbits, two dozen and a half of sack, and one dozen claret.

≈ Godalming to Gosden Common

As you walk along the High Street, pop into Crown Court as you pass. Once an enclosed courtyard with just a narrow passage to the street, it was opened out in 1950 to provide an exit from the car park. The 'ancient' archway was in fact constructed from material salvaged from the demolished buildings. Under the archway, on the left, is a useful map of the town showing many of its historic features and buildings.

At the end of the High Street, bear right into Wharf Street (still walking), and cross the new relief road at the traffic lights to reach Catteshall Lane on the far side (by the Police Station). You can get back in the saddle now.

Follow Catteshall Lane to its end, turning right at the mini roundabout on the way. It passes through a curious mix of modern industrial units, housing, and a few rural remnants. At the far end, when the road bends to the left and becomes Catteshall Road. Catteshall Lane continues straight ahead, but there is a one-way system. Either walk past the 'No Entry' signs or work your way round the one-way system, then continue along the final length of Catteshall Lane to the Ram cider house.

The Ram must come close to being most people's idea of the perfect country pub with its timber beams and cottage garden, but at a first glance you could almost mistake it for a private home.

 *The Ram Cider House, Catteshall Lane. Free house. 01483 421093. Food G (also serves other beverages)*

Turn right at The Ram into a lane which leads to the entrance of Catteshall Manor; at its gates turn left onto another track signed 'Public Bridleway'. This is tarred at first, but after the entrance to Catteshall Farm it becomes rough in places and you may have to get off and push.

As you climb towards the top of the hill, note the great lumps of stone which can be seen in the surface of the track. This is the famous Bargate stone which has been quarried since Roman times and has been used in many local buildings. It occurs as large boulders (called 'doggers') in otherwise soft sand.

The track ends after almost a mile – the far end is used as a driveway to some cottages and is metalled. Turn left into Munstead Heath Road and begin to descend the hill. The view to the right over the surrounding

The Ram Cider House, Catteshall

country will give you a good idea of the height you have climbed since leaving Godalming. A mile down the road (13½ miles from the start) keep straight ahead at the T-junction, taking the road signposted 'Shalford & Guildford'. Another mile of generally downhill riding will bring you to the A281 Guildford to Bramley Road.

△ Gosden Common to Chinthurst

Turn right onto the main road for about 400 yards past Gosden House School and then turn left into Tannery Lane (although the road sign says 'Gosden Common'). The road climbs up over two bridges. The first crosses the Bramley Stream, and it is well worth trying to look over its high parapets. The second bridge is a complex affair which crosses both the disused Guildford to Horsham railway (now a footpath and cycleway) and the derelict Wey and Arun Junction Canal alongside it.

The canal was built 50 years before the railway and the old hump-backed bridge which crossed it was built into the much larger bridge needed to clear the rail tracks. It can still be seen by going down the footpath at the far end of the bridge.

The lane continues to a T-junction. Ignore the turnings to left and right and take the bridleway going straight ahead past Chinthurst Farm instead. Where it passes the farm the bridleway can be muddy but it should be passable even after wet weather, and it is worth the effort for the view to be had a little further on. Continue for about 500 yards until you reach a sharp right turn.

Pause here for a few moments to enjoy the splendid panorama of the North Downs which can be seen only from this spot. To the left, on top of the ridge, is the tower of

the Hog's Back Hotel at Tongham, over 7 miles away, and even further to the left the Downs can be seen sloping down to the River Wey at Farnham. In the centre is the gap in the Downs in which Guildford is situated; the cathedral tower can be seen peeking out from behind Guildown. To the right is the Tillingbourne valley, with the Downs stretching away towards Newlands Corner and beyond.

The bridleway continues for another 400 yards to a junction with another path. To the right is the way to the top of Chinthurst Hill. This is well worth the steep climb, but lock up your cycle and leave it here to collect on the way back. The views from the top of the hill are magnificent – on a good day you can see the South Downs in the distance. The tower on top of the hill is of no great age; it was built as a folly in 1936 by Lord Inchcape.

⑧ Chinthurst to Blackheath

From the path junction, turn left down the hill. The way into the car park is immediately on the right. Continue along the track, which has recently been superbly resurfaced, down to the main road, the B2128 from Shalford to Wonersh, and turn right.

☞ *From the B2128 the ride heads for Blackheath along a bridleway, which shouldn't normally give any problems, but an alternative route along a country lane is described on page 112.*

Turn left off the B2128 after 75 yards or so into the bridleway signposted 'Great Tangley Manor Farm'. The first part of the bridleway is tarred and in good condition. After about 400 yards it passes the driveway leading to Great Tangley Manor itself.

Great Tangley Manor: *Sadly, this historic and beautiful building is not open to the public,*

GREAT TANGLEY MANOR.

and in summer it is hard to see much of it through its boundary hedges. It was described by the noted local writer Eric Parker as "one of the most perfect timbered houses – perhaps it is the most perfect – in the county". According to legend, it is the site of one of King John's hunting boxes. The original building was a fairly simple open hall around which John Caryll built the basis of the present house in around 1582; this date appears on a carved timber bracket in part of the later construction. The whole house is surrounded by a moat.

Considerable additions were made to the house late in the 19th century. They were designed by Philip Webb, who worked on it for 20 years, on and off. It has been said that his aim was to reproduce the spirit of the building but not to copy the detail. The end of his covered way leading across the moat to the house can just be seen from the bridleway. The house is now divided into separate homes.

150 yards or so beyond the entrance to the Manor there is a junction of paths, in the centre of which is a large tree. Possibly the best view of the manor can be had by looking back from here. To the left, another bridleway heads off through ancient farm buildings and cottages, one of the which is converted from the old Granary. Tucked round a corner is Great Tangley Farm House; amid the other historic buildings it comes as a disappointment as it is quite modern.

Continue straight ahead from the tree. As the sign shows, the bridleway is part of the Downs Link path, joining the North and South Downs Ways. It now becomes a sandy track running between hedges, heading uphill towards some woods.

After passing a field gate it narrows, but fortunately the undergrowth has been cut back and the worn, sandy surface has been remade with stone chippings, even if they are a little loose for comfortable cycling. There is a good view towards St Martha's Hill and the Downs on the left as the track winds up the hill towards the woods.

The track broadens as the slope flattens out, and eventually you come to a small clearing where there is a padlocked gate on the right. A narrower path emerges from behind on the left, crosses the bridleway, and forks off to the right. Ignore this and stay on what is obviously the main track. Just after you pass a large house called Tangley Way, the track curves to the left.

Continue on the track until you reach the public road at the edge of Blackheath (about 200 yards further on), turn right down the hill to the crossroads in the village, then left to reach The Villagers pub (17½ miles).

Blackheath: *The village owes its existence to squatters who built themselves homes in* the early 19th century and tried to eke a living out of the poor soil. Before the century ended a prosperous Victorian middle class village had been established. The church, dedicated to St Martin, was designed by Charles Harrison Townsend in 1895 in the curious style of a Spanish roadside church. The village hall and the Franciscan monastery (the latter situated off the Chilworth road) were built in the same year.

The Villagers, Blackheath. Free house. 01483 893152. Food Acc

⑨ Blackheath to Shere

From the pub, continue straight on to the Blackheath Common car park, which is at the end of the public road. Pass through the car park and onto the broad bridleway (number 302) which begins at its far end.

The condition of this bridleway varies; some parts are very sandy but elsewhere the council has resurfaced it to repair some muddy patches. Although you are unlikely to have any real problems in getting through this stretch, the deep, soft sand will mean you have to get off and walk in places. (There is no convenient road diversion on this section.)

After leaving the car park ignore a wide, unsigned track which branches off to the right, then keep straight on at a crossways of tracks. In some places on this and the next stretch the centre of the track is very sandy and you will need to ride along the edge of the track, but be careful not to cause further wear and tear.

About half a mile from the car park watch out for the waymark post which stands in the fork where a narrower path veers off to the right. Follow the bridleway numbered 232 to the right. After gradually veering away from the other track, it crosses an open area of very sandy heath. Then, after descending a short hill, and about half a mile from the fork, it merges with another

Shere village

track leading from a small group of houses. Keep going until you come out on Farley Heath Road. Turn left onto the road and head into Farley Green.

☞ *For information on Farley Green, see Ride E. Between Farley Green and Little London rides E and F share a stretch of route (although in opposite directions), so it is possible to link the two rides together.*

From Farley Green take the road which is signposted Albury. Half a mile further on, shortly before the level crossing and at the bottom of the dip, just after the phone box, turn right into Brook Lane.

After passing under the railway the lane changes its name to Dark Lane and passes through the hamlet of Little London, so-called, it is said, because of the Londoners who fled there from the Great Plague in 1665. Parts of the William IV pub are claimed to be over 600 years old.

▦ *William IV, Dark Lane, Little London. Free house. 01483 202685. Open eves from 5.30 excl Sun. Food C G*

☞ *If you want to avoid the next length of bridleway, turn right at the T-junction at the end of Dark Lane, then left into Sandy Lane at the next junction.*

At the T-junction at the end of Dark Lane, go straight ahead onto the bridleway on the other side of the road, the old extension of Dark Lane across the heath. After a short while another track merges in from the right, and then the track divides. Take the right fork, which soon emerges from the cutting and passes behind some gardens. When it reaches the road continue to the junction with Sandy Lane, then turn left into Shere.

Shere *is one of those places in Surrey which have managed, against the odds, to remain all that an English country village ought to be.*

William Morris certainly thought so: "No written description can possibly do justice to the manifold beauties of Shere" he wrote, but he tried nevertheless. It must have helped that the Bray family have been Lords of the Manor of Shere since 1497, ensuring continuity throughout the centuries.

A low bridge carries the main street across the Tillingbourne river – not much more than a broad stream at this point – around which both people and ducks gather. Although the Normans were responsible for building the grey-towered church, it seems they used the site of an earlier Saxon church, and succeeding generations have certainly added to and altered the building.

The church is linked to the main street by the tiny village green, triangular in shape but always known as The Square. Its old elm trees were lost to Dutch Elm disease some years back, but a young oak will one day provide shade for future generations to sit beneath. Apart from its couple of pubs, the village also has a good selection of shops.

The White Horse Inn was built as a single storey farmhouse in 1475, and became an alehouse when the farmer began brewing his own beer. A second floor was added later to provide accommodation, a hole for a ladder being cut in the bar ceiling to provide access. The pub has two early fireplaces, one with the original wattle and daub above it, the other with a Tudor carved mantelpiece of chalkstone. A hidden second cellar containing smuggled casks of brandy was discovered in 1955 when the main cellar was damaged.

The Shere Museum has a fascinating collection of artefacts of both local and wider interest. A little further down the road is the late 19th century fire station of the Albury and Shere Volunteer Fire Brigade.

🍺 Prince of Wales, Shere Lane. 01483 202313. Open all day. Food (not Sun, Mon, Tue eves) C G

🍺 White Horse. Chef and Brewer. 01483 202518. Open all day from 11.30. Food

☕ Asters Tea Shop, Middle Street. 01483 202445. 10–5 (6 Sats, 6.15 Suns), closed winter Mons.

🛒 The Newsagency, Middle Street. 6–1, 2–5.30, Suns 8–2.

🛒 Alldays, Middle Street. General shop/off-licence. 8–10 every day.

⑩ Shere to Newlands Corner

The road comes to a T-junction soon after the bridge over the Tillingbourne. Turn left and go up the hill, under the footbridge, past the junction with Rectory Lane, and on to the junction with the A25 road. Cross the main road to reach Combe Lane almost opposite. After some initial bends, the lane climbs steeply on a broad curve through a wood called West Hanger. After a considerable amount of climbing the road comes to very steep, sharp bend, followed by a road junction. Combe Lane bends to the right, heading for East and West Horsley.

☞ *To link with Ride A continue along Combe Lane from this junction and follow the signs for West Horsley.*

Continue straight ahead at the junction into Staple Lane. About 100 yards further on turn left onto the North Downs Way at the small car park. The climbing is over now, and the final 1½ miles is a level ride along a track through the trees on the top of the North Downs. The track eventually comes out onto the A25 road at Newlands Corner. Cross the road to reach the car park and the start point. The refreshment facilities will no doubt be welcome, but take great care in crossing the main road because it is not easy to see the traffic (or vice-versa) at this point.

Alternative sections of route

☞ *These alternative sections of route avoid bridleways which may not be in good condition.*

③ Compton to Hurtmore

Turn right out of Down Lane and then left at the roundabout, following the B3000 signs. At the next roundabout, take the turning signed for Hurtmore and Charterhouse to rejoin the main route at Prior's Field School.

√ Hurtmore to Eashing

At the end of Hurtmore village near the Squirrel pub, turn right onto the link to the A3 (signposted Petersfield and Portsmouth) and follow the A3 for just over half a mile to the exit to Eashing, to rejoin the main route at Eashing Bridges. Keep in to the side of the road and you should be perfectly safe.

⑧ Chinthurst to Blackheath

Turn right out of the Chinthurst car park and continue along the B2128 road for about half a mile to the outskirts of Wonersh. Turn left into Blackheath Lane. The first part of this road runs through suburban housing (with a handy phone box) but this soon ends and the road becomes a narrow country lane climbing up the hill. Take care: some motorists drive as if it were a major road. At the top of the hill the road passes the Barnett Hill Conference Centre of the Red Cross (once owned by the family of Thomas Cook) and then heads on to Blackheath village. Continue over the crossroads at the far end of the village, about a mile from the turning off the main road, and head up the hill towards The Villagers pub.

Ride G:
Cobbett Country

Tilford • Whitmead • Charles Hill • Cuttmill • Littleworth • The Sands •
Crooksbury Hill • Waverley Abbey • Sheephatch • Tilhill • Tilford

Distance: About 8 miles
Landranger Maps: 186
Pathfinder Maps: 1225

The area through which this ride makes its way is associated with many
notable men and women, but there is one from whom it is inseparable –
William Cobbett. This farmer, soldier, and radical politician, who was born at
Farnham in 1762 and after whose book, 'Rural Rides', this series is named,
knew this corner of Surrey from his boyhood and loved it dearly. It's easy to
see why.

The distance covered by this ride may seem short, but don't be deceived.
There is a great deal to see and do on the way, so you definitely won't want to
hurry it. You should also bear in mind the nature of the countryside hereabouts.
The noted Surrey historian H E Malden described the landscape of these
Lower Greensand hills as like 'a miniature Highland country'. He was right,
and not just because they're clad in pine and heather – the area is quite hilly
too. But don't let that put you off; just allow enough extra time so that you can
take it easy if you want. It's splendid countryside for walking as much as for
cycling.

This is a good half-day's ride, and you could easily take longer, but for those
who want a longer ride, you can combine this one with Ride H, taking a break
at Tilford in the middle.

Starting Points

The obvious place to start is at Tilford (grid
reference SU 873434). You can park
between the green and the river, but not
on the green itself. It can become rather
full during hot summer weekends.

There are alternative car parks around
Puttenham Common, including one by
The Tarn, just off the Puttenham (Hogs
Back) to Elstead road (SU 910455).
Waverley Abbey might seem like another
good place to start, but you should be
aware that car parking in that area is
extremely restricted.

⇄ The only railway station near the
route is at Farnham. Leave the station by
the exit on the Alton-bound platform and
head out of the town on the B3001
Waverley Lane, which is to the left of the
Waverley Arms. Waverley Abbey is just
over a mile and a half away. If this road is
too busy for comfort or pleasure, try the
Tilford Road instead. It is straight ahead as
you leave the station. Tilford is about 2½
miles away.

Ride G
Cobbett Country

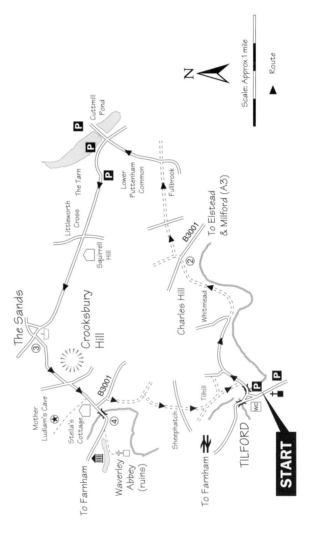

Scale: Approx 1 mile

▲ Route

N

To Farnham

Mother
Ludlam's Cave ✤

Stella's
Cottage

Waverley
Abbey
(ruins)

Sheephatch

To Farnham ⇌

The Sands

③

Crooksbury
Hill

B3001

④

Tilhill

WC

Littleworth
Cross

The Tarn

Squirrell
Hill

P

P

P

Cuttmill
Pond

Lower
Puttenham
Common

Fullbrook

Charles Hill

B3001

②

Whitmead

To Elstead
& Milford (A3)

TILFORD

✝
■

P

P

START

The Route in Brief

① From CP TR then R again, SP Elstead, Milford & Godalming, and cross bridge. Take next on R, Whitmead Lane. At hairpin (L) bend, take track to left of white gate of Whitmead (BY). Follow track to crosstracks just beyond houses, then TR down hill to Donkey pub.

② From entrance to pub CP cross road to BW opposite. After about 20 yds TR onto another BW and climb steep, sandy slope. Continue on BW as it joins driveway, then at entrance to 'Amina Heights' turn to L down drive past Lodge to road. Cross road and continue on BW on far side. At end TL onto road and climb rise to Lower Puttenham Common.

At XR by the Tarn TL. The road climbs steadily for two miles (keep SO at Littleworth XR) to The Sands, then downhill past pub to XR in village.

③ TL at XR into Botany Hill, SP Waverley, Crooksbury & Tilford. Substantial climb follows over flank of Crooksbury Hill. Once over top TL at dog-leg junc with Crooksbury road then immediately R into Camp Hill. At bottom of hill, TL onto B3001 to continue route (optional diversion to R for Waverley Abbey).

√ After 250yds TR onto unsurfaced BY through woodland. At junc of tracks after 500yds TR up short, steep slope. At Sheephatch Farm cross road to continue on BY on far side. Keep SO until track becomes tarred drive to Tilhill House. Pass house then diverge to R onto narrow path (BW). At road TR and cross bridge to reach Tilford CP.

Tilford

The Ride

① Tilford to Charles Hill

From the car park at Tilford, take the road signposted 'Elstead, Milford & Godalming'. Cross the bridge and head up The Street past the Post Office and the garage next door to it. Shortly after Upper Street Farm turn right into Whitmead Lane, a narrow country lane which winds and undulates along the hillside above the river. After half a mile the road suddenly comes to a hairpin bend. Ahead is the white-painted gate of Whitmead; a prominent sign makes it clear that the driveway which passes through it is private. However, to the left of the gate you will see a grassy trackway, indicated by a signpost with a red arrow.

The track climbs at first, and as you reach the crest of the hill there are some marvellous views to the right. The surface is occasionally sandy but mostly in good condition, as it makes its way through the woods along a ledge cut into the hillside. The river is only just below you, although it's not easy to see it through the trees. When the track eventually becomes a tarred drive serving some large houses, keep going until you come to a crossing of ways just beyond the houses. Turn right down the hill and you'll come out beside The Donkey pub, 1½ miles from the start.

You may not have come very far yet, but it's worth making a stop at The Donkey, and not just because it's some way to the next source of refreshment.

The Donkey: *The origin of the pub's name is fascinating. The building, which was two cottages before it became a pub in about 1850, is sited next to the main road between Godalming and Farnham at the foot of a steep climb out of the river valley. In the days before the roads were surfaced they could be extremely sandy in these parts, making it hard going for heavy horse-drawn carts. Many of them had great difficulty on this hill, so the pub kept a number of donkeys which could be hired to give assistance.*

The assisting donkey was attached ahead of the wagon's own horse, and the landlord (whose father and grandfather both kept the pub) recalls that the tackle for this survived in an outbuilding for many years after it was last used. If you look on the outside wall nearest the road you will see one of the rings used for tethering the donkeys between spells of work. Back in the 1960s the pub still kept a donkey, but as a pet rather than a beast of burden, and it was quite common to see it in the bar having a pint!

🍴 *The Donkey, Charles Hill. Morlands. 01252 702124. Food (not Sun eves) C G*

② Charles Hill to The Sands

From the entrance to The Donkey car park cross the busy road to the bridleway opposite; it starts on the left of the gate leading to a private house. After only 20 yards or so, turn right onto another bridleway. It is very sandy and steep, so you are strongly advised to walk. At the top of the slope the path emerges onto a tarred driveway serving a private house. Keep going until you come to the entrance to 'Amina Heights', previously Three Barrows Place. You might think you have wandered into someone's garden, but there is no need to worry; you are still on the public bridleway. Turn to the left, smile for the video surveillance camera, and continue down the drive and past the lodge to the road.

Cross the road (2 miles) and continue along the bridleway on the far side – a delightful path which climbs gently along a ridge, giving excellent views over the countryside on both sides. There are one or two stretches which are either a little bumpy or sandy, but nothing too much to worry about. The track narrows as it passes Fullbrook Farm (on the left) where, sadly, the occupants have planted conifers along the fence, which will soon block the view. When you reach the road (Suffield Lane), turn left and climb the slight rise to reach the open expanse of Lower Puttenham Common. The land is owned by the Hampton Estate, but looked after by Surrey County Council. The road is broad but there isn't a great deal of traffic.

The route turns left at the crossroads by The Tarn (just over 3 miles), but before you turn off, continue straight ahead for another hundred yards or so to the point where the road runs beside the Tarn, from where there is a superb view along the length of the lake. On the other side of the road Cutt Mill Pond can be seen dimly through the trees. Having taken this short diversion, return to the crossroads and turn right past the Tarn car park. There is another small car park a short distance further on, opposite Whitefield Cottages. To the right, hidden behind the trees, is Hampton Park.

The next stretch of road presents a climb which may not be particularly steep but seems to go on for a distance. Sadly the scenery, although pleasant enough, is a little limited, and the roadside view is not improved by the long wall on the left-hand side further on (4 miles).

The climb continues beyond Littleworth Cross, the junction with the Elstead–Seale road. Just after the crossroads watch out for a house called Squirrel Hill on the left. The older part of it was designed by Lutyens in 1890, one of his earliest works. It was in this house that he first met Gertrude Jekyll, the renowned Surrey garden designer. The two of them subsequently worked together on the design of many of the substantial houses built in this corner of Surrey around the turn of the century. As the road

approaches The Sands it is lined by houses set in large gardens, but mostly hidden behind tall hedges (5 miles). There is a welcome descent into the village, which has a pub, a small post office, and an off-licence.

The Barley Mow, Littleworth Road. Courage. 01252 782200. Food G

③ The Sands to Waverley Abbey

Continue past the Barley Mow to the main crossroads a little further down the hill and then turn left into Botany Hill, signposted 'Waverley, Crooksbury, & Tilford'. Rising up on the left is Crooksbury Hill which, at 534 feet, is the highest point hereabouts. Fortunately, the road does not go right over the summit, but there is a substantial climb nevertheless.

When Eric Parker, the Surrey writer and naturalist, wrote of Crooksbury around the turn of the century, he praised the pine trees which 'clothed the hill in a dozen different wardrobes of greens and greys, purples and blacks'. But then came the 1914–18 war and to satisfy the demand for timber for the trenches, all the trees, except for a few near the summit, were felled. For Parker, this hill – the 'constant companion of travellers for many miles around' – became a sad memorial. Of course, the trees were later replanted and now clothe the hill once more, but today the natural magnificence of the scenery is marred by the radio transmitter which dominates the hilltop – a sad reflection of our own age perhaps!

The uphill climb eventually comes to an end and the welcome descent begins. At the junction with Crooksbury Road go left and then immediately right into Camp Hill. There's quite a steep slope, so keep your speed under control because you suddenly come to a busy junction at the bottom. In fact, stop at Stella Lodge just before that junction (a little over 6 miles) and turn off the road onto the footpath which runs past the Lodge.

You'll have to dismount and walk along the path. The footpath leads through the grounds of Moor Park and from there almost to Farnham.

Moor Park: *The house is about a mile away along the path. It was once called Compton Hall, but was bought in 1680 by Sir William Temple and renamed by him in honour of the similarly-named house in Hertfordshire, which he much admired. Sir William had spent his life in the diplomatic service of both Charles II and James II. He had been ambassador to the United Provinces and brought about the Triple Alliance between England, Holland and Sweden in 1668, as well as the marriage of William of Orange and Mary.*

He retired to Moor Park, and dedicated the rest of his life to gardening and writing. His 'Essay on the Gardens of Epicures' brought together these two activities; in it he praised the Dutch style of gardening, which he had so much admired in Haarlem and The Hague. He laid out the gardens of Moor Park in this style, and they, in turn, were much admired by William Cobbett in his boyhood. Today they are mostly gone, partly through changes to suit the tastes of later times, but also partly because of neglect.

Other than this, Sir William did not prove to be a literary giant. However, in 1688 he employed as his secretary and amanuensis the 21-year-old Jonathan Swift. Young he may have been, but Swift had already acquired quite a reputation. 'An eccentric, uncouth, disagreeable young Irishman, who had narrowly escaped plucking at Dublin', was Macaulay's description of him. Swift soon

Stella's Cottage

quarrelled with Sir William, went back to Ireland and was ordained as a priest. Then he made it up with his employer and returned to Moor Park, where he wrote 'The Battle of the Books' and 'The Tale of a Tub', He became Dean of St Patrick's in Dublin in 1713, where he later wrote 'Gulliver's Travels'.

Sir William and Swift feature in Moor Parks's two tales of true romance. The first concerns Dorothy Osborne, who waited for seven long, and at times seemingly hopeless, years to marry Sir William. In that time she sent to him what Eric Parker has described as 'some of the most graceful girlish letters ever written'. Happily, they have been preserved.

Sir William's steward was a man named Johnson. His wife was a confidential servant to Sir William's sister, Lady Giffard, and the Johnson's daughter, Esther, also served her as a maid. Swift, who acted as a tutor to the girl, developed a hopeless but long-lasting passion for her, and recorded its story in his 'Letters to Stella'. Stella's Cottage at the bottom of Camp Hill, sometimes known as Swift's Cottage, is where Esther lived with her parents.

Make your way along the footpath beside the garden wall of Stella's Cottage. You will either have to contort your bike through the barrier which blocks the path, or chain it up and leave it there.

Continue for about another 100 yards along the path and you will come to a cave in the sandstone hill on the right. The entrance arch is lined with stone, but the iron railings which once barred it have now gone. There is nothing to stop you entering the cave, but be careful if you do because the roof is collapsing.

In 1825 Cobbett wrote that the cave was no longer the enchanting place it was when he first knew it as a boy. The stream which previously ran out of it through a clean paved channel had become a dirty gutter instead, he bemoaned! It has deteriorated a lot further since then and it is doubtful how much longer it will last.

Mother Ludlam's Cave: *The natural cave in the sandstone is reputed to be have been the home of Mother Ludlam, a white witch. It is said that anyone who needed to borrow an item, no matter what it was, could go to the cave at midnight, turn thrice around, repeat thrice the name of the item, and promise to return it within two days. Next morning the item would be there for them to collect at the cave entrance.*

All went well until someone borrowed a large cauldron made from a single sheet of beaten copper and failed to return it within the stipulated time. With that the borrowing came to an end. The cauldron is said to have been taken first to Waverley Abbey and then, when that place was dissolved, to Frensham church, where it remains today.

Talk to local people nowadays and they might be prepared to accept that the story of Mother Ludlam is only a folktale, but ask them about the stream that flows through the cave, and they will probably tell you, with a completely straight face, that the water comes all the way from Guildford!

Having visited the cave, return along the footpath to Stella's Lodge, and turn right into Camp Hill. At the junction just beyond you have a choice. The route continues to the left along the Farnham–Milford road (the B3001), but if you have never visited Waverley Abbey, you cannot come so close and not go there.

To reach the Abbey go straight ahead at the junction – follow the sign for 'Farnham'. This stretch of road is narrow and busy, so be careful. Pass Waverley Mill, cross the bridge, and follow the bend around to the right. Just after the bend, pull in to the gravelled entrance in front of the gates of Waverley Abbey House.

The land on which the Abbey stands is private property, although the ruins themselves are in the care of English Heritage, and the public has the right of access along the track provided. The entrance to the track is barred by a large wooden gate – a kissing gate is provided for pedestrians – and there is another locked gate further on. Unless you feel strong enough to lift your bikes over the top of these gates, we suggest you leave them chained up out of the way near the entrance. If you do decide to take them with you, please do not cycle on the access track. The ruins are a very pleasant 400-yard walk from the entrance along the edge of the lake in the grounds of Waverley Abbey House which overlooks the scene. The lake may have been one of the Abbey's fishponds. Along the way, an old bridge crosses the lake to the house, which is of 18th century design but was completely rebuilt after a fire in 1833. It is now a Christian study centre and is not open to the public.

Waverley Abbey was established beside the River Wey in 1128 by William Giffard, the second Bishop of Winchester. It was the first house of the Cistercian order (known as the White Monks) to be founded in England. The order itself had existed for only a few years. It was started in Citeaux, France by an Englishman, Stephen Harding, in protest at the corruption which affected the Benedictine order at the end of the 11th century.

Waverley began with a small group of monks who arrived from D'Aumône in Normandy. By 1187 their numbers had grown to 70, but there were also 120 lay brethren who were offered the chance of a monastic lifestyle (which compared well with that of a peasant) in return for their labour.

Life was austere and could be very hard. The buildings were still incomplete when floods inundated the Abbey in 1201 and destroyed the crops and part of the building. Work on a new church started in 1203, but there was another great flood in 1233 which left eight feet of water in the Abbey. Another, in 1265, took the monks days to clean up the silt.

With all these setbacks it is hardly surprising that the new church was only completed and dedicated in 1278. Nicholas de Ely, Bishop of Winchester, hosted the occasion and paid for nine days of feasting. It is said that on the first day there were over seven thousand guests. Earlier, in 1208, King John had paid a visit and, to be on the safe side, he brought his own wine for the four-day stay – 500 gallons of it! Life was not always austere.

Waverley was among the first of the small monasteries to close at the Dissolution, its end coming in July 1536. The derelict buildings proved a useful source of ready-dressed stone for local builders. Sir William More took many wagonloads when he was building his new mansion at Loseley near Guildford in the 1560s. Even so, when John Aubrey visited in 1672 he found the extensive walls of a church and cloisters, a chapel being used as a stable, a window with glass in it still, and painting on a wall.

The White Monks always chose wild and lonely spots for their houses. Waverley was no exception and it has retained those qualities down through the years – it was in this remote place that Cobbett claimed to have seen a wildcat, probably the last sighting of one in Surrey. The ruins have now been cleared of the ivy, ash and thorns which once choked them, and the tall elms which populated the meadows have all gone, leaving the grey walls to stand alone, quite stark against the dull green of the pine-clad hills. Be sure to come when it is quiet, when you can be alone and experience the real peace of this remarkably beautiful spot.

The Abbey ruins are open every day until about 4.30pm. There is no charge – a welcome change these days.

√ Waverley Abbey to Tilford

Return along the track from the Abbey ruins to the gates of Waverley Abbey House and then turn right onto the B3001 road. Follow this back past Waverley Mill, around the sharp corner at the junction with Camp Hill and along the straight section of road which follows.

About 250 yards after the Camp Hill junction, as the road bends away to the left, turn right onto a broad but unsurfaced track which is marked by a signpost with a red byway arrow.

The track runs through the woodland along the hillside above the River Wey, and when you come to a cleared area where four yew trees grow beside the track (roughly 7 miles), pause for a moment – there is a good view looking down over the loop in the river towards the Abbey ruins. Parts of the track may be sandy on this stretch but otherwise it is in good condition.

After about 500 yards or so you will come to a junction which should be easily recognisable because of the profusion of waymark arrows on the adjacent post.

Turn right up quite a steep but mercifully short slope. From the top it's a pleasant ride through the woods. At Sheephatch Farm cross the road onto the continuation of the track on the other side. This was once an old road from Waverley Abbey to Tilford but today is virtually deserted. Cycling through here on one occasion, a deer suddenly leapt out just ahead and bounded away along the track before diving back into the undergrowth. It's hard to know who was most startled!

Continue straight ahead along the track through the woods until it becomes a tarred drive serving Tilhill House from where, now you are out of the trees, there are some marvellous views across the valley of the Wey. Just beyond the house (note the attractive cast-iron dovecot in its garden) turn off the drive onto the narrow path which diverges to the right down the hillside. (There is a sign marking it as a bridleway.)

The path is surfaced at first, but watch for the sudden step down where the tarmac ends. As the path descends towards the level of the river meadows you can see Tilford Bridge slightly to the right. The path passes some old pillboxes – they seem to have been built all along the Wey valley – before coming out onto the road beside Tilford Post Office. Turn right over the bridge to return to the car park.

Tilford is one of those villages which have a good claim to be the prettiest in Surrey. The best time to see it is on a warm summer's afternoon when a cricket match is in progress on the green. Locals and visitors gather outside the pub with glasses in hand, applauding the progress of the play, and children splash about in the river down by the bridge. But it can be equally charming at dusk on an autumn or winter's evening, with the lights of the Barley Mow sending out a welcome across the green, and drifting smoke from cottage chimneys telling of blazing fires within.

The sloping green is Tilford's most immediately obvious feature, but the complaints of opposition cricket teams that you cannot see the bowler as he starts his run are not entirely justified. The village's most celebrated feature, though, is the Tilford Oak, situated at the north-west corner of the green. Tradition has it that this tree is the King's Oak (or 'Kynghoc') mentioned as a boundary marker in a charter given to Waverley Abbey in 1128, but, as far as is known, Tilford has never been on the boundary of the Abbey lands.

Cobbett extolled the virtues of the Tilford Oak: 'by far the finest tree that I ever saw in my life' he said. He claimed its girth to be thirty feet at a point eight or ten feet above the ground. In 1907 Eric Parker measured it and found it to be only twenty four feet nine inches. He came back in 1934 and found it was exactly one foot more, so Cobbett may have been indulging in a typical bit of exaggeration. Today the tree is rather decayed, and some drastic but necessary surgery has robbed it of much of its splendour, but look around the green at the other commemorative oaks which have been planted to continue the tradition.

Tilford is at the confluence of the two branches of the Wey, and the loops which the river makes mean that two medieval bridges were needed to cross it. That on the road to Farnham now carries northbound traffic only. Alongside it has been built a structure of concrete and steel, the only remarkable feature of which is its supreme ugliness. A similar construction at Elstead has recently been replaced with something more in keeping, so maybe Tilford will be next to benefit.

The Barley Mow, Tilford Green. Courage. 01252 792205. Food (not Sun eve) C G

Ride H:
Hymns, Ponds and a Devilish Murder

Tilford • Frensham Little Pond • Frensham Church • Frensham Beale Manor •
Frensham Great Pond • Graywalls • Rushmoor • Pitch Place • Thursley •
Ridgeway • Rushmoor • Tilford

Distance: Just over 15 miles
Landranger Maps: 186
Pathfinder Maps: 1225 & 1245

The south-west corner of Surrey is extremely popular with tourists and visitors,
the two well-known ponds at Frensham being among the main attractions.
Much of the Common land which surrounds the ponds is now owned by the
National Trust and Waverley Borough Council and, as the Frensham Country
Park, is visited by up to 500,000 people each year! This means the area can
be busy at times, but fortunately most visitors don't stray far from their cars.

That leaves an immense amount of beautiful countryside to be enjoyed by
those who are willing to seek out the less accessible spots. This ride will take
you to many of them. As well as visiting quiet corners of the two main ponds
and passing other smaller but pretty ponds and lakes which most people never
see, you'll ride along ancient lanes around the picturesque villages of Thursley
and Churt, call at a churchyard with a story of murder most foul to tell, and
pass a house where many famous hymns were penned.

The ride is fairly demanding, but most people should be able to do it without
difficulty. You could complete it in half a day but, with such beautiful countryside
to enjoy and so much to see along the way, it would be a pity to rush it. Why
not take things easy and make a day of it?

Starting Points

As with Ride G, start at Tilford, leaving
your car on the parking area between the
village green and the river (grid reference
SU 873434).

There are also a couple of car parks on the
north side of Frensham Little Pond
(reached by the lane from Millbridge to
Rushmoor) as well as the Frensham
Common car park on Bacon Lane
(signposted from the A287 Hindhead–
Farnham road). However, all these get

packed at busy times. If you do park at
Frensham Common, join the ride at the
Frensham Pond Hotel, farther along
Bacon Lane.

≋ The only rail station at all convenient
for the ride is that at Farnham. Leave the
station by the exit on the Alton-bound
platform (Platform 2) and head south-east
on the Tilford Road, which starts
immediately outside the station. Tilford is
about 2½ miles away.

Ride H
Hymns, Ponds and
a Devilish Murder

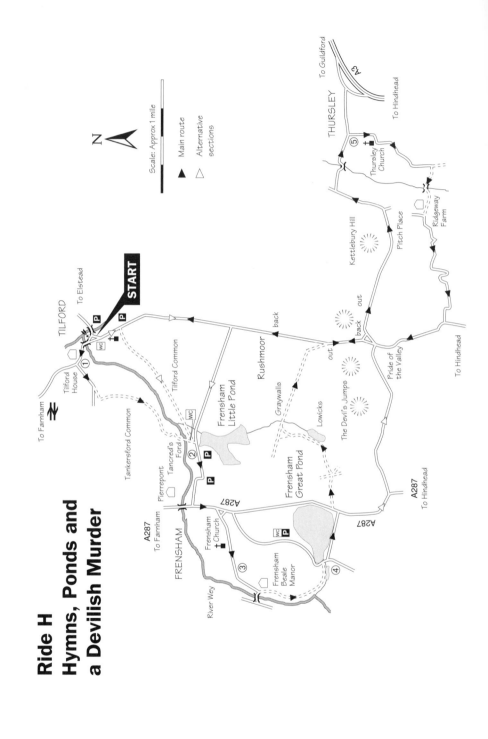

The Route in Brief

① Pass the Barley Mow pub, then TR, SP 'Frensham, Bourne & Farnham'. At next junction TL into The Reeds, SP 'Frensham & Rural Life Centre'. Just before top of hill TL onto BW signed 'Tilford Reeds'. Follow BW over Tankersford Common and through yard of Pierrepont Home Farm. Cross river and continue on BW to road at Frensham Little Pond.

② From Frensham Little Pond TR along lane. At TJ at Millbridge TL onto A287, SP 'Churt & Hindhead', then after 200 yards TR into lane, SP 'Frensham & Dockenfield'. Continue through village, past church.

③ Continue through Frensham until the Mill House. TL onto BW which runs through the forecourt and then runs beside river. Ignore all footpath side turnings, staying on BW until it ends at Frensham Great Pond.

√ At Frensham Great Pond TR into Bacon Lane, then TL into Pond Lane at Frensham Pond Hotel. TL at TJ with A287, then R after 50 yards onto BW. SO at junction of paths following waymark post numbered 42. Stay on BW when it bends sharp R 200 yards after Lowicks House. SO past Graywalls along driveway, then TR onto Sandy Lane, over ford, to Rushmoor.

TR at TJ with Tilford Road. At next junction TL, SP 'Elstead & Thursley', then L again into Thursley Road. Continue through Pitch Place, past junction with Sailors Lane, then TR at next junction (Dye House Road), SP 'Thursley & Hindhead'. Continue to Thursley village.

⑤ TR into The Street, which becomes Highfield Lane by church. At end of surfaced lane at Little Cowdray Farm TR, SP 'Punchbowl Farm'. At bend take path to right of cottages, SP 'Ridgeway'. CAUTION is needed here because the slope is steep and rough.

At bottom of slope cross stream by footbridge and continue up track on far side past Ridgeway Farm. SO past junction with Sailors Lane and continue to TJ with Hindhead–Tilford road. TR and continue past Pride of the Valley Hotel and through Rushmoor to Tilford.

The Ride

① Tilford to Frensham Little Pond

☞ *The route from Tilford to Frensham Little Pond is extremely pretty and interesting but there is one short stretch which can be very muddy even in dry weather. If you want to try it (and we heartily recommend you do), you can walk through (wear suitable footwear or even cover your feet and lower legs with plastic bags held up by elastic bands) or simply ride straight through; we haven't tried it, but we've seen it done! If you would rather avoid this stretch, there are two alternative routes on page 140.*

From the car park at Tilford, take the road which passes the Barley Mow pub and the famous Tilford Oak, which is described in Ride G. Just after the Oak turn right for 'Frensham, Bourne & Farnham', crossing the bridge over the Wey's south branch, after which the road turns sharp left. About 200 yards after the bridge the road passes Tilford House.

Tilford House, with its ornate sundial on the front wall, was built in 1690 for the Abneys, a prominent family of Dissenters (a group of religious non-conformists) who previously lived in Stoke Newington in London. From 1712 until his death in 1748, the family provided a home at Tilford House for Dr Isaac Watts who, while living there and working in the gazebo, wrote many famous hymns, including 'O God our help in ages past'. Another famous hymn written in the house was 'Rock of Ages', by Augustus Montague Toplady, who was born in nearby Farnham in 1740.

When Elizabeth Abney, the unmarried daughter of the family, died she left the house and estate to her chaplain, the Rev Thomas Taylor, directing that the chapel in the yard should be kept up for Dissenters. A subsequent resident of the house was Charlotte Smith, well-known in her day as a novelist and poet; she died there in 1806, and is commemorated by the reredos in Tilford Church.

Just after Tilford House turn left into The Reeds, signed 'Frensham & Rural Life Centre', and climb the slope towards the belt of trees ahead.

When the road bends to the right just before the top of the hill, branch off to the left onto the bridleway indicated by the sign to 'Tilford Reeds'.

The Rural Life Centre *is at the Old Kiln Museum, about 650 yards further along The Reeds. Started as a private collection of farming tools and implements, it is now a complete museum of rural life during the last 150 years. There are two working forges, a collection of carts, wagons and gigs, a narrow gauge railway (operates Suns only), and a wheelwright's shop, plus an Aboretum with 100 varieties of young trees from all parts of the world.*

The last Sunday in July is Rustic Sunday, when the attractions include a range of craftspeople demonstrating country skills (different charges apply).

The Centre has been a Pride of Place Award winner. It is open Wed–Sun and bank holidays 11–6 from April 1 to September 30. Entry costs £2.50 (OAPs £2, children £1.25). Car parking is free. There is a café and a picnic area. ☎ 01252 795571 or 792300.

At first the bridleway follows a drive to some houses – fork left just after some stables or you'll end up in someone's garden! After another house the track follows the line of a fence, becoming quite narrow. A little farther on the boundary banks on both sides show it was once much broader than it is today, forming an important link between Frensham, Tilford and Waverley Abbey. Local tales say it was also a favourite route for smugglers.

Frensham Ponds

The two ponds at Frensham were built in the 13th century to ensure a regular supply of fresh fish for the Bishop of Winchester's palace at Farnham Castle. (In those days fish brought from the coast would have gone off by the time it arrived.) There used to be a third pond near the Duke of Cambridge pub on the road south from Tilford, built for the monks of Waverley Abbey and called the Abbot's Pond, but its dam burst in 1841.

The Great Pond covers 108 acres, the Little Pond – not so little – about half that. The Great Pond was created by enlarging a small natural pool and has a sophisticated water supply system to prevent swollen winter streams from clogging it with silt. The Little Pond, which is also known as Tancred's Mere (and shown on some old maps as Crowsfoot Pond), is artificial.

In 1940 the ponds were drained in case they were used as landmarks by German bombers. They became so overgrown with saplings and undergrowth there were fears they would never recover and, in one respect, they haven't. In his book *Highways and Byways in Surrey*, Eric Parker tells how the northern corner of the Little Pond, by the boathouse, was once a sheet of waterlilies covering almost 1000 square yards. 'There cannot be as many people see them as there are lilies' he said, writing of the days when the spot could be reached only on foot along sandy tracks. Some of the lilies survive today, but in nothing like the number that used to pack this quiet corner.

Paths run round the Little Pond and make for a pleasant walk (no cycling please). Among the reeds at the far end you may well spot the blue flash of a kingfisher in flight, as well as some other rarely-seen birds.

The next stretch of the bridleway crosses Tankersford Common, now used for commercial forestry. The pines, with their tendency to suppress all other growth, can be monotonous, but they finally come to an end and the track winds through a belt of broad-leaved trees before emerging into open fields. Ahead are the buildings of Pierrepont Home Farm. To the right you can just see Pierrepont House, about half a mile away in the trees.

Pierrepont House: *The present building, now a school, was designed by Norman Shaw in 1876, but the estate itself is much older.*

In 1761 Evelyn Pierrepont, the second Duke of Kingston, bought the estate, gave it his family name, and enlarged the stately Georgian house that stood on a knoll beside the river at Tancred's Ford. He sold it 10 years later when his health began to fail, and during the next 13 years it passed through the hands of three different owners. Local historians have suggested that the reason for the rapid turnover was that the track which crossed the ford and ran past the house was regularly used by smugglers, and the new owners may not have been keen on that.

A less romantic reason may be that the house was situated close to damp and marshy land by the river, and may not have been too healthy. In 1785 Ralph Winstanley Wood bought the estate and pulled down the old house, having built himself a new one called Highfield about half a mile away near Millbridge. (The bricks of the old house were apparently re-used to build the workhouse in Farnham.)

In 1862 Wood's grandson sold the property to Richard Henry Combe, who had Highfield House demolished and the present Pierrepont House erected in its place, reviving the former name of the estate. When Mr Combe's son died in the 1940s, the estate was broken up.

The bridleway passes right through the farmyard of Pierrepont Home Farm, so if it's milking time you may well have to wait while the farm's large herd of cows pass through. Go through the gate, then head slightly to the left across the farmyard and follow the track around past the farmhouse, after which it becomes a narrow path heading across the meadows towards the river at Tancred's Ford. The higher area of ground on the right of the path is the site of the original Pierrepont House.

At the river you have a choice of crossing by the ford or the footbridge. A sign asks horses to use the former, but we recommend the latter for cyclists!

The low-lying land on the far side of the river is marshy and the track can be like a quagmire even in dry weather, although there is a firm bottom to the track under a few inches of mud. You can ride straight through if you don't mind getting mud-splattered. If you prefer to stop and walk through, be prepared for your feet to get muddy.

Follow the track up the slope past the cottage, and keep straight on at the top of the hill until you come to some toilets. From there you'll be able to see Frensham Little Pond ahead. The best way to reach it is to push your bike along the track leading straight to it. The dam, from which the most extensive views can be had, is to the left.

② Through Frensham

From the Little Pond head west along the road (Priory Lane), past the entrance to the National Trust car park. A quarter of a mile further on there is another car park by a sharp right-hand bend (2 miles). The road beyond this point is lined by some wonderful old cottages, idyllically situated with the river at the bottom of their gardens. The present Pierrepont House can be seen through the trees on the far side of the valley.

The Priory, Frensham

Priory Lane ends at a junction with the A287 Frensham Road at Millbridge. The bridge itself is just to the right of the junction, and beyond it is The Mariners pub.

Millbridge: *Several picturesque and historic houses are clustered around Millbridge, so do pause for a few moments before riding on.*

The Mariners is said to have got its name because it was used as a distribution centre by smugglers. The original 400-year-old Three Mariners Inn was demolished in the 1900s and the present rather characterless and much-extended building put up in its place. The house on the left of the road junction is The Priory which, despite its name and looks, has no ecclesiastical connections whatever. The 15th century cottage on the opposite corner of Priory Lane is now called the Old Post House. This name reflects its former use which came to light only during the 1930s when heavy ivy growth was cut back to reveal the words 'Post Office' in large black-painted letters.

Warren Cottage, a little farther up the hill towards Churt, later took over this role; it served as a small shop with a blacksmith's forge alongside until the 1930s.

The Mariners Hotel, Frensham Road, Millbridge. 01252 792050 or 794745. Food C G Rest Acc

At the end of Priory Lane turn left into the main road, following the signpost for 'Churt & Hindhead' – take care because the road is busy and the traffic fast-moving. Go up the hill for about 200 yards and then turn right into the road signed 'Frensham & Dockenfield', along the side of the green.

Today the triangular green is overlooked by St Mary's village school; at one time it was overlooked by The Cricketers Inn, but the remains of that establishment now form part of the adjacent School House – surely a unique adaptation! On the third side of the green, beside the main road, is

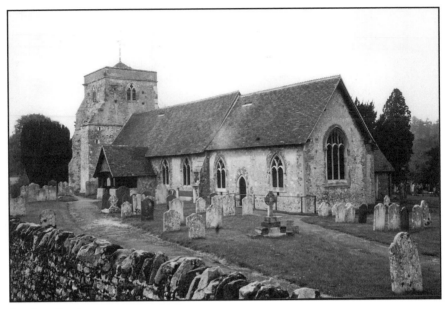

Frensham Church

the substantial Celtic Cross – a rather unusual type of war memorial for this part of the country. Made of Cornish granite and topped with a miniature church, it carries the 58 names of those who died during World War I, a large number for a rural area with a small population. Twelve more names had to be added in 1945.

The road leaves the green behind and becomes The Street. The substantial building on the right is the Old Vicarage, considerably altered in 1883 and again after a fire in 1895, while on the left is the Toll Cottage. Beyond them the scene is dominated by the village church with a row of neat cottages facing it (3 miles).

St Mary's Church, Frensham: *The Annals of Waverley Abbey for the year 1239 give us an exact date for the building of the church, but they also set us a puzzle: 'The Church of Fermesham has been moved this year from the place where it was first sited to another place with the advice and help of Luke*

Archdeacon of Surrey, and in the same year it has been dedicated.' We can only wonder where the church was originally sited and why it had to be moved. Nothing has ever been found of it to help solve the mystery. Maybe it was destroyed by the furious storms which did so much damage to Waverley Abbey and the bridges over the Wey in 1233 (see Ride G).

The church is built of local sandstone, flint and rubble. The first things you notice about it are the massive buttresses supporting the 14th century tower. The different architectural styles of the buttresses suggest they may have been added at varying times. The rest of the church has been much altered and added to over the years, with a major restoration – almost rebuilding – in 1868. Its story is fully described in a booklet available inside.

In the church you can see the early medieval font made of Purbeck marble, a stone coffin, and the cauldron which is said to have belonged to Old Mother Ludlam (again, see Ride G). The church booklet is circumspect, not wishing to upset local tradition while not wanting to give

Frensham Great Pond

The sandy northern shores of the Pond belong to the National Trust and are now part of the Frensham Country Park. The beach and car park (where there are toilets and an information centre) are half a mile up the lane to the left. To the right the lane crosses the outflow of the Pond and passes into Hampshire. On the far side of the outflow is the site of a water mill which existed here around 1550. It is said the stones which can be felt in the ground beneath the old oak tree are its remains.

A little farther down the lane, behind the brick parapet on the right-hand side of the road, is a 19th century sheepwash (as distinct from a sheep dip), used to wash grease out of the wool to make it easier for shearing. The sheep were pushed into the wash on the left-hand side and came out on the other through a narrow ramp which has now been filled in because of subsidence. The water level was raised by slotting boards into the recesses in the outflow.

This corner of the pond is a favourite with wildfowl, because a lot of visitors bring bread to feed them. The resident geese can sometimes be a bit intimidating, especially if you happen to meet them in the middle of the road, but it's amusing to see them waddle off at speed whenever there's a tit-bit on offer! There are sometimes herons around, but usually you'll have to look a little farther away as they're not so keen on company. You may be lucky enough to see two or three together on other quieter waters in the area.

Although the ponds attract a huge variety of wildfowl, both resident and migrant, some species that were once seen in these parts are no more. In the bar of what is now the Frensham Pond Hotel there was once a case containing two stuffed blackcocks and a grey-hen which were shot in 1889, said to have been the last of their species in this part of Surrey. (They may be the same ones which were later displayed in the Frensham British Legion Club.)

Sadly our ancestors took a great delight in shooting anything that flew, regardless of – indeed, often because of – its scarcity. In a letter of May 7th, 1779, published in his book 'The Natural History of Selborne', the pioneering naturalist Gilbert White told how the pondkeeper at Frensham had shot five of a flock of six exceedingly rare long-legged black-winged stilts, members of the plover family. The sixth survived only because the pondkeeper had by then 'satisfied his curiosity'. His book also records the shooting of an osprey at the pond seven years earlier. A Times correspondent, Anthony Collett, reported that a pair of ospreys nested by the Great Pond around 1890, but they, too, were shot by the keepers. Thankfully, today's keepers satisfy themselves with noting their sightings on a board by the information centre.

A slightly different sort of bird was seen on the Pond in 1913. The first-ever seaplane, built at Farnborough, was brought here for trials and proved highly successful. It was kept in a hangar built for it on the north shore.

credence to superstition, so it describes the cauldron as being of 'origin unknown'! Measuring 8ft 8ins in circumference and 1ft 2ins depth, it has been estimated that it would hold over 100 gallons.

From the church continue along The Street and down the hill. On the way look across to the right and you'll see the oast houses of Pitt Farm on the hillside beyond the river.

Farnham Hops: *Hops and the oast houses in which they were once dried are now more readily associated with the countryside of Kent than Surrey, but hops were grown very widely all around Farnham until quite recently. They were first introduced into the area in 1642, and thrived on its rich loam soil and chalky sub-soil.*

Farnham hops were always reckoned to be among the very best. In Cobbett's time, they fetched seven pounds a hundredweight, when those from Kent and Hampshire sold for only five.

③ Frensham to Frensham Great Pond

Continue down the hill past the gates of Frensham Beale Manor and on to the old Mill situated on the River Wey. The road curves across the mill race and around the edge of the pool into which it empties in a scene which is quite delightful. Few passers-by can resist stopping to lean on the parapet of the wall to gaze into the water below or watch the birds swooping low across the surface of the pool.

Turn off the road by the entrance to the Mill House; a signed bridleway passes through a narrow opening next to the wall-mounted post box. Cross the forecourt of the Mill House, and go through the gate at the far side. From there the path winds around the garden of the Mill House and climbs towards the buildings of Frensham Beale manor house.

This timber-framed house mostly dates from the 16th century but it also has some 20th century additions. The stone-built section at the north end was once a chapel. The manor's unusual name is derived from that of its first owner, James le Bel, who acquired it in 1241.

The path continues along the side of the Manor House garden, set on a ledge up above the River Wey, but at the far end of the garden it returns to the water's edge.

The ride through the riverside woods and meadows is quite superb and is, without doubt, the best way of getting to Frensham Great Pond. Along the way a footbridge branches off to the right across the river, but it doesn't seem to be marked on any maps and the destination of the path it carries is a mystery.

About a quarter of a mile after this bridge continue straight ahead along the bridleway, ignoring the footpath which branches off beside the main river as it curves away to the south-west.

You are now in the farthest corner of Surrey – the little stream beside the path marks the Hampshire border. Soon you'll arrive at a pretty pool hidden away among the trees (4 miles), which is fed by the overflow from the Great Pond. Few of the thousands of people who visit the Ponds each year know this lovely spot exists, so it's a popular haunt of the shyer forms of wildlife.

At its far end of the pool the path climbs a slight rise and comes out onto the dam of the Great Pond, with a truly magnificent vista immediately in front of you. The great sheet of water stretches away into the distance with the open heathland of the King's Ridge behind it, providing a purple-tinged backdrop when the ling and bell-heather are in flower in late summer. Sometimes the water will be busy with boats from the local sailing club.

Frensham Great Pond from Pond Lane

√ Frensham Great Pond to Thursley

On leaving the bridleway turn right into Bacon Lane, which runs across the top of the pond's dam, then, immediately before the Frensham Pond Hotel, turn left into Pond Lane. On the left, opposite the hotel's dining room, are the old stew ponds, which were used for rearing and stocking fish.

The Frensham Pond Hotel has had a long and varied career. The original building, parts of which are said to date from the 13th century, was a farmhouse. It subsequently became the White Horse Inn, and around the turn of the century had a reputation as a gambling den popular among young army officers from Aldershot. According to a local historian, it was also the 'scene of many a meeting of the Pond Club, whose celebrations too often degenerated into orgies of intemperance, and free-fights between the

champions of neighbouring villages'! Things are different now; since the 1960s the hotel has been vastly developed and expanded. It now has over 50 rooms and a restaurant with superb views over the pond.

Frensham Pond Hotel, Bacon Lane, Churt. 01252 795161. Food Rest Acc

Despite its name, Pond Lane curves away from the water's edge, which is occupied by the Frensham Sailing Club. The ride re-enters Surrey just beyond the club's grounds where the pond's main inlet stream, which marks the border, passes under the road in a culvert. The pond itself can be seen through the trees on the left, with the popular sandy beach on the far bank.

At the far end of the lane, watch for a second culvert which carries another small stream under the road. This is the stream which fed the original pond from which the Great Pond was developed. It comes from a small dammed pond on the right just before Pond Cottage.

☞ *At the junction where Pond Lane meets the A287 Farnham Road there is a choice of route to be made. The most scenic way crosses the heathland of Frensham Common, but it is extremely sandy and you will almost certainly have to walk for much of the next mile. It is well worth it though, as the countryside is very beautiful and quiet, and we think it is not to be missed. However, if you would rather stay on made-up roads, you will find an alternative route described on page 140.*

At the end of Pond Lane turn left onto the main road, but just 50 yards further on turn right onto the signed bridleway. Be careful not to go too far along the main road – the turning is immediately before the parking restriction signs.

The bridleway is very sandy and you may need to dismount straightaway. Follow the bridleway for about a quarter of a mile to a junction where several paths meet (5 miles). The track you want is marked by a blue-painted post with the number 42, which you will find slightly to the left of straight ahead.

The glories of the surrounding country-side should provide ample compensation if you have to walk along this stretch. Great efforts are being made to ensure that a mixture of different types of landscape will exist here. In some places scrub and saplings are being cleared to ensure the survival of parts of the ancient open heathland. In other areas broadleaved woodland is being encouraged, while elsewhere the stately Scots Pine dominates.

To the left are the heights of the King's Ridge, the western slopes of which could be seen from the dam of the Great Pond. Evidence of prehistoric man's activities has been found all over this area. There are

burial mounds from the Bronze Age on top of the ridge, and Stone Age tools around 10,000 years old have been found on nearby sites.

On the right of the track is a small lake in the private grounds of Lowicks House, and the house itself is passed a short distance further on. Notice the summerhouse beside the track, with its somewhat out-of-scale weathervane. After Lowicks House the bridleway follows a raised causeway which is much better for cycling, but it turns off (sharply) to the right at a junction about 200 yards beyond the house – a footpath continues straight ahead. The blue-painted posts marked '42' will show you're on the right route.

Another sandy length of path follows, but you soon come out onto the gravelled drive of a house called Graywalls. Keep going until you come to a tarred lane – inappropriately named Sandy Lane.

Turn right onto the lane, and almost immediately there is a ford through the stream that feeds Frensham Little Pond (almost 6 miles). The bottom is lined with concrete blocks and, as they would probably give you an uncomfortable ride (and even tip you off into the water), it seems better to use the footbridge alongside.

The lane passes through a pleasant stretch of woodland before it reaches the the heathland settlement of Rushmoor. At the top of a sudden climb the lane bends sharply to the right and about 400 yards after that it ends at a junction with Tilford Road, by a phone box. Turn right into Tilford Road; the road is not too busy, but its straightness can encourage traffic to speed, so take care.

A little further on the road passes between two of the Devil's Jumps. Tradition tells of the Devil jumping about between these three unusual conical hills, scooping up handfuls of earth from what became the Devil's Punchbowl to throw at Thor, who lived at nearby Thursley. Thor, thoroughly annoyed by these antics, retaliated by picking up a stone and throwing it back, knocking the Devil off his Jumps. You can still see the stone today!

At the next junction (just over 7 miles) take the turning on the left signposted 'Elstead & Thursley'. After a short, steep climb; turn left again into Thursley Road. (If you're gasping for refreshment by this stage, continue along the Tilford Road for another few yards to the Pride of the Valley Hotel, then, after your break, take the road signposted 'Thursley' opposite the hotel – it forms the third side of a triangular junction.)

The next stretch of road is level riding as it passes Churt Place, which occupies the site of Bron-y-de, built in 1921 as the retirement home of Lloyd George, where he became a farmer and fruit-grower. (It burned down in the 1960s.)

On the left,opposite Churt Place, are a couple of small ponds formed by damming a stream. This stream runs through a deeply-cut valley and there is a stiff uphill stretch ahead as the road climbs nearly 100 feet in the next 500 yards or so as it approaches Pitch Place (just over 8 miles). To the left, as you reach the crest, is Kettlebury Hill, the highest of the sandy peaks hereabouts, and then the road undulates and bends for the next half mile.

Pitch Place has given its name to this small hamlet, which now consists of a mixture of old timber-framed farmhouses and cottages and large turn-of-the-century houses. Pass the junction with Sailors Lane and half a mile further on turn right into Dye House Road, which is signposted 'Thursley & Hindhead'.

The Dye House, a large Georgian mansion, is on the right at the start of a steeply

curving descent into a valley. At the bottom (9 miles) the road bends sharply over a small bridge. The stream which flows under the bridge, the Smallbrook, is fed by the springs which carved out the Devil's Punchbowl.

After the bridge the road bends one way and then the other, climbing steeply all the while. Then, all of a sudden, the way ahead is straight and level as the road approaches Thursley village. The flat expanse of the village cricket ground comes as something of a surprise after the hilly landscape of the last half-mile or so.

Stop at the small green at the junction with The Street. Before turning off up The Street there are two short diversions you might care to take. The first is down The Lane, a short side turning which also starts by the green. The 16th century timber-framed Olde Hall (on the left as you go down the lane) is especially outstanding.

The other diversion you may like to make is along the main road for another 100 yards or so to The Three Horseshoes pub, one of the all-too-rare opportunities for refreshment on this ride. The plain Victorian frontage of the building hides a much older structure behind. There are some interesting old photographs of the area in the bar.

🍺 *The Three Horseshoes, Dye House Road, Thursley. Free house. 01252 703268. Food (not Sun eve) G Rest*

Thursley: *The 'No Through Road' sign at the end of The Street belies the fact that before the turnpike road was built this was the London–Portsmouth road. Fortunately, Thursley was bypassed long before the motor vehicle had any llow the old road over the heath all the way to Hindhead. It gives a good idea of how rough travel was more than 200 years ago.*

The unknown sailor's gravestone

The idyllic cottages which line The Street may have witnessed many famous men and women passing by their doors – kings and queens like Henry VIII and Elizabeth I on their way to inspect their fleets at Portsmouth, admirals with thoughts of great sea battles uppermost on their minds, and men of letters and learning like Pepys, whose duties with the Admiralty often brought him along this road. Pepys' diaries record the perils of 17th century journeys in this area. For August 6th, 1668 he wrote: 'So to coach again, and got to Liphook, late over Hindhead, having an old man, a guide, in the coach with us; but got thither with great fear of being out of our way, it being ten at night.'

Then there were the ordinary folk, many of them sailors heading home after a long voyage or returning on foot, money spent, back to their ships. Dickens' Nicholas Nickleby and Smike, having fallen on hard times and little better than penniless, passed through on just such a journey to seek work and their fortunes in Portsmouth.

One sailor came this way on 24th September 1786. Why he was walking is far from clear, for he had money. Enough money, in fact, for him to pay the expenses of food, drink and board of three fellow travellers with whom he fell in on the way. They made their way to Thursley, where they were seen together leaving the Red Lion.

A while later two local men walking to Hindhead noticed something in the roadside bushes which they discovered to be the stripped body of the sailor. His throat had been cut so badly that his head was almost severed from his body. The men raced back to the Red Lion to raise the alarm and a party set off in pursuit of the murderers. They were apprehended in an inn near Petersfield in the very act of selling their victim's clothes.

Tried and convicted at Kingston, the three of them were brought back to Hindhead to be hanged and afterwards gibbeted in chains, at the spot known today as Gibbet Hill. The gibbet, with its gruesome load, stood there until it was blown down in a storm in December 1791.

The identity of the sailor was never discovered, and he was buried in Thursley churchyard. His tombstone, which was paid for by public subscription, can be seen in the north-west corner of the churchyard. A memorial stands beside the old road at the spot where the murder took place, and a Celtic cross on the summit of Hindhead marks the site of the gibbet.

The name of Thursley comes from the Anglo-Saxon name Thor's Leah, a clearing or grove sacred to Thor, the pagan god of thunder, who was usually depicted as wielding a hammer and may thus have been linked with the local iron industry.

William Cobbett was a regular visitor to Thursley, which he usually made his first or last stop on his journeys into Hampshire or Sussex. But he would never take the road over Hindhead if he could help it. The bare sandy

IN THURSLEY VILLAGE.

heath was, he said, "certainly the most villainous spot that God ever made".

The architect Sir Edwin Lutyens (1869–1944) spent his boyhood years living in The Cottage (now Lutyens House) near the green and the style of his work owes much to the traditional Surrey buildings with which he grew up. His first work was the conversion of The Corner, a row of cottages opposite the end of The Street which he made into a single house when he was only 19.

⑤ Thursley to Tilford

The Street is absolutely delightful, and we recommend you get off and walk so as not to miss any of its charms. At the far end of The Street the road bends to the right towards the cluster of buildings by the church and becomes Highfield Lane.

The Church of St Michael and All Angels, Thursley *is well worth a look, even though it has suffered at the hands of Victorian 'restorers'. The original building is Saxon, and in 1927 the vicar, noticing an outline on the north wall of the chancel after heavy rain, chipped away at the rendering and uncovered two Saxon windows, complete with wooden frames to which sheets of horn or cloth, the latter oiled to make it translucent, would have been fixed as glazing.*

The dominant feature of the church is the immense timber structure which supports the belfry. Built in the late 15th century, it is so unnecessarily massive that it has been suggested that it may have originally been intended as a support for something far more substantial than just a wooden belfry. Fortunately the restorers left this unique structure alone, as they did the attractive sundial on the south face of the tower, with its inscription 'Hora pars vitæ' – 'an hour is a part of life'.

Hill Farm, next to the church, also deserves a closer look. From the front it could be a typical country house of the 18th century, but from the side you can see that the front

was put on a much older building to bring it up to date with the latest fashion.

After a pause to visit the church, continue up the lane as it begins its steady climb towards the heights of Hindhead and the Devil's Punchbowl, although this ride won't take you quite that far! The lane narrows beyond the church, and although there are some modern houses along the first part of the road, they remain hidden behind the high banks and hedges (10 miles).

The climb is continuous from this point, but at least it's not too steep. As you make your way up the hill, glance back at the church spire to see how far you've climbed. At Little Cowdray Farm the road divides and a sign warns that conditions beyond are unsuitable for motor vehicles.

Turn right, following the sign for Punchbowl Farm, but after a few yards the lane bends left past some cottages. It is vital you stop here. Dismount, and take the cinder path signposted 'Ridgeway' to the right of the first cottage. Another notice warns of its unsuitability for motor vehicles. The path is steep with a loose surface and you could lose control if you tried to ride down it. (It also has some steps cut into it.) The descent leads into the valley of the Smallbrook, which it crosses by a footbridge. You will most probably have to push your bike up the steeply-climbing track on the other side of the valley.

When you reach Ridgeway Farm at the top, have a look at the construction of the wall of the outbuilding beside the track. Set into the mortar round the lumps of Bargate stone are small, dark chips of carstone, a hard iron-bearing sandstone. This technique is known as galleting and can be seen in many buildings in this area, especially churches. It dates back to medieval times, but its purpose is unknown. It may simply be decorative, or it has been suggested that the idea is to create a ring of iron to keep out the devil.

From the farm go straight ahead, crossing Sailors Lane, and up the slope towards Upper Ridgeway Farm. The road curves to the left, so that the farm, with its two magnificent timber-framed houses, appears quite suddenly. The road curves around a small, neatly-kept pond and then begins to twist and turn as it crosses the spurs of high ground which jut out from the Hindhead ridge. Beyond Upper Ridgeway Farm there is a dip in the road (11 miles). Watch out for Glenhead Farm – although the house is modern, note the terracotta work on its exterior. After yet another dip the road passes Hyde Farm, parts of which may date from the 14th or 15th centuries. During recent renovations a well more than 100 feet deep was discovered inside the house. This small belt of fertile land in the midst of sandy heaths has a long history. It is thought Hyde Farm may be the property mentioned in a Saxon charter of AD 688, in which the gift to the church of two 'hides' of land in Cert (Churt) is recorded.

Just beyond Hyde Farm the road curves around the rim of a valley and, after passing an area of coppiced woodland, bends steeply and sharply to the left. Soon after the stone quarry near Stock Farm (just under 12 miles) the road ends at a junction with the Hindhead–Tilford road. Turn right and enjoy the downhill run, with its views ahead towards the Devil's Jumps and the surrounding countryside.

Pass the junction with Hale House Lane, just after which is the Pride of the Valley Hotel, on the corner of the Jumps Road. The hotel, which dates from 1870, was built by the Marden family who also ran the White Horse (now the Frensham Pond Hotel). Part of the building was originally a butcher's shop.

The hotel sign features the area's most famous resident; the staff are no doubt tired of being asked if their fathers knew Lloyd George. They (or more likely their grandfathers) may well have done, because he had a shop opposite the hotel where he sold his farm produce. (It was later a restaurant but is now a private house.)

Pride of the Valley Hotel, Jumps Road, Churt. Free house. 01428 605799. Food Rest

From the Pride of the Valley continue along the main road between the Devil's Jumps (follow the sign for Tilford); you'll recognise this stretch from having travelled along it in the opposite direction on your way to Thursley. Pass the end of Sandy Lane (13 miles), and continue through Rushmoor on the long, straight, and fairly level stretch of road. There is a Tilford village sign just after the junction with Grange Road (14 miles), but this is a bit misleading, as there is still more than a mile to go.

The Hankley (previously the Duke of Cambridge), Tilford Road, Tilford. Free house. 01252 792236. Food G.

The road crosses the unmade Elstead–Frensham track (15 miles) and then it is only a short downhill run past the church and down to the green and the car park near the Barley Mow.

For information on Tilford, please see the notes in Ride G.

Alternative sections of route

① Tilford to Frensham Little Pond *off-road via* Tilford Common

From the car park at Tilford, ride up the hill away from the pub and the river and turn left into Tilford Road by the school, continuing uphill. Pass the church with its war memorial, and then turn right onto a track immediately after the entrance to The Little House. Its byway sign is missing but the entrance is beside a small hut bearing British Gas signs.

This was once the main route between Frensham and Elstead. (It crossed the Tilford Road to continue past Stockbridge Pond and across Hankley Common.)

The surface is tarred for the first few yards but then becomes sandy. At the fork a few yards further on take the left-hand branch. There is a lot of flinty stone in the track so go cautiously and, if necessary, get off and walk. There are quite a few dips and sand accumulates deeply at the bottom of them. The track passes open fields on the left which are used as a forestry nursery; aerial photographs of this area have shown the remains of a Celtic field system which existed here more than 2,000 years ago. The fenced-off woodland on the right is used for keeping free-range pigs, as the churned-up ground and sparse vegetation may indicate.

After 1½ miles the track comes to the public toilets near Frensham Little Pond. To reach the road and the pond dismount and walk along the path which is blocked by an old tree trunk on the left.

① Tilford to Frensham Little Pond *by road*

Leave Tilford as in the alternative above, but continue along Tilford Road past the byway turning. Then, about 1¼ miles from the car park, turn right into Grange Road. Pass the Tilford Park Nursing Home and follow the road straight on through the regimented fields and plantations of the local forestry industry. After a mile of easy, level riding you will enter more traditional woodland, and shortly afterwards the road dips to a small ford, which is not usually more than a few inches deep. The stream is the outflow of Frensham Little Pond, which you can glimpse through the trees on the left.

√ Frensham Great Pond to Thursley

Turn right out of Pond Lane onto the A287. This road can be busy but it should be safe provided you're careful. After a little more than half a mile on this road, turn left into the Jumps Road. Follow this for about 1½ miles until you come to the Pride of the Valley Hotel. From there, take the road virtually opposite which is signposted for Thursley, and then continue as for the main route.

Ride I:
Fold Villages of the Surrey Weald

Dunsfold • Stovolds Hill • Lakers Green • Alfold Crossways • Alfold • High Bridge • Knightons • Furnace Bridge or Upper Ifold • Durfold Wood • Hazel Bridge • Chiddingfold • Hambledon • Pockford • Dunsfold

Distance:	Between 9½ and 21 miles
Landranger Maps:	186
Pathfinder Maps:	1245 and 1246

On its southern flank Surrey extends into a region known as the Weald, which is (broadly speaking) the area between the North and South Downs. Two main types of countryside dominate the area – the Lower Greensand hills, close to the downs, and the central belt of Weald Clay. At one time the clay was covered with a great and near-impenetrable oak forest called the Andredesweald, which stretched from Kent, through Surrey and Sussex into Hampshire. Habitation was slow to come to the area, but finally small settlements were established in clearings in the forest – folds, as they were known. The names of the villages and farms through which this ride passes reflect these origins.

Looking at the peaceful scenery, it is incredible to think that, until the coming of the Industrial Revolution, this was one of the country's industrial heartlands. Iron and glassmaking flourished throughout these woods, and the remains of these industries, which must once have covered the area in a pall of smoke, can still be seen at many places along the ride. Since the war another major industry has dominated the area, and you will certainly encounter signs of it on the ground, if not in the air. The wartime Dunsfold airfield is now a British Aerospace factory and test flight base.

Allow a full day for the complete ride, especially if you choose to tackle the more difficult bridleway stages (see the special note below).

Special Note

In centuries past, the thick, sticky clay of the Weald caused immense problems for transport. It was so bad that oxen were the favoured draught animals of the region for hundreds of years, their cloven hooves being better suited to the clay than those of horses. On unsurfaced tracks these conditions still exist, making off-road cycling an interesting experience, to say the least. Some bridleways are simply routes – hardly visible – across fields of pasture, bumpy but exhilarating! Others are well-used paths. But their use, especially by horses and in winter, churns up the clay into an almost impassable morass, and matters may be little better when this mess has been baked hard by the summer sun. It makes cycling pretty well impossible and even pushing a bike can be hard work.

Ride 1
Fold Villages of the Surrey Weald

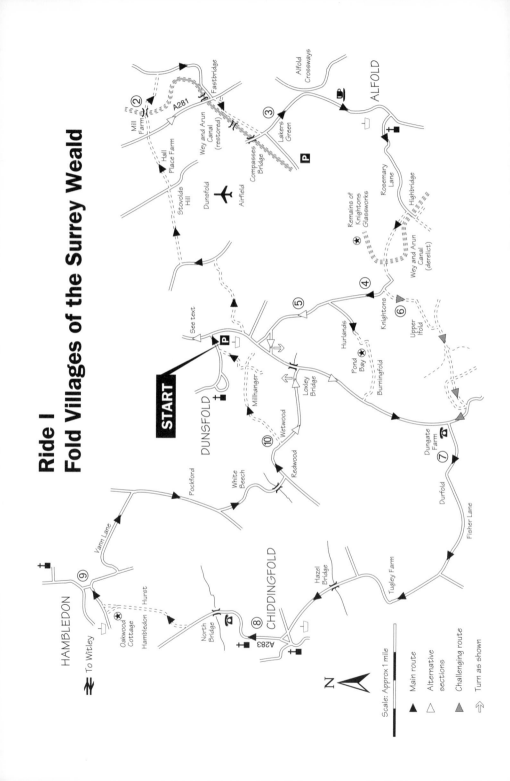

START

HAMBLEDON

To Witley

Oakwood Cottage

Hambledon Hurst

⑨

Vann Lane

North Bridge

CHIDDINGFOLD

⑧

A283

Hazel Bridge

Tugley Farm

Fisher Lane

Durfold

⑦

Dungate Farm

Pockford

White Beech

Redwood

Wetwood

⑩

Millhanger

Loxley Bridge

Burningfold

Pond Bay ✸

Hurlands

⑤

Knightons

④

Upper Ifold

⑥

Wey and Arun Canal (derelict)

Remains of Knightons Glassworks ✸

Highbridge

Rosemary Lane

ALFOLD

Alfold Crossways

③

Lakers Green

P

Compasses Bridge

Wey and Arun Canal (restored)

Airfield

Dunsfold

Scovolds Hill

Hall Place Farm

Mill Farm

②

A281

Fastbridge

DUNSFOLD

P

See text

N

Scale: Approx 1 mile

▲ Main route
△ Alternative sections
▲ Challenging route
⇧ Turn as shown

Our recommended route avoids paths *which are likely to give severe problems. However, there are some difficult bridleways which pass through countryside which is well worth exploring, and we have offered one of these as a 'challenging alternative'. By all means try this section if you have a suitable bike and the weather has been reasonable. Just be prepared for the conditions you may find.*

There is one other important point to note. On parts of this ride bridleways run through private property – even through gardens and along drives. Don't worry about this and don't be put off! Although it may feel odd to cycle through someone's front gate, on public bridleways you have an unquestionable right to walk, cycle or ride a horse! We have researched these rides carefully to make sure you will not be trespassing if you follow our directions.

Starting Points

Start at the car park on the green at Dunsfold, near the shop and post office. Informal parking is possible in villages such as Hambledon and Chiddingfold and there is also a car park on the Dunsfold to Alfold road; it's off the route but not too far from Dunsfold. There are also some lay-bys and wide verges along the roads – be sure not to block farm or forest gates – and some pubs, if asked, may let customers park while they go cycling.

⇌ Witley station is on South West Trains' Waterloo–Guildford–Portsmouth line, a mile or so west of Hambledon.

The Route in Brief

① Head S through village then TL on BW just after village hall. Pass small pond and Pound Farm, then TR onto gravelled track

by gate of New Pound Farm. Follow track between fields then down slope into woods. At bottom of hill cross stream and continue beside airfield fence. At road TL.

TR through gate about 100 yds after turn to High Billinghurst Farm onto BW across field. Aim for gate on far side 100 yds in from RH edge of field. Through gate and TR onto concrete track. When concrete track goes off to L after broken old gate, keep SO up path through pines, past fenced enclosure. Beware – old manholes!

At end of woods path enters field. Keep to RH edge, then take narrow path between old gateposts. Pass pond and through gate into farmyard. Follow concrete farm road SO past cowshed to road. Cross over, heading slightly R, into drive of Hall Place (BW). At Hall Place Farm pass through small gate to L of main entrance. Keep to L and follow track along side of farm then down slope. Pass cottages to reach A281.

② Cross to Mill Farm drive opposite (BW). At farm pass first buildings to farmyard, then out through gateway in far RH corner. Go through second gateway onto track, which soon crosses course of old canal and adjacent stream bridge. After a while go through gate into short field. SO to gate ahead leading into larger field. Follow hedge on R to wooden 5-bar gate and leave field, passing wooden shed. Follow driveway through garden to road.

TR onto road and continue to A281. Cross road to BW opposite (loop of old road), turning R onto narrow grassy track. Follow track through gateway into field, aiming for L end of buildings in distance. Leave field through gate along track past mobile home park, then SO along access road to road at Lakers Green.

③ TL out of BW onto road then SO at junc. At Alfold Crossways TR onto B2133 Alfold road. In centre of Alfold TR by Crown pub into Rosemary Lane. After about 1 mile TR immediately before isolated house at High Bridge onto BW into Forestry Commission woods. Go round gate onto BW then keep SO on main track as another BW diverges to R. Keep SO at crossways of paths, then go round end of another gate. Pass old wooden garage then cross bed of old canal. Pass entrance to Sidney Court, then track becomes metalled road – Knightons Lane. At bottom of dip after Old Knightons (at junc of lane to Upper Ifold) choose which route to follow next (see text).

√ *To Durfold via Furnace Bridge*
Keep SO along Knightons Lane for ½ mile, then TL at next turning, SP Hurlands & Howicks. Follow lane through farm gate then SO past farm buildings and out of farmyard by gate at far end. Follow gravelled track down hill, then round to right, over bank, and through one gate on far side, then another. Leave track by gates of Burningfold Manor and follow BW across grass and into wood. BW heads to R and over bridge, heading towards tarred drive, but turns L just before it. After 200 yds it merges into drive. At end of drive TL onto road. At phone box by Durfold Farm TR into Fisher Lane, SP Chiddingfold. Continue from stage Δ.

⑤ *To Durfold via Loxley Bridge*
Follow Knightons Lane for about 1 mile then TL into Chapel Hill. At TJ at end TL into main road down hill to Loxley Bridge. Immediately after bridge TL into Plaistow Lane. Follow this for 1½ miles to phone box near Durfold Farm then TR into Fisher Lane, SP Chiddingfold. Continue from stage Δ.

≈ *To Durfold via Upper Ifold*
At bottom of hill after Old Knightons TL onto BW to Upper Ifold Farm. Follow track past farm and outbuildings, then through short belt of woods. After Upper Ifold House keep SO past stables, then FR when track divides. Pass more stables then track enters woods and splits three ways. Ignore

indistinct path on L, but veer L at following fork. Next section is in bad condition.

At gravel forest track TR then immediately L along edge of wood. At TJ of paths by Dungate Farm, TR to reach road. TR onto road for about 400 yds then TL into Fishers Lane, SP Chiddingfold.

Δ Follow the road for over 3 miles straight through to Chiddingfold.

⑧ At Chiddingfold TR onto A283 for about 1 mile through North Bridge. Pass gates of Northbridge House then TR opposite sign for North End Farm onto BW. At Hurst Cottage veer slightly L then follow track through woods. Cross bridge over stream, then after 400 yds FL onto a drive, passing a pond and some cottages, to reach the road by the cricket green.

⑨ TR onto road (Vann Lane) and head E. Pass the end of Woodlands Road, then follow lane sharp L by brickworks entrance. Keep SO for about 2 miles, past junc with Upper Vann Lane, then, after Pockford Farm TL into White Beech Lane, SP Dunsfold. At next TJ TL, again SP Dunsfold. After less than ½ mile TL at Woodside Cottage onto BW, SP Duns Copse and Wetwood Rough.

⑩ Almost immediately veer R onto farm track, then veer R again after 400 yds at gate. At bottom of hill by Mill House TL over bridge and follow drive to road. TR then R again for Dunsfold or TL then L again for church.

Dunsfold

The Ride

① Dunsfold to Mill Farm

Dunsfold straggles along a village green which is over half a mile long, and, as the buildings are set well back from the road, it has a very spacious look. The heart of the village is towards the south, where the green merges with the Common. The village church is some distance away. Apart from the green, one of the village's claims to fame is its number of ponds. Once there were seven, but a couple have now been filled in. One, on the opposite side of the road to The Sun pub, has a cobbled bottom, allowing carts and cattle to be driven through to wash off the mud.

Have a walk around the village, taking a good look at Forge Cottage, between the pub and the shop. It is a rare example – only three are known in Surrey – of an aisled hall house,

built like a barn with two rows of posts dividing the building into a nave and aisles. Note how the chimney doesn't seem to match the style of the rest of the building. That's because it was added much later; the original would have had only a smoke hole.

In 1992, to celebrate the fiftieth anniversary of the opening of the airfield, a fascinating book entitled 'Dunsfold – Before the Airfield' was written and published by Alan Siney (4 The Riddens, Loxwood Road, Rudgwick, Horsham, West Sussex RH12 3DR). It covers the general history of both Dunsfold and the neighbouring villages, and looks at those places which were lost or dramatically altered by the airfield's construction.

⊞ *The Sun Inn, The Common. Friary Meux. 01483 200242. Food G*

⌂ *Dunsfold Village Stores & PO, The Common. Open Mon–Fri 6–1, 2–5.30ish, Sat 6–1, Sun 7–11.*

☞ *The first stage of the ride uses a number of bridleways across fields and through woods. It's a fascinating route to follow, but if conditions are bad, you may prefer the alternative road route given on page 160.*

Head south through the village and turn left onto the bridleway just after the village hall. It begins as a tarred drive running along the right-hand side of Dunsfold Free Church. Follow it down the slope by an ancient barn and around the edge of a delightful little pond, past the old and highly picturesque Pound Farm.

At the corner of the farm buildings, turn right onto a gravelled track, as indicated by another bridleway sign. (Don't make the mistake of continuing into the entrance of New Pound Farm.) The track, which runs between two fields, is in a reasonable, if slightly bumpy, state, but watch for patches of clay which could be slippery in wet weather, particularly on the slope down into the woods (about 1 mile). Get off and walk if necessary. At the bottom of the hill cross the footbridge over the stream.

On the far side of the stream, the track runs beside the airfield's chain-link fence until it comes to a tarred but deserted lane. This is one of the old roads blocked off when the airfield was built and it is a real joy to cycle along it. Turn left along the road and pass through the private woodlands which surround it. As you come out of the wood, continue for about 100 yards past the turning to High Billinghurst Farm and then go through the gate on the right, by the bridleway sign. This leads into a field from which there are superb views towards Hascombe Hill, about a mile away.

The course of the bridleway isn't obvious on the ground, but it heads straight across the middle of the field in the direction

indicated by the sign. By the time you get to the woods on the far side you want to be about 100 yards in from the right-hand edge of the field. You should be able to see the gate by the time you're halfway across the field. As this is a bridleway, you can cycle across the field if you wish. Go through the gate and turn right onto the concrete track on the other side (2 miles).

After a very short distance, go through a broken-down old gate. The concrete track turns away to the left; don't follow this, but instead continue straight ahead up the path through the pine trees, passing a fenced enclosure on the left. This area was once part of the airfield and old concrete manholes and other remains are scattered along the way, so take care.

At the end of the woods the path comes out into another field. Keep to the right-hand edge and then take the narrow path between the two old gateposts, which almost seem to be tucked away in the bushes. Pass the pond – an old sandpit – and go through the gate into a farmyard. From there the concrete farm road running straight ahead will take you past the cowshed and down to the public road.

This road was the original Guildford–Horsham road which was bypassed when the airfield was built. It now comes to a dead end at the main gate of the airfield. Cross the road, heading slightly to the right, and turn into the drive of Hall Place (as the sign shows, it is another bridleway).

Follow the drive right through to the gates of Hall Place Farm. The bridleway passes through a narrow gate on the left of the main entrance – press down the spring-loaded button to release the catch. Keep to the left and carry on down the track which runs along the side of the farm. After a while the track heads down a hill and passes a small group of cottages before coming out onto the A281 road – built to bypass the airfield (3 miles).

② Mill Farm to Lakers Green

☞ *If you wish you can turn right onto the A281 and take a short cut to Fast Bridge, passing the end of the airfield on the way, but the road is very busy.*

Cross the road to the driveway of Mill Farm opposite. The farm keeps a large flock of geese, which you will probably see either in the fields or in one of the barns. As you approach the farm itself, go past the first of the buildings and into the farmyard. Head for the far right-hand corner of the yard and go out through the gate there (it may be open or closed). Immediately after that is another gate, which leads onto a somewhat overgrown track. On the right is a hedge bordering the farmhouse garden, at the far end of which the track

crosses the dried-up course of the old Wey and Arun Canal. The bridge over the canal has long been filled in, but a few yards further on a similar brick-built bridge over a neighbouring stream survives.

Continue along the track and through a gate leading into a short field. Cross the field to another gate immediately ahead and go through it into a second, larger field. Keep to the right-hand edge of this field, following the hedge as it curves around to the right. Leave by the wooden five-bar gate in the far right-hand corner, beyond which is a large wooden shed.

This is one of those somewhat unnerving places where a bridleway goes through someone's garden; in this case that belonging to a magnificent half-timbered house called Great Garson. Go past the wooden shed in the garden, down the drive, and turn right onto the lane outside

Great Garson

The Wey and Arun Junction Canal
London's lost route to the sea

The idea of building a canal to link the River Wey and the River Arun, and so provide an inland water route between London and the south coast, was first put forward in the mid-17th century. Nothing became of it at that time, but a hundred years later the Wey had been made navigable as far as Godalming and the Arun to beyond Pulborough, and a scheme was promoted for a canal to fill the 20-mile gap between them. However, work did not start until 1813 and the canal was not completed until 1816.

The new canal was a failure right from the start. The through traffic which had fondly been expected failed to materialise. The coastal route proved more attractive, especially now that the war with the French had ended and Channel shipping was no longer threatened. Local traffic was insufficient to pay the costs of running the canal, although the benefits to agriculture in the area were considerable.

The supply of water to keep the canal topped up was always a problem. The company had enlarged Vachery Pond, just south of Cranleigh, to act as a reservoir, but even so, there were often restrictions in dry periods. This meant the carrying capacity of boats had to be reduced, further undermining the venture's usefulness.

The canal had been in operation for only a couple of decades when the railways began to spread across the south of England. In 1865 the line from Guildford to Horsham via Cranleigh opened for business, depriving the canal of even its local traffic. By 1871 it was bankrupt and was abandoned after a working life of just 55 years. It was already in a poor state of repair, and it did not take long for nature to begin to reclaim its course. Most of the bridges were demolished once the canal had been drained, and even brickwork from the locks seems to have been scavenged. Parts of the canal bed were sold off and have now been built over, but its old course can be traced for considerable distances.

Interest in the canal was revived in the 1960s with the publication of the poignantly-titled book *London's Lost Route to the Sea* by Paul Vine. With several schemes to restore closed canals being promoted in other parts of the country, local enthusiasts set up a Trust to attempt the 'impossible'. Progress has been slow, but parts of the canal have now been restored and rewatered, although it will still be many years before there is any chance of it reopening as a through route.

Fast Bridge

the front gates. The lane descends a slight hill before curving to the right (about 4 miles), after which it bends left and runs beside a restored and rewatered stretch of the old canal as it approaches Fast Bridge. The original bridge over the canal, which leads to a farm, can still be seen on the right, just before the lane joins the A281.

Cross the main road to reach the bridleway almost opposite. This follows a derelict loop of old road for the first few yards, before turning off to the right onto a narrow, grassy track. This is Farnhurst Lane, an old green lane which runs parallel to the canal. Keep your eyes peeled and you'll see the beautifully-restored Farnhurst canal bridge, half-hidden among the trees on the right.

Follow the track through a gateway and into a field. Its course across the field is quite faint, but aim for the left end of the

buildings in the distance and you'll come to the gate which lets you out. From there another grassy track passes the side of a mobile home park. At the far end, continue straight ahead along the tarred access road to reach the road by the Three Compasses Inn at Lakers Green (5 miles).

The Three Compasses Inn. Courage. 01483 275729. Open all day from 11.30 (exc Mon 2.30–4.30.) Food (very reasonably priced) 12–2 and 7.30-9.00 G

Lakers Green: *The road through Lakers Green which passes the Three Compasses was once the old Guildford–Horsham road, but today it ends at the back gate of the airfield which was built across its route. Just inside the airfield perimeter you can see a section which is still in the condition of a pre-war A-road, complete with its original surface of flint chippings. Immediately outside the gate is Compasses Bridge over the canal from which* there is a good view of the restored section; there was a wharf just here where the inauguration of the canal took place on September 29th, 1816.

There were once four acres of grassy open common land at Lakers Green before the trees encroached. Lakers Green House, just off the Dunsfold Road, had to be demolished when the airfield was built because it was on the approach to a runway. Several other buildings in the area suffered a similar fate.

The airfield was built in 1942 by Canadian forces. Eight years after the war ended it was sold to Hawker Aircraft Ltd, now part of British Aerospace, and production facilities were added to the wartime hangers. The Hawk and the Harrier were among the famous aircraft built at Dunsfold.

③ Lakers Green to Knightons

Turn left out of the bridleway by the Three Compasses Inn and at the junction go straight ahead in the direction of Alfold Crossways, about half a mile further on. At the junction at Alfold Crossways, turn right onto the B2133 Alfold road.

Alfold Crossways: Notice the tollhouse on the right just before the junction. If you look closely, it seems to be back-to-front – and it is! In 1757 the road from Guildford to Alfold, through Lakers Green and the airfield site, was made into a turnpike, with a tollhouse facing onto the road at Alfold Crossways. At that time the roads to Fast Bridge and Horsham, which are now part of the A281, were both just small country lanes. In 1809 the new road to Horsham opened, but its junction with the existing road, just south of the tollhouse, was awkward because it had to twist its way between existing buildings.

As the Horsham road grew in importance compared with that to Alfold, it was decided to change the junction layout. The road from Guildford through Lakers Green was realigned to run through the garden behind the tollhouse

so that the back of the house now faced the road. As a result, the tollkeepers found that their well, previously at the bottom of the garden, was now across the road! When the airfield was built in 1942, the old Guildford road was blocked off and a bypass built via Fast Bridge, connecting with the Horsham road at Alfold Crossways. This left the present rather strange road layout at the Crossways, where there seem to be two separate roads running parallel.

The road on from the Crossways is not particularly inspiring, but the village of Alfold is less than a mile away. The school, on the left on the approach to the village, is about 6 miles from the start.

🍺 *Alfold Farm Shop & Tea Room, Loxwood Road. 01403 752028*
🍵 *Alfold Stores*
🏢 *The Crown. Morlands. Food G*

In the centre of Alfold turn right into Rosemary Lane, just by the Crown pub. The scene here is possibly one of the most delightful village cameos in the whole of Surrey, with the pub, the row of tile-hung cottages which follow on from it, and the church, with the village stocks by the churchyard entrance.

Alfold: The main feature of the village is the church of St Nicholas which is well worth a visit. In the churchyard look for the slab of Sussex marble which is said to mark the grave of Jean Carré, one of the leading French Huguenot glassmakers who settled and practised their trade in this area. He died in 1572.

Alfold church, like most others in the area was built in the 13th century, which must have been about the time these villages were established. It is built of Bargate stone rubble, and rendered. Inside it has much fine timber work as befits a church in the oak forests of the Weald. It has a similarity to the church at Thursley, some 10 miles to the north-west, in that the spire at Alfold is also supported on massive timber beams.

Alfold

Continue from the church along Rosemary Lane. It soon seems as if you have left the village, but there are several old cottages and farms, as well as some more modern properties, along the lane.

At Velhurst Croft, just after Rosemary Cottage (a little over 7 miles), the road turns sharply to the left. About three hundred yards after this, the lane ends at a rather isolated house at High Bridge. The name derives from the bridge which once crossed the old canal, the dry bed of which can be seen in the garden of the house.

Turn right onto the bridleway which curves off past the front of the house. It runs through Forestry Commission land and most of it has been maintained in an excellent state, although some recent repairs have involved large quantities of loose flints and shingle, which can be difficult to cycle on.

A gate blocks the entrance to the bridleway but you can ride around the end of it. The wood on the right-hand side is Glasshouse Copse, commemorating the industry which used to be based there. Shortly after the gate another bridleway diverges to the right, but the main track is quite obvious.

At the crossways of paths keep straight on into a thicker part of the wood, and go around yet another gate across the track. Soon after this you'll pass an old wooden garage on the left, and then the driveway of Old Lock Cottage joins the track (about 8 miles).

At this point keep an eye out for the fence and fir hedges of Sidney Court, a house which has almost the look of a small French chateau – but stop about four or five yards before you come to the corner of the fence. Look to the left and right and you will see the marshy hollow which is the bed of the old canal. You are on the site of a bridge which has been demolished and levelled. From here you can make a short detour off to the right along the old canal towpath, but you may find it easier to leave your bike behind.

The canal bed is now overgrown but still damp in wet weather. It heads into Sidney Wood, which is named after the de Sydenie family of Alfold, who also lent their name to a small settlement in Australia! After about 150 yards there is a path down some steps into the woods on the left. Follow this for a few yards to the display board which marks the site of Knightons Glassworks, which existed here more than 400 years ago. Foundations of the furnaces can be seen in the undergrowth beyond the fence and on some of the stones you can still see drips of molten glass.

Before you retrace your steps to the track, you may wish to continue a little farther along the towpath to a derelict lock, the site of which can be recognised by the sudden rise in the path. The lock chamber is very overgrown, the gates have long since rotted away, and even the brickwork has gone, presumably taken for hard-core.

Back on the track, pass the entrance to Sidney Court, and then the track becomes a metalled road – Knightons Lane – by the next house. At Old Knightons, a lovely half-timbered cottage, the road bends to the right and then heads down a short but quite steep hill, and at the bottom you have a choice to make about the next stage of the ride.

☞ *There are three possible routes between Knightons and Durfold. All have their attractions and it may not be a bad idea to try a different one on separate occasions. The recommended route is via Furnace Bridge. It uses a track which is* *mostly in excellent condition, although there is a short length which may be messy in very wet conditions. It is described in stage √ .*

The route via Loxley Bridge stays on roads for the entire distance but it is a quite delightful ride, as described in stage ⑤. It includes the option of ending the ride early by taking a short cut back to the start at Dunsfold.

The route via Upper Ifold is the challenging alternative. It involves a bridleway which is in very poor condition and nigh-impossible to ride. The clay tends to be rough and sticky in all but the driest of weather, which makes even walking quite hard work, and you will need suitable footwear. It is best kept for good weather – see stage ≈ .

√ Knightons to Durfold
via Furnace Bridge

Continue along Knightons Lane for about half a mile after the farm-track to Upper Ifold Farm, until you come to a turning on the left, where there is a brick-built pillar box on the grassy corner. The signpost is a bit worn but points to Hurlands and Howicks – it is more readable on the other side.

After about 500 yards the lane ends at a farm gate but a bridleway continues straight ahead. At the farmyard keep going straight ahead. Pass the farm buildings and leave the farmyard by the gate at the far end of the yard, from where a gravelled track leads down the hill to Furnace Bridge. At the bottom the track curves to the right and crosses a raised bank.

Furnace Bridge: *The embankment which the track crosses is an old pond bay – the dam of a hammer-pond of an old ironworks which once occupied the field on the right. You'll notice the raised bank along the far edge of the field.*

The works itself was in the copse on the left of the track, where charcoal dust and glassy slag has been found. The pond fed waterwheels which powered bellows to produce the heat in the furnace and drove a hammer which beat the iron into the required shape and removed impurities.

The track crosses the bridge itself and goes through a gate on the far side, from where Burningfold Manor is visible on the hillside to the right. After another gate the track curves towards the Manor gates, but the bridleway carries straight on across the grass and into the wood ahead. At first the way is not very obvious, but later it becomes a more distinct clay path. After about 100 yards a blue arrow on a post confirms you are heading in the right direction. Follow the bridleway round to the right and over a small stream, heading towards a tarred drive. Just before it reaches the drive the bridleway turns left

to run alongside it for a couple of hundred yards before merging into it. (Watch for the unmarked speed humps.)

At the end of the drive turn left into Plaistow Lane and continue for just under a mile to the phone box beyond Durfold Farm (about 10 miles), then turn right into Fisher Lane, signposted Chiddingfold. Continue from stage Δ.

⑤ Knightons to Durfold
via Loxley Bridge (road route)

From Old Knightons continue straight along the road past the junction with Rams Lane (on the right) then, at the bottom of a dip about 700 yards further on, turn left into Chapel Hill. The lane passes a number of splendid houses and cottages and then emerges onto an open green with the prestigious gates of a large house on the left. At the junction with the

Chapel Hill, Dunsfold

Chiddingfold road turn right if you want to go back to Dunsfold and end the ride.

To continue, turn left down Wrotham Hill to Loxley Bridge, but just after the bridge, turn left into Plaistow Lane. Follow this for about 1½ miles as far as the phone box beyond Durfold Farm, then turn right into Fisher Lane, signposted 'Chiddingfold'. Continue the ride from stage Δ.

≈ Knightons to Durfold
via Upper Ifold

At the bottom of the hill from Old Knightons, turn left onto the track – a bridleway – to Upper Ifold Farm, which runs on a ledge along the side of a shallow valley towards the farm and some woods.

After the farmhouse come some extensive outbuildings and a few more houses. They are separated by a short belt of woodland from Upper Ifold House and the Barn House (about 9 miles). From there, keep going past some stables, but then when the track forks, take the branch on the right (it's not quite straight ahead).

Pass some more stables, this time on the right, and then the track heads into the woods. Just inside the trees it splits into three. Ignore the indistinct path which turns off quite sharply to the left and then take the left branch at the following fork. It's the more obvious of the two paths.

The condition of the track soon begins to deteriorate and the next stretch may not be a lot of fun. Although attempts have been made to repair the surface in places, the soft clay soon oozes up, making the going very hard work, even on foot.

After a while, the bridleway comes out onto a gravel and sand forest track. Turn right, then immediately left, to stay on the bridleway, which runs along the edge of the wood. This section is in very bad condition, even in good weather.

Note: the forest track runs parallel to the final length of the bridleway, but it is on private land and, strictly speaking, you should not use it.

Eventually the bridleway emerges through a gate at a T-junction of paths at Dungate Farm. Turn right onto the path which, as the faded sign indicates, marks the border with Sussex, and come out onto the road. Turn right and follow the road for about 400 yards to the junction by the phone box at Durfold. Turn left into Fishers Lane for Chiddingfold.

Δ Durfold to Chiddingfold

Fishers Lane provides a gentle amble along the southern edge of Surrey through Durfold and Fisherlane Woods. The corner by Durfold Hatch Cottage is particularly delightful. Watch out for the unexpected industrial premises on the left (11 miles via Upper Ifold); they were built as a walking stick factory, an industry established here over 100 years ago.

Keep straight on at the junction to Shillinglee and again at the next junction (High Street), which is just after Tugley Farm (about 12 miles). At Hazel Bridge (13 miles) there is a steep descent into the valley and an equally steep climb back up. That apart, this stretch offers easy cycling.

The name of Chiddingfold House heralds the approach of that village; the owners of the house usually open their garden for charity one day each summer as part of the National Gardens Scheme. For a booklet listing the Surrey gardens in the scheme, send a large s.a.e. to Lady Heald, Chilworth Manor, Guildford, GU4 8NL. (Contributions towards the cost of the booklet are gratefully accepted.)

Just along the road, shortly before the village green is reached, watch out for the unusual dovecote in front of the house called Greenaway.

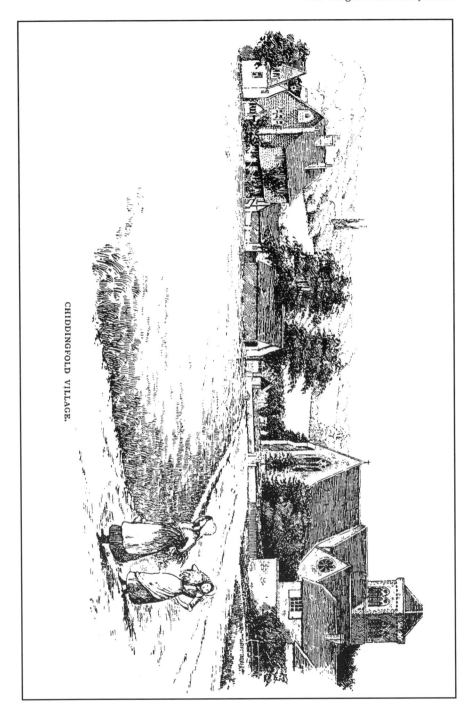

CHIDDINGFOLD VILLAGE.

Chiddingfold: In 1225 a Norman called Laurentio Vitrario (from the Latin word *vitrum*, which means glass) was granted 20 acres of land in the parish and set up the first-known glassworks in the country since Roman times. The works established Chiddingfold as England's main centre of glass-making for almost the next 400 years. Glass from here was used in both Westminster Abbey and Windsor Castle. A map in the Palazzo Vecchio in Florence dating from 1556 shows only two places in Surrey – Guildford and Chiddingfold – indicating the importance the industry gave to the village.

At one time the village green itself was the site of no fewer than eleven glassworks, but this led to a local outcry and they were closed down. However, many others continued in the surrounding woods. The end finally came because of worries about the amount of Wealden oak being burned to fuel both the iron and glassmaking industries, and its use for glass production was banned completely in 1615.

In Haslemere Museum there is a reproduction of one of the old Chiddingfold glassworks, and there are samples of the glass in the museum at Guildford. But the most impressive relic of the industry is to be found in a lancet window in St Mary's church, by the green. It was made in 1916 using 427 fragments of glass gathered from three sites around the village by the Rev Stephen Cooper, a former curate. It is said that during World War I old slag from the glassworks was used to surface the roads around Cranleigh, which then glittered in the sun when newly-repaired!

The Crown Inn reckons it is one of England's oldest public houses, claiming to have been founded around 1250 as a guesthouse for travellers to Waverley Abbey. This, however, can only be conjecture. The earliest documentary evidence is dated March 22nd, 1383, a title deed, a copy of which hangs in the inn. It is also claimed that King Edward VI and Queen Elizabeth I stayed there while they were on their travels. The Swan Inn, just around the corner, cannot boast such illustrious visitors, but it does keep pigs in its outbuildings and garden!

The village green comes complete with a not-so-unusual pond and a rather-more-scarce working blacksmith's forge. The milestone on the green notes that the village is just 38 miles from Hyde Park Corner.

🏨 The Crown Inn, The Green. Free house. 01428 682255. Open all day. Food (also serves afternoon tea) Rest Acc (some rooms with four-poster beds)

🏨 The Swan, Petworth Road. 01428 682073. Food G C

🛒 Forrest Stores (Spar), The Green. 8.30–10 (Sun 9–9)

🏪 The Old Bakery, The Green. 9.30–5.30 (Sun 10.30–5.30)

🛒 Roberts Stores, Petworth Road.

⑧ Chiddingfold to Hambledon

From the green, turn right onto the main A283 road. This is quite busy, but there is no better alternative and you will be on it for only a mile. Pass the unusual Catholic Church of St Teresa of Avila (14 miles), built as recently as 1961, and continue along the main road to North Bridge (where there is a telephone box) and up the hill on the far side of the bridge.

🏨 The Winterton Arms, Petworth Road. Friary Meux. 01428 683221 Has a No Smoking room.

Pass the gates of Northbridge House and turn right onto the bridleway opposite the sign for North End Farm.

This gravelled track is now the drive to Hurst Cottage, but it was once part of the Godalming–Chichester turnpike road. When it was replaced by the A283 via Milford and Witley, the stretch across Hambledon Hurst was abandoned. At the entrance to Hurst Cottage, veer slightly to

Oakwood Cottage

the left; don't go across the raised ridge which was the old road. Other than that, the track follows the line of the old road throughout. The ride through the woods is splendid.

After crossing a bridge (about 15 miles) the track runs beside a stream. About 400 yards further on, as you approach a house on the right-hand side, the track divides.

Strictly speaking, the bridleway continues roughly straight ahead, as did the old turnpike. However, it is extremely swampy beyond this point and is not to be recommended. Instead, most people seem to use the drive.

Pass the small pond and a group of cottages, and follow the drive round to the right and up to the road (Vann Lane) by the cricket green. There is a shop with post office and phone box just to the left.

🛒 *Hambledon Village Shop & Post Office, Cricket Green. 9–5.30 (9–1 Tue, 9–4 Sat). Closed Sun.*

Hambledon: *Oakwood Cottage, a small timber-framed building facing the cricket green, is owned by the National Trust and has been restored and furnished as a cottager's dwelling with an appropriate garden. It is thought it was originally a barn dating from the 16th century, adapted and added to over the succeeding centuries.*

Remarkably, in an area where country cottages are in great demand and readily snapped up for modernisation, this one managed to survive in 19th century condition and, on becoming vacant in 1980, was bought by the National Trust for preservation and restoration. It can be visited between April and October on Wed, Thur, Sat, and Sun (plus BH Mon) between 2 and 5, but by prior appointment only. ☎ 01428 684733

(Mrs E Hardy) to arrange it. An entrance fee is payable.

Hambledon is something of a scattered village with at least three separate parts – that around the cricket green, a cluster at Beech Hill, and one further to the north around the church, higher up the hill. Oddly, the pub, The Merry Harriers (renowned for advertising 'Warm Beer and Lousy Food') is almost the last building in the village, north of the church.

The Bargate stone church of St Peter's is well worth a visit, as much for its surroundings as for itself. Eric Parker, the Surrey writer and naturalist, lived nearby and is buried in its churchyard, in the midst of the countryside he loved so much. Fortunately the land around the lane to the church is owned by the National Trust and is therefore protected.

Incidentally, you may have noticed that by the time you get to Hambledon the landscape has changed. You have moved into the sandy soils of the Greensands, leaving the Weald clay behind for the moment.

The Merry Harriers, Hambledon Road. Friary Meux. 01428 682883. Food G Camping site

⑨ Hambledon to Wetwood

From the cricket green head east along Vann Lane. (If you go the wrong way, the sign for 'Vann Lane & Pockford' will put you right.) Just beyond Goodbrook House (about 16 miles) a bridleway crosses the road; it is the continuation of the old turnpike from which you diverted a while ago. The road passes the end of Woodlands Road (turn left to reach the church and pub), and then, shortly after Hambledon House, there is a sharp left bend by the entrance to a brickworks. Just beyond the Piggeries a steep hill into a dip (17 miles) is

Hambledon

followed by a more gentle climb up the other side. Much of this stretch of road is lined by hazel hedges, and if you come this way in September you might be able to gather a good crop of nuts if the squirrels haven't got to them first. Look over the hedge on the right and you can see the characteristic shape of Black Down, just over the Sussex border.

Follow Vann Lane around to the right at its junction with Upper Vann Lane. Shortly after Pockford Farm (18 miles), almost at the top of the hill, branch left into White Beech Lane, signposted 'Dunsfold'. Beyond White Beech Farm the road dips sharply to cross a branch of the River Arun, with a steep but short climb up the other side to a junction with the Chiddingfold road (19 miles). Once again, turn left in the direction of Dunsfold, pass Redwood Place, and follow the road for just under half a mile as far as Woodside Cottage. (A sign on the right of the road indicates 'Duns Copse' and another on the left is 'Wetwood Rough – Private'.)

⑩ Wetwood to Dunsfold

☞ *The bridleway route described below should be in good condition since part of it is tarred and much of the rest had major repairs in 1995. However, if you prefer it, an alternative route is given on page 160.*

At Woodside Cottage turn left into the entrance which is signed as a bridleway. Almost immediately it veers to the right onto a rough farm track. After about 400 yards, just before the track heads through a gate towards a modern barn, the bridleway branches to the right onto a much narrower pathway.

There is a lot of hard core in the surface of the path on this section which makes for rough riding, so you may find you need to walk. The scenery, though, is splendidly pastoral, with views over open fields

giving way to hedges and trees. A junction with a footpath leading to Duns Copse follows after a few hundred yards. Beyond this point, the bridleway was brought up to a very high standard during 1995. Roadstone was laid on a special matting which is designed to allow water to drain away while preventing wet clay forcing its way up – hopefully this treatment will provide a successful long-term solution to the poor ground conditions previously found here. Take care at the bottom of the slope as you approach the Mill House because the track there is covered with deep gravel.

At the Mill House (about 20 miles) turn left, cross the small bridge, and follow the tarred drive as it bends its way across the fields which cover the bottom of the valley. Dunsfold Church is hidden away among the trees on the hill to the left and from here it is clear just how isolated the church is from the rest of the village. To reach it turn left when you come to the road at the end of the drive, then turn left again after just a few yards.

St Mary and All Saints, Dunsfold, is built away from the rest of the village, giving rise to the idea that it might have taken over an earlier pagan site. The mound on which it stands could be artificial. The church dates from the 13th century and its quality suggests that royal masons may have been responsible for its construction.

William Morris went so far as to describe it as 'the most beautiful country church in all England'. The pews are unusual in being as old as the church itself – most churches didn't get them for another century or two, and these are the oldest in the country. The door is just as old, and shows that graffiti is not just a modern problem!

Look at the base of the wall just to the right of the porch, where you will see a chained oak plug, provided to allow water to drain away when the floor was washed. There are a couple more elsewhere in the walls. The yew tree in the churchyard, now heavily cut back, is probably older even than the church.

To reach the Holy Well, turn right out of the lychgate at the churchyard entrance and follow the track for about 100 yards to the bottom of the hill, where the well is on the left. Its water is said to have excellent healing properties for diseases of the eye. The shrine was erected by the Dunsfold Amateur Dramatic Society in 1933.

The well stands beside one of the branches of the River Arun; Himalayan balsam, or policeman's helmet as it is often known, grows in profusion here. Its delicate white or pink flowers can be seen between July and October. A footpath continues past the well and along the riverbank, leading to the Mill House.

From the church and continue along the road past the farm and its neighbouring cottages. At the T-junction turn right down the hill and follow the road through until you come to Dunsfold Green, opposite the school.

Alternative sections of route

① Dunsfold to Lakers Green

☞ *This alternative avoids several lengths of bridleway which may give problems after wet weather. However, it does involve using fairly busy A and B roads instead.*

From Dunsfold head north out of the village. At the T-junction, after a little more than half a mile, turn right onto the B2130 in the direction of Cranleigh. Three quarters of a mile after this junction, the road turns sharply to the left. If you wish you can turn right here onto the road leading to the airfield and resume the main route at the driveway leading to Hall

Place. Alternatively, continue along the main road until its junction with the A281. Turn right there and continue for about 1½ miles to Fast Bridge, passing the end of the airfield on the way. From there you can either turn off onto Farnhurst Lane to get to Lakers Green, or you can continue on the A281 to Alfold Crossways.

⑩ Wetwood to Dunsfold

From Woodside Cottage continue along the Chiddingfold road past Blacknest Farm – which has a well reputed to be over 1,000 feet deep – to Loxley Bridge. From there a climb up Wrotham Hill brings you to Dunsfold Common, past the end of Chapel Hill, and it is then only a short ride back to the start. If you want to visit the church turn left into Shoppe Hill, opposite

Ride J: Thameside Travels

Chertsey Bridge • Weybridge • Walton Bridge • Sunbury Lock • West Molesey • Lower Green • Esher • Weston Green • East Molesey • Hampton Court • Hampton • Sunbury • Lower Halliford • Shepperton • Chertsey Bridge

Distance:	between 4 and 24 miles
Landranger Maps:	176
Pathfinder Maps:	1190

This ride breaks three of the key rules of these guides: it involves the use of more roads than we would like (and some busy ones at that); a few of the places through which it passes are not exactly rural; and, because of a lack of bridleways in the area, we have had to use some footpaths. The route cheats a little bit, too, by taking a slightly extended view of the Surrey boundary! All of these were necessary if we were to include a ride within easy reach of the northern part of Surrey and its neighbouring areas. Certainly, the ride is different in character to the others in this guide, but most people will agree it has its own special appeal.

The proximity of the Thames guarantees some first-class scenery, but there is much more to this ride than simply a trip along the river towpath. It also ventures away from the immediate vicinity of the river to seek out some of the delightful, but often overlooked, locations nearby. We think they will charm and maybe even surprise you.

The route is easy, mostly level riding. There is a great deal to see, though, and you should allow most, if not all, of the day for the complete ride. For those who want something a little longer, Ride K extends the ride north and west from Chertsey Bridge, taking in the villages of Laleham and Thorpe. For shorter rides, see page 178.

Starting Points

There is a small free car park (max height 6 feet) about 200 yards on the east side of Chertsey bridge (grid reference TQ 056666), but there are many car parks, mostly free, on this route. Indeed, there are too many to mark them all on the map.

At the other end of the route the car park at Sandown Park racecourse near Esher is available for public use on all but race days. If you want to tackle the ride in two separate halves, a convenient place to start either half is the Cowey Sale car park near the south end of Walton Bridge.

≷ The ride runs by or close to railway stations at Esher and Hersham on the South West Trains' Waterloo–Woking main line, as well as Hampton Court, Hampton, and Shepperton on various SW London branch lines. Chertsey station is also reasonably convenient.

Ride J
Thameside Travels

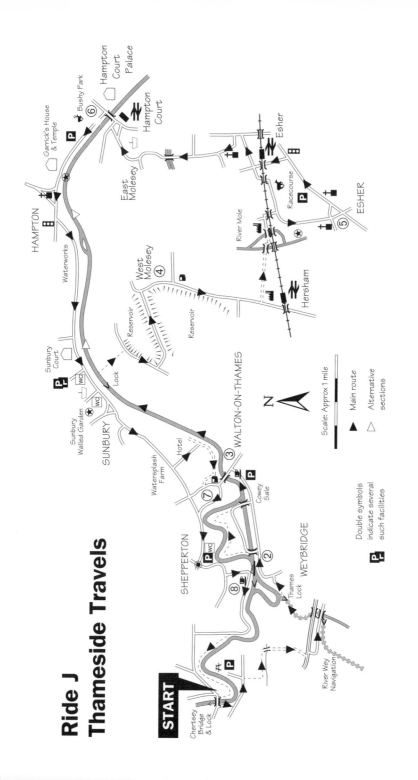

START

Chertsey Bridge & Lock

River Wey Navigation

Thames Lock

WEYBRIDGE

SHEPPERTON

Cowey Sale

WALTON-ON-THAMES

Watersplash Farm

Hotel

SUNBURY

Sunbury Walled Garden

Sunbury Court

Lock

Reservoir

Reservoir

West Molesey

HAMPTON

Waterworks

East Molesey

Garrick's House & Temple

Bushy Park

Hampton Court

Hampton Court Palace

Esher

ESHER

Racecourse

River Mole

Hersham

N

Scale: Approx 1 mile

▲ Main route

△ Alternative sections

Double symbols indicate several such facilities

The Route in Brief

① Cross to the Chertsey side of the bridge and TL beside entrance to boatbuilders' yard. By marina gates turn half R onto path between fences. At end TL onto road across Meads. At start of dead-end road to Dockett Eddy TR onto footpath over field (walk bikes). At far side of field TL.

At corner of field TR over concrete bridge and follow track to locked gate. Squeeze bike through gap. Follow road through mobile home park to junc with A317. Cross to far side into old Addlestone Road. Follow road to L through business park. Opposite Weybridge Town Lock TL onto steep narrow footbridge to reach towpath to Thames Lock.

Cross far end of lock then follow concrete path away from river. At end join road. Pass garages and cross bridge into Jessamy Road, then L into Thames Street. At R bend leave road through small CP on left and join river towpath at far end.

② Follow towpath past Shepperton Ferry steps and footbridge. When river divides at start of Deborough Cut, climb steps up onto bridge and cross onto Island. Join towpath on L at end of bridge. Keep to path as close to water's edge as possible. Pass sports fields then join road past reservoir and out through gates. Cross bridge and TL at TJ to Cowey Sale.

③ Follow towpath under Walton Bridge and over bridge at marina inlet. Continue SO past pubs to Sunbury Locks. About 250 yds beyond locks TR onto narrow path between fences. At far end TR into Hurst Road, then after 600 yds TL into Walton Road (B369), SP Molesey & Hersham, between reservoirs. At XR TR into Molesey Road.

√ SO at junc with Rydens Road, then after 400 yds TL at SP 'North Weylands Industrial Estate' beside factory, leading to path between fences (BW). At far end, cross river and follow path to R beside railway and over narrow bridge to reach Mill Road. At far end road bends R under railway. At junc TR and follow road round edge of racecourse and up hill. At Esher Green dismount and walk against traffic flow to XR in centre of town.

⑤ TL onto A307 past racecourse. At traffic lights TL into Station Road, then under railway and R into Weston Green Road. At main road TL then L again into Alma Road. Pass church then TR (SO really) at junc with Ember Lane. Cross bridges then TR at roundabout by Police Stn into Bridge Road. At end, by river, TR and cross bridge over Thames. At far side TL into A308 Hampton Court Road.

≈ Continue to Riverdale Waterworks then TL at traffic lights into Lower Sunbury Road. SO for over 3 miles through Sunbury. Just after Watersplash Farm TL into Felix Lane, SP Shepperton Moat House Hotel. Through gateway marked 'Private Estate' and TR at TJ. At far end of road go through narrow gate in fence. Cross bridge over marina inlet and follow unmade Penny Lane to A244 Walton Bridge Road and TL.

Δ TR into Walton Lane (B376) just before bridge. At end by Halliford Green TL into Russell Road. At roundabout TL into Church Road. Continue past Church Square into Chertsey Road, then after 200 yds, TL into Ferry Lane.

⑧ Pass ferry slipway and follow road to R. Pass Shepperton Lock and continue to start of No Entry section. Walk bike along edge of river until grass towpath resumes as road bends away. Follow towpath back to Chertsey Bridge.

The Ride

① Chertsey Bridge to Shepperton Ferry

From the car park cross the bridge to the Chertsey side of the river. Immediately after the bridge turn left into the road beside the entrance to Bates' boat-builders yard. Follow the road – which leads into an industrial estate – until its end at the gates of a marina, then turn half right onto the narrow tarred path between chain-link fences. At the end of the path turn left and follow the narrow road out across Chertsey Meads.

You cannot see the river from the road, but keep an eye out across the field to the left and you may well see the odd sight of a boat apparently sailing across the grass. The Meads are now cared for by Runnymede Council and are being restored as riverside grass meadows. The field on the right between the road and the River Bourne is cut for hay, but the meadows on the left are left to encourage grassland wild flowers to flourish, and walkers are asked to keep to the paths.

Pass the private road leading to Chertsey Meads Marine, and continue to the next junction. The dead-end road ahead leads to the delightfully-named Dockett Eddy, while to the left the road leads to a car park, a riverside picnic site, and Dumsey Eyot. Ignore these roads, dismounting instead and walk your bike along the public footpath which runs to the right across the field towards the Bourne.

At the far side of the field the footpath turns left, officially along the river bank, but as this can get very overgrown most people walk along the field edge instead.

Continue to the far corner of the field, where several power lines come together.

(What a great pity it is that the National Grid cannot be persuaded to bury these power lines and vastly enhance the beauty of the Meads.) The path turns right and crosses a concrete bridge over the river. After the bridge you find yourself on a partly-surfaced vehicle track. There is probably no harm in cycling from here, but do not stray from the track. It ends at a locked gate leading into an estate of mobile-type homes. There is a stile for walkers, but there is also a gap between the fence and gatepost through which a bike may be squeezed. Otherwise you will have to lift your bike over the gate.

Follow the road through the estate, minding the speed bumps, to the junction with the A317 dual carriageway. Cross to the far side to reach the old Addlestone Road, which now serves the local business park – turn left onto the main road, then right at the traffic lights, or cross at the pedestrian lights if you prefer. As you enter the business park, follow the road as it bends to the left.

On the right, just beyond the last offices, you will see the Wey Navigation. Continue along the road or (the better choice) join the towpath and follow it until you come to Weybridge Town Lock, the name of which belies its fairly rural setting (just over 2 miles). There is a break in the towpath at the lock, beyond which the navigation goes through a bridge under the road. Towpath users have to cross the road and go down a steep, narrow footbridge over a backwater on the other side; the entrance is marked by a National Trust sign.

The towpath resumes by the wide pool where the Wey Navigation rejoins the natural river. This pool was once known as Weybridge's port; cargo barges and boats moored at a wharf on the opposite bank where houses have recently been built. The main river passes under the iron bridge of 1865, the predecessor of which gave the town its name. The Navigation passes through a less dignified hole in the wall. Notice the upright roller on the corner of the towpath – it guided boats' towropes to help them manoeuvre around the tight corner.

The river's setting is very rural considering that the centre of Weybridge is close by, so take care along the towpath – not only is this a popular walk, but there are lengths which may be overgrown with nettles; bare arms and legs may suffer!

After half a mile the towpath leads to Thames Lock, the final lock on the Wey Navigation, with its picturesque lock-keeper's cottage. Cross the bridge at the far end of the lock and follow the concrete footpath away from the river. At the end of the path join the road and pass a row of garages. Cross the weight-restricted bridge

into Jessamy Road (3 miles), and at the end of this short road turn left into Thames Street. There you will find pubs and some toilets, although the latter were padlocked on one of our visits, so it may be best not to rely on them.

Old Crown, Thames Street. Courage.
Lincoln Arms, Thames Street. Ind Coope.
01932 842109. Food C G

Continue along Thames Street to the bend where it becomes Walton Lane, then leave the road and go through the small car park which overlooks the river at the confluence of the Thames, the Wey and the Bourne. River channels seem to run in all directions, but only one of them is navigable – the Wey Navigation. (The navigable channel of the Thames passes through Shepperton Lock, which is hidden from view.) Join the Thames towpath at the far end of the car park; it

The bridge at Weybridge

Thames Lock, Wey Navigation

has recently been upgraded and is in very good condition.

Just around the corner from the car park are some steps in the river bank from which the Shepperton Ferry departs. This, one of the last remaining ferry services on this part of the river, provides a link for pedestrians and cyclists at a point where the towpath crosses to the other bank. On this ride you can use the ferry to shorten the ride by turning back here – for the route back see stage ⑧. Alternatively, you could cross the river and complete the next part of the route in reverse order, making the ride a 'figure of eight'.

Shepperton Ferry: *services operate*

Mon–Fri:	*every hour 0900–1700*
	plus 0830, 0930, 1630, 1730
Sat:	*every half hour 0900–1730*
	(1830 May–Aug inclusive)

Sun/BH:	*every half hour 1000–1730*
	(1830 May–Aug inclusive)
Fares:	*single 60p, return £1.00*
	(under 14s and cycles half fare)

The ferry runs only if called by the bell at the scheduled times. Please ring the bell long and hard if you require a ferry. For information ☎ *Nauticalia Boats 01932 254844*

② Shepperton Ferry to Walton Bridge

From the Shepperton Ferry steps continue along the towpath, passing a footbridge to an island, shortly after which the river divides. In the 1930s the Thames Conservancy bypassed the sinuous loops of the river past Shepperton Church and Lower Halliford by building a new straight channel called the Desborough Cut. Opened in 1935 it was named after Lord

Desborough, the Conservancy's longest-serving chairman (1904–1937).

The towpath beside the Cut is a fine, broad path but mildly uninteresting. The alternative is to follow the old towpath along the original course of the river. Climb the steps onto the bridge over the entrance to the Cut, then cross the bridge to reach Desborough Island. The towpath entrance is on the left at the far end of the bridge, just as the road curves to the right – it is only a rough path but its condition is reasonable.

As you follow the towpath you'll see Shepperton Church and Ferry Square on the opposite bank (about 4 miles). Shortly after this the towpath leaves the very edge of the river for a hundred yards or so, but watch out – if you find yourself in a field with a barbed wire fence between you and the river's edge, find a gap in the fence to get back to the water's edge.

After passing some sports fields the path eventually emerges onto a road. Continue down the road past the reservoir and the water pumping station, and out through some gates. Then cross another bridge over the Desborough Cut and carry your bike back down the steps onto the main river towpath, or alternatively you can stay on the road and turn left at the T-junction just beyond the bridge. A few hundred yards along either the towpath or the road will bring you to the open area of Cowey Sale (5½ miles).

Cowey Sale *is a popular grassy stretch of the riverside south-west of Walton Bridge. The site is said to be the place where Julius Caesar crossed the Thames during his invasion of Britain in 55BC. The British defenders are*

Cowey Sale

reputed to have driven sharpened stakes into the river bed in an unsuccessful attempt to block the ford, hence the alternative name for the area of Cowey Stakes.

🍴 *There is a refreshment kiosk serving hot and cold drinks, sandwiches and hot meals on the towpath at Walton Bridge.*

③ Walton Bridge to West Molesey

Continue along the towpath under Walton Bridge, which at this point is used as a roadway leading to Walton Marina. Beyond the bridge the towpath parts leaves the roadway and continues along the riverbank, crossing a bridge over the inlet to the marina. On the opposite bank is a similar bridge at Shepperton Marina, which you will cross later.

About a quarter of a mile further on a road comes down to the riverside, marking the site of another lost ferry across the river. There are two large pubs, one of which sets out tables on the towpath, while the other has a terraced garden overlooking the river. There is a phonecard callbox just up the road.

🏠 *The Swan, Manor Road. Youngs. 01932 228922/2255964. Open all day Sats. Food C G Rest.*
🏠 *The Angler's Tavern, Hillrise, Manor Road. Free house.*

The next stretch of the towpath is bordered by the gardens of houses in the outskirts of Walton, and then by a small park. After that, a suburban road comes down to the riverside, giving access to a nearby works, and runs beside the river to the Elmbridge Leisure Centre. On the other bank is a large river authority yard.

🏠 *The Weir Hotel, Sunbury Lane*

Just after the Leisure Centre there is a large weir across the main river channel.

From this point the towpath follows the straight artificial channel leading to Sunbury Locks, passing a footbridge on the way. There are two parallel locks at Sunbury, the newer of which was opened in 1927. The path runs beside the edge of the lock and, for safety reasons, you must dismount and walk for a few yards.

The next eight miles of the ride are a complete mixture. There are some truly delightful stretches but these are balanced by a few lengths where, to be frank, the scenery is uninspiring. If you'd rather give this part of the ride a miss continue along the towpath for another three miles to Hampton Court, where you rejoin the main route at stage ≈ .

To continue with the main ride, turn right about 250 yards beyond Sunbury Lock onto the path which runs between the fences of a land-fill site and a Thames Water works. The path is very narrow and there could be problems if it became overgrown, but it seems that someone cuts back the weeds from time to time.

At the end of the path turn right into the fairly busy Hurst Road and pass the entrance to Apps Court Farm (8 miles). After 600 yards, turn left into Walton Road (the B369) where the signpost indicates 'Molesey Industrial Estate & Hersham'. The road runs between two embanked reservoirs and the sheep grazing on their banks add a welcome rural touch. At the crossroads about three-quarters of a mile further on, turn right into Molesey Road.

√ West Molesey to Esher

The next mile or so past the giant Queen Elizabeth II Reservoir is a touch monotonous, but at least the road is flat and you can speed along. The only feature worth noting is a petrol station, where you can buy refreshments.

River Mole backwater

At the junction with Rydens Road at the end of the reservoir continue straight ahead, but about 400 yards after that watch out for a sign for the 'North Weylands Industrial Estate', about 400 yards before the railway bridge at Hersham station. Turn left into the industrial estate on a road along the side of a factory. When this bends to the right behind the factory, continue straight ahead onto a bridleway – a tarred path through open but derelict land, sadly lined with unsightly chain-link fences.

After almost half a mile the path emerges beside the railway at a modern bridge over the River Mole (11 miles). On the right-hand side of the bridge are large sluice gates which were built as part of a 1980s flood prevention scheme for the River Mole. A small backwater was widened, straightened and deepened to become the main river channel. Running between banks of concrete and steel, it may be effective but is hardly attractive.

Cross the bridge and bend to the right, following the path beside the railway. The path crosses the old course of the river on another concrete bridge, but this one is narrow and has mellowed with age. Beside it is an attractive brick-built railway bridge, and there are water lilies and arrowhead (so-called because of the shape of its leaves) growing in the river.

If it wasn't for the backdrop of modern industrial units on the site of the old mills and an unfortunate amount of rubbish, this could be a very pleasant spot.

The path leads out onto Mill Road. Continue straight along this road beside the railway line. There is a useful general store on the left, just before the road bends to the right, passing under the railway line by a low bridge.

"WOLSEY'S TOWER," ESHER.

Beyond the bridge is Lower Green, presenting a complete contrast to the scene on the other side of the tracks. Just ahead is a small triangular green, and across the way is an entrance into Sandown Park racecourse. To the right are ornate gates leading into part of Esher Place, where the Metropolitan Police have a dog training facility.

Turn to the right and follow More Lane up the hill. After passing another entrance into the racecourse and a small area of woodland known as The Warren, the road comes out on Esher Green. On your right, overlooked by the large Victorian Christ Church are the 18th century lodges framing the entrance to the private estate of Esher Place.

Esher Place: The modern residential estate is built on the site of a palace of the Bishops of Winchester, built between 1450 and 1480. Most of it was demolished in 1670 to make way for a new mansion, but the gatehouse – known as Waynflete's Tower, after Bishop William of Waynflete who had it built – survives on the banks of the River Mole. It is a four-storey quasi-fortified building, one of the first in England to be built of red brick.

The most famous resident of the palace was Cardinal Wolsey – hence its alternative name of Wolsey's Tower. He was sent there in 1529 in disgrace, having been deprived of his position as Henry VIII's Lord Chancellor. He hated its 'moist and corrupt air', and persuaded Henry to allow him to go to York. Later Sir Richard Drake (it is not certain if he was related to Francis, but he may have been his father) kept high-ranking Spanish prisoners of war there after the defeat of the Armada.

The Tower is privately owned and underwent major restoration in 1994. It is not open to the public. It can be reached only through the private estate of Esher Place, and is mostly screened from view by hedges.

Dismount at the Green if you want to reach the crossroads at the very centre of

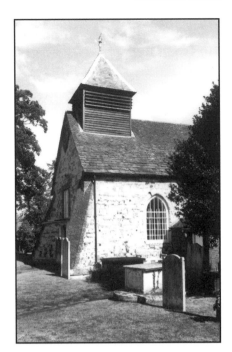

St George's church, Esher

Esher (12½ miles), as the obvious route along Church Street is one way in the wrong direction.

Esher sits astride the old Portsmouth road and was once an important stop for stagecoaches. The Bear, a coaching inn which once provided stabling for 100 horses, is a prominent reminder of this trade. Tucked away behind the Bear is the old church of St George which served the parish until 1854. It is one of the few churches in the country which date from Tudor times. For years it was left to become derelict, but it is now cared for again and is open on Saturday mornings 10.30 to 12.30, April to September.

Christ Church, built to replace it in 1854, was paid for out of the rents accumulated from an unusual source – the Church owned the freehold of Sandown Park racecourse. (In 1899 it was decided it was improper for the Church to be the landlord of a racecourse, and the freehold was sold for £12,000.)

Sandown Park had other religious connections. It was built on the site of Sandown Farm, which was once the land of Sandon Priory and Hospital. Founded in the 12th century, the Priory's end came when the Black Death claimed all its brethren.

Sandown Park was the first racecourse in the country to be fully enclosed. Until then racecourses were open (as is Epsom today) and anyone could turn up, including undesirable and criminal elements. Because it could exclude such people, Sandown became the favourite course of Victorian ladies.

Just to the south-west of the traffic lights is a water fountain, which, as its inscription points out, was given to the people of Esher by Queen Victoria, who often stayed at nearby Claremont.

Esher has a wide selection of pubs, shops and other facilities.

⑤ Esher to Hampton Court

From the centre of Esher go down the hill along the A307 Portsmouth Road past the gates of the racecourse, with the unusual 'Traveller's Rest' nearby. At the traffic lights turn left into Station Road. (The huge milepost on the corner is known as the 'White Lady'.)

About a hundred yards or so after the railway bridge, turn right into Weston Green Road. Follow this across the golf course to Weston Green (almost 14 miles). Turn left onto the main road (Hampton Court Way) and then, within yards, turn left again into Alma Road.

Don't be in too much of a hurry to press on but take the opportunity to look around the delightful surroundings of Weston Green first.

Weston Green: *The green remains, even if it is now rather sadly bisected by the main road. The village is now overshadowed by suburbia, but the many historic houses and cottages help it to retain a rural feel.*

Marney's Pond, in Alma Road, was restored in 1993, and a fine job has been made of it. Floating nesting boxes have been provided for waterfowl, together with seats for human visitors. Next to the pond is the distinctive All Saints' Church, built in 1939 to the design of Sir Edward Maufe, the architect of Guildford Cathedral. With its whitewashed brick and tall

Weston Green

bell tower, it would hardly look out of place in the Mediterranean. The interior is very tall, simple and spacious.

▦ *The Greyhound, The Green. 0181-398 1155*
▦ *The Cricketers, The Green. 0181-398 3982. Courage.*
▦ *The Lamb and Star, Hampton Court Way. 0181-398 0834.*
▦ *Marney's Pond Village Inn (formerly The Alma Arms), Alma Road. 0181-398 4444. Free house. Open all day Sats only. Food G*
☐ *Post Office and Store*

Leave Weston Green along Alma Road, which becomes Chestnut Avenue as it bends past the church. Turn right – go straight ahead, really – at the junction with Ember Lane. The area is mostly suburban, but on the left is Imber Court, now the Metropolitan Police horse training centre and sports club. Continue along Ember Lane to the two river bridges. The first is modern and crosses the River Ember while the older one beyond crosses the River Mole. This area was once much prone to flooding, and the solution adopted was to divert and straighten much of the river, which now flows through a concrete trough.

At the mini-roundabout by East Molesey police station turn right into Bridge Road and follow it through to its end on the riverside at Hampton Court, where there are plenty of pubs and shops, too many to list individually. At the river, turn right, then left onto the bridge over the Thames. At the far side of the bridge, assuming you don't plan to visit the Palace on this occasion, turn left into Hampton Court Road (the A308).

≈ Hampton Court to Walton Bridge

Hampton Court Road runs between the Thames on the left and Bushy Park on the

right. The road is busy but wide and if you take care you should have no problem; alternatively, there are public gardens along much of the riverbank and if you prefer you could walk through them with your bike.

It has to be said that the route cheats on this stage. It hardly qualifies as a 'rural ride' with all the traffic, in addition to which you may notice that the next mile or so is not even in Surrey. In crossing the Thames you also crossed the county boundary into what was once Middlesex and is now part of the London Borough of Richmond.

▦ *The Cardinal Wolsey, The Green, Hampton Court Road. Free house. 0181-979 1458. Food Acc*

Garrick's Temple: *On the approach to Hampton, you will see on the open space between the road and the river the 'Temple to*

Garrick's Temple

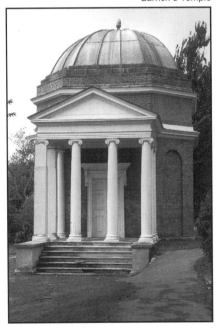

Shakespeare', a domed summerhouse erected in 1755 by the famous actor David Garrick to house Roubilliac's statue of Shakespeare. (Garrick bequeathed the original statue to the British Museum in his will, and a copy was made to replace it.) If you want to look inside the temple you must telephone in advance to Richmond Council on 0181-892 0221. Sadly, it is beginning to show signs of age. The columns which support the portico are not stone, as they may at first appear, but are clad in wood, which is gradually rotting.

Just across the road from the temple is the home in which Garrick lived from 1754 to his death in 1779. His occupation of the house resulted in its name being changed from Hampton House to Garrick's Villa.

As the main road enters Hampton it becomes Thames Street (16½ miles); were it not for the traffic this would be an extremely pleasant location.

A sign on the wall of the Bell Inn, next to the parish church, notes that there has been an inn on the site since 1512. Dr Johnson described it as 'neat without and clean within', an accolade indeed for those days. The pub's name recalls the old practice by which ferries and river boats were summoned by ringing a bell (as is still the case today at Shepperton).

The Bell Inn, 8 Thames Street. Taylor Walker. 0181-941 2364.

The Red Lion, Thames Street.

Continue along Thames Street until it becomes Upper Sunbury Road. On the left is the first of the many waterworks you will pass in the next mile or so.

Riverdale Waterworks: Until 1852 London's water supply was drawn straight from the grossly polluted Thames and its tributaries within the city. However, persistent outbreaks of cholera forced the government to act and the abstraction of water for drinking was banned below Teddington, the limit of the tidal river. As a result, London's local water

companies had to move west. The Riverdale Works in Hampton, as the legend on the building shows, was built for the Southwark & Vauxhall Water Company. The coat of arms bears the dates 1582 and 1897. The first is the year when drinking water was first pumped out of the Thames (by a tide mill built into the old London Bridge).

At the traffic lights, turn left into Lower Sunbury Road. The surroundings are almost industrial as the road passes through the huge water treatment works, but the trees which line the road help to lessen their impact. The traffic is also much less busy than on the main road.

About 500 yards from the junction a private footbridge crosses to Platt's Eyot, the height of which may come as a surprise, unless you happen to know that its hill was built up with spent gravel from the nearby water filtration beds.

The road becomes Lower Hampton Road as it crosses back into Surrey. On the right-hand side pine trees on the slope of the Stain Hill reservoirs help to give a rural feel to the scene, a feeling which is enhanced at the far end of the reservoir by the open space between the road and the river. Just beyond the Sunbury Cricket Club ground (almost 18 miles) is the mansion of Sunbury Court, built in 1770 and now used as a youth centre and conference venue by the Salvation Army.

On the approach to Sunbury itself there is a toilet (of the automated variety) and a car park on the left. At the mini-roundabout the road's name changes yet again, now to Thames Street. Keep straight on.

The narrowness of the street is enhanced by the height of the surrounding buildings and their closeness to the road. For years Sunbury suffered from the effects of too much traffic and decline set in. Now traffic calming 'speed tables' have been installed

Sunbury Walled Garden

and heavy lorries banned, and the situation is improving. Most of the buildings in the street are listed and many of their owners have made a commendable effort to brighten up the properties. Thames Street could do with a few more shops to give it that extra touch of life. Instead they are to be found in a modern parade in a side turning, The Avenue, where there is also a car park.

White Horse, Thames Street. Courage. Food Patio

The Phoenix, Thames Street. Free House. *01932 785358. Food G*

Skinners, The Avenue. Newsagents and PO. Open to 5.30 (1.00 on Suns)

Pavitts, The Avenue. Supermarket. Open 8am–8pm including Suns.

Threshers, The Avenue. Off-licence.

The Magpie, 64 Thames Street. Gibbs Mew. 01932 782024. Open all day. G F

On the right-hand side just beyond The Avenue is Sunbury Park. There are toilets and a car park at the entrance to it.

Sunbury Park and Walled Garden: *The 12-acre park, once the grounds of a now-demolished mansion, was purchased by Surrey County Council in 1975 and leased to Spelthorne Borough Council.*

In 1985 it was decided to develop the former walled kitchen garden into a two-acre formal one. It includes various popular styles of garden through the centuries, including Tudor knot gardens, parterres, and two rose gardens, one based on varieties popular in Victorian times, the other using modern varieties. Four island beds display plants and shrubs from all parts of the world.

The centrepiece is the recreated Lendy memorial, commemorating two local brothers killed in the South African wars early this century. The portico which frames the northern

gate of the garden was saved when Benwell House, the offices of the old Sunbury-on-Thames Urban District Council, was demolished. The garden is open 11–5 daily, admission free, and is well worth a visit.

Unlike many municipal open spaces, the park itself is allowed to grow wild, giving it much more of a rural feel. Look out for the 'ha-ha' – a deep ditch with a wall on one side to allow uninterrupted views while excluding unwanted intruders.

🏠 The Flower Pot Hotel, Thames Street. Free House. 01932 780741. Open all day May to October. Food (cold food available right up to closing time) Acc.

The grounds of Sunbury Park divide Sunbury into east and west ends. St Mary's Church is at the west end. Charles Dickens featured it in Oliver Twist, when Bill Sikes and Oliver slept under the yew tree in its churchyard the night before committing the Shepperton robbery. Opposite Church Street are some phone boxes and another free car park.

From this point the road runs away from the river and becomes Fordbridge Road as it leaves the town to pass nurseries and market garden farms. The name of the road and that of Watersplash Farm, a little further on, owe their origins to the River Ash, which today is crossed by a concrete bridge. There is a river authority depot on the left just before the bridge.

Shortly after Watersplash Farm turn left into Felix Lane (almost 20 miles), sign-posted 'Shepperton Moat House Hotel'. Follow the lane past the Marina and the hotel entrance, then pass through the gateway marked 'Private Estate' and turn right when you come to the T-junction at the end.

Although there may appear to be no way out of the estate, look for the narrow gate in the fence at the end of this road. Go through the gate. A sign on the white

brick building beyond it tells you you are on land which is the property of the Walton Charities; that there is no right of way and that to ensure this, the gate is closed each Good Friday. Hopefully you have not chosen this day to do the ride! Beyond the building is an open area with the local Sea Cadets centre by the river on the left, and just ahead a bridge crosses the inlet to the marina.

On the far side of the bridge follow the unmade road called Penny Lane. Don't be tempted to enter the side turning called Riverside to find a way through along the river – there isn't one. The temporary structure of Walton Bridge can be seen clearly to the left, while on the right is a large gravel pit.

Penny Lane finally emerges onto the main Walton Bridge Road (A244). Turn left and follow the road for a short suburban stretch round the curve which leads to a wide open area on the approach to the river. On the left is a garage with a shop, after which is the junction with Walton Lane on the right, and the approach to Walton Bridge straight ahead.

Walton Bridge: Walton hasn't had a lot of luck with its bridges over the Thames. The first, built in 1750, was of an unusual but short-lived design. Its ends and supporting piers were of stone but the span was of Chinese-style open woodwork. It was the subject of two paintings by Canaletto. The replacement bridge was the inspiration for one of Turner's works, but it didn't last long either. The third bridge, an iron one, was built in 1863 but only 14 years later it needed major repairs.

In 1952 this bridge was declared unsafe as a result of war damage, and the present temporary structure was built alongside it; the 1863 bridge was later demolished. The 'temporary' structure has now lasted for over 40 years, and is now lacking not just elegance but structural strength as well and a weight restriction has been applied to it. It is planned *to build a new dual carriageway, Walton Thames Crossing, a little downstream of the present bridge. A new bridge for pedestrians and cyclists will be built on the upstream side of the present bridge.*

Δ Walton Bridge to Shepperton Ferry

Turn right into Walton Lane (B376) at the junction just before the bridge. The road runs past large properties hidden away behind high walls before emerging onto the green at Lower Halliford. On the left is Halliford House, and next to it Peacock House, its blue plaque announcing that this was the home of the author and poet Thomas Love Peacock from 1823 until his death in 1866.

Turn left at the junction into Russell Road. A loop in the Thames brings the river right alongside the road here; it is overlooked from the opposite side by some quite startling modern buildings.

🍺 *The Red Lion, Russell Road. Courage.*
🍺 *The Ship Hotel, Russell Road.*

Russell Road passes Halliford School and approaches a roundabout, passing a car park with toilets. Turn left into Church Road, which leads to the original riverside settlement of Shepperton, with its old houses and cottages lining the road. The village centres around Church Square, where the church is accompanied by two hotels and a tiny inn, the King's Head. The sign on the latter depicts Charles II, who is said to have stayed in Shepperton with Nell Gwynne.

St Nicholas' Church was built in 1614, after its 12th century predecessor was damaged by floods. Material from the old building, including much of the flint, was salvaged and re-used. The brick tower was

Chertsey Bridge

added in the early 18th century after Queen Anne, the patron of the parish, suggested it would improve the look of the church.

The church's unusual features include two flights of outside stairs, one beside the tower leading to the bell-ringing chamber and the gallery, the other leading to a small gallery in the north transept known as the manor house pew. Inside, there are box pews dating from the 19th century, the period when most other churches lost theirs.

🏠 *The Anchor Hotel, Church Square. 01932 221618. Food*
🏠 *The King's Head, Church Square. Courage. Food G*
🏠 *Warren Lodge Hotel & Restaurant, Church Square. 01932 242972.*

On the river's edge at the far end of Church Square, beyond the hotel, is Ferry Square, given for public use by the lord of the manor in 1970. Leaving Church Square, turn left into Chertsey Road. About 200 yards further on turn left again into Ferry Lane, leading to the slipway from where the Shepperton Ferry operates. The timetable is on page 166. (20½ miles)

☕ *Riverside Refreshments, Shepperton Lock. Usually open 12–5.30 April to September.*
🏠 *Thames Court Hotel, The Towpath. Free house. 01932 221957.*

⑧ Shepperton Ferry to Chertsey Bridge

From the ferry slipway follow the road round to the right as it becomes The Towpath, which, despite its name, is a properly made-up road. On the left is Shepperton Lock, where there are toilets, a phone box, and refreshments. Soon after the lock the road becomes one-way in the wrong direction; to stay within the law you must dismount and walk.

As the road turns away from the river, join the towpath along the riverside. It is

signed as a footpath, but as it is the towpath there is a presumption that you can ride on it. It begins as a grassy track, but later narrows and has a stony surface. Houseboats are moored along this section. The towpath comes out by Chertsey Bridge, just over 24 miles from the start. There is a kissing gate at the end of the towpath but it is possible to get through by standing your bike on its back wheel. There is a ladies' toilet on the far side of the bridge but not one for gents.

Chertsey Bridge: *Built in the 1780s, it has been extensively restored by Surrey County Council. The bridge's seven arches of white stone rise from the banks to a peak in the centre. As part of its restoration, bronzed street lamps were fitted on its graceful parapets. It is a great pity that lamps are needed at all, for they tend to spoil the bridge's proportions and its elegant simplicity.*

🏠 *The Boat House, Bridge Road. Free House (Family Fayre). 01932 565644. Open all day. Food (all day) Rest C Riverside Terrace Acc (Toilets open to public 8–6)*

Shorter Options

The ride heads out on one side of the Thames and back on the other. Shorter rides are possible by crossing the river by bridge or ferry and turning back. Rough distances between the various points are:

Chertsey Bridge –	
Shepperton Ferry & back	5 miles
Shepperton Ferry –	
Walton Bridge & back	4 miles
Walton Bridge –	
Esher & back	15 miles

Ride K:
Monks' Tracks and Gravel Pits

Chertsey Bridge • Laleham • Chertsey Bridge • Chertsey Abbey • Penton Hook • Thorpe • Chertsey • Chertsey Bridge

Distance: 11 miles
Landranger Maps: 176
Pathfinder Maps: 1190

This ride can be regarded either as an extension to Ride J, or as a stand-alone ride. It involves a route across the Thameside meadows along tracks which may well have been created by the monks of Chertsey Abbey to link the abbey with the villages of Laleham and Thorpe. Sadly, one vital link in the route to Laleham – the ferry across the river – no longer exists, so the ride begins with an out-and-back trip along the east bank of the river to visit that village. With its sandy river beach, caravan and camping park, and sports grounds, it is still a popular spot for the weekend crowds.

The village of Thorpe is almost entirely surrounded by gravel pits, one group of which now forms the Thorpe Park theme park, and the busy M25/M3 interchange is less than half a mile away, but it somehow retains the qualities for which the writer Eric Parker praised it more than 60 years ago.

Many of the comments in the introduction to Ride J apply equally to this one, particularly regarding the occasional use of busier roads than we would like and the need to use the odd footpath. With motorways and main roads criss-crossing the area and the remains of the gravel working industry all around, this part of Surrey is never likely to qualify as an Area of Outstanding Natural Beauty, but it has some surprises to offer and some corners which are well worth exploring.

Starting Points

There is a small free public car park on the B375 Chertsey–Shepperton road 100 yards east of Chertsey Bridge (see Ride J). There is also a large free car park on Thames Side, halfway between Chertsey Bridge and Laleham, and there are car parks in Chertsey itself.

≋ The most convenient railway station is at Chertsey, about half a mile from the town centre. It is on the Virginia Water–Weybridge. Virginia Water, on the Waterloo–Reading line, is just over 1 mile from Thorpe village along the B389 road. Both are served by South West Trains.

Ride K
Monks' Tracks and Gravel Pits

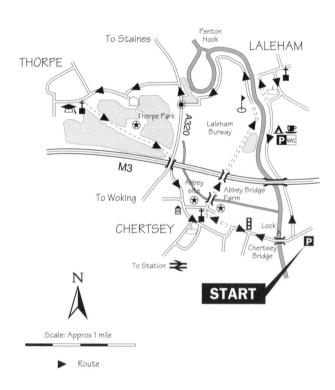

The Route in Brief

① From Shepperton end of Chertsey Bridge turn into Thames Side beside lock. Follow road under M3 and past CP. At R bend keep SO along towpath, then take 3rd on R – Blacksmiths Lane. At War Memorial TR onto main road, then R again into Ferry Lane. Return along riverside to Chertsey Bridge.

② Cross Chertsey Bridge and follow road towards town. SO at traffic lights then R, TR into Willow Walk (BW) immediately before Vine pub. Follow path when it bends R past cottages, then L into Church Walk. TR past island in road then cross over into Colonel's Lane, past Abbey site.

At end of lane pass round gate into Ferry Lane, past farm. Cross bridges over Abbey River, then M3. SO on track until it joins unmade road beyond reservoir, then on to river's edge and entrance of golf course. TR along golf club drive, then through gates, and follow road round Penton Hook. At far end, after sharp L turn into Penton Park estate, TR at mini-roundabout, over bridge and out into Mixnams Lane. At end TR at roundabout onto A320 for ¼ mile, then TL, SP 'TASIS', into Norlands Lane. After ½ mile, TR at roundabout by RMC House, and keep SO to Church Approach.

③ Lift your bike over stone stile on L in Church Approach and walk along path. Cross low (metal) stile then follow path through middle of Thorpe Park. Continue until motorway fence, then TL onto concrete track under road bridge.

At far end of bridge follow path up zigzag to L to A320. TL onto road and cross bridge over motorway. At far end TL down zigzag path to road. Follow Staines Lane into Chertsey. Leave town along London Street to return to Chertsey Bridge.

Chertsey Lock

Laleham Reach

The Ride

① Chertsey Bridge to Laleham and back

From the east side of Chertsey bridge cross the main road (if necessary) and join Thames Side, the road which passes beside the lock and runs along the bank of the river, passing under the M3. After the motorway bridge the road moves slightly away from the river's edge to leave an open space on the bank. This is a popular spot for outings and on sunny weekends it can become crowded. About half a mile beyond the motorway there is a free car park, with toilets and refreshments, and a caravan and camping ground. Behind it are the extensive sports fields of Laleham Park. The river has a sandy bank along this stretch and it is favourite spot for

bathing. It is also a favourite spot for water birds, as the state of the riverbank indicates!

☕ *Laleham car park, Thames Side. Open daily during summer until 6pm (8pm on Sats, Suns, and B Hols)*

Further ahead, as the road bends to the right, continue along the towpath and take the third turning on the right. This is Blacksmith's Lane – the Old Forge is one of the last buildings on the left – which emerges by the War Memorial opposite the church.

Laleham: *The village rather turns its back on the river, focusing itself instead around the junctions of the roads to Staines, Shepperton, and Ashford. To find the river from the centre of the village you have explore one of the small side roads.*

Laleham Abbey was built in the early 1800s for the Earl of Lucan. It is approached from

Willow Walk, Chertsey

Abbey Drive, off Ferry Road. The Rev Dr Thomas Arnold lived in Laleham and taught there before he went on to become the renowned headmaster of Rugby School. His son Matthew, the poet, was born in the village and his grave can be found in the churchyard.

▦ *The Three Horseshoes, Shepperton Road. Fullers.*

🏠 *Post Office and Shop, Shepperton Road.*

Turn right onto the main road for a short distance before turning right again into Ferry Lane. This leads you back down to the riverside, from where you return along Thames Side to Chertsey Bridge.

② Chertsey Bridge to Thorpe

Cross to the west side of Chertsey Bridge and continue along the main road towards the town. Go straight ahead at the traffic lights, but watch out because the left-hand lane is only for traffic turning left. About 250 yards after the traffic lights the road bends to the left and then to the right to skirt the boundary of the long-disappeared Chertsey Abbey. Just before the right-hand bend (immediately before the Vine pub) turn right into a bridleway called Willow Walk.

▦ *The Vine, Bridge Road, Chertsey. Courage. 01932 563010*

Don't be put off by the fact the bridleway looks like an alley along the back of a factory. It quickly opens out again, giving a view on the right of a magnificently restored barn which is now used as offices by a computer company. As the path turns to the right you may think you're entering the gardens of some half-timbered cottages, but don't be put off; you haven't taken a wrong turning!

Follow the bridleway until it comes out into the open area of Church Walk. On the left one of the cottages has a reproduction of one of the famous Chertsey tiles on its front. Turn right here (past the shrub-filled island) to come out onto the road proper.

On your left, just inside the Abbey Green park is a depression in the ground running parallel with the road. This is the remains of the moat which once surrounded Chertsey Abbey.

Take the lane almost straight across from Church Walk (it is part of Colonel's Lane). A short distance up the lane a gateway on the left leads into the park where there is an information board and the ruins of some walls. The walls are almost the only remains of the Abbey left above ground.

Chertsey and its Abbey: *The Benedictine Abbey was founded in 666 when Frithwald, who was sub-King of Surrey under the King of Mercia, Wulfer, gave the land to Erkenwald., who became the first abbot and was later Bishop of London. The Abbey was built on the 'Isle of Ceorot' (Cirotesige), from which the name of Chertsey is derived. (The medieval town and the abbey site are situated on a slight hill, as was shown in 1947 when they were the only areas left above the waters of the floods.)*

The first abbey buildings were probably of wood, and did not survive a Danish attack 200 years later, when the then abbot and his monks were slaughtered. However, the abbey was rebuilt, and, having become ruinous, rebuilt again in the early 12th century, becoming one of the greatest religious establishments in the country. John de Rutherwyk, who died in 1347, was a noted abbot who carried out many improvements to the vast lands owned by the Abbey (some 50,000 acres at Domesday).

The area occupied today by the Abbey Green park formed the domestic area of the abbey. Tile kilns, the remains of bread ovens, and signs of lead smelting were discovered here in the 1930s. In the centre of the park area can be seen the remains of some of the fish ponds built by Rutherwyk. The religious buildings were on the east side of the lane. The church itself was 275 feet long and was lined with Purbeck marble. Its fabulous decorated floor tiles, illustrating romantic legends, were produced on site. Examples of the tiles are on display in the Chertsey Museum.

As Shakespeare recounts in 'Richard III', the body of Henry VI was brought to Chertsey Abbey after his murder in London in 1471.

The Abbey was dissolved by Henry VIII at the Reformation in 1537 and the main buildings were dismantled over a period of time. It is said the builders of Hampton Court (and probably other nearby buildings too) took advantage of the ready supply of stone in its construction.

Continue along the lane from the park gateway, passing the side wall of a large barn (was it built of stone from the Abbey?). A gate ahead blocks the lane to motor traffic, but cyclists and walkers can pass around the side of it to gain access to Ferry Lane, a bridleway which runs out to the Thames opposite Laleham. It also leads to Abbey Bridge Farm.

Abbey Bridge Farm *is owned by the Surrey Bird Rescue and Conservation Centre. In fact, the centre is involved in the rescue of animals as well as birds, and there are several varieties of goats, a pig and other animals to be seen. One rescuee, Roger the fox, is reputed to be the only fox to have been entered in a dog show. In the centre of the yard is a huge dovecot dating from 1880 which was restored and resited here in 1991. The centre is also working to restore the barn.*

From the farmyard continue down the lane and cross the bridge over the Abbey River, a sidestream of the Thames. Ahead, as the traffic noise indicates, is the M3 motorway, which the bridleway crosses on a bridge. At the start of the bridge approach, the bridleway follows a separate gravel track fenced off from the lane. This is to avoid possible conflicts with lorries which use the lane.

The surfaced lane ends at some works, the bridleway continuing as a gravelled track. This area, known as the Laleham Burway, is criss-crossed with streams and drainage ditches which the bridleway crosses on crude bridges made of concrete slabs. Be careful because the ends of some slabs are raised above the surface of the track.

The track runs past an embanked reservoir, at the end of which it joins an unmade road. Follow this forward to the edge of the river at the point from which the ferry to Laleham used to depart. The view of the village on the far bank is rather attractive, but one which is seen by

Abbey Bridge Farm

few people. Follow the unmade road until you come to the entrance to a golf course.

The bridleway comes to an abrupt end at this point; the Rights of Way authorities are obviously unaware the ferry no longer operates across the river. For walkers, a footpath crosses the golf links, but it doesn't seem a good idea to go that way with a bicycle, even if you're pushing it. Instead, turn to the right down the golf course entrance drive. Strictly speaking, this is not a right of way, but you are unlikely to have any problems.

Go through the golf club entrance gates, and past a boatyard on the right. This area is called Penton Hook, with its riverbank homes on the right-hand side. They may seem idyllic on a summer's afternoon, but one wonders how they seem on a dark winter's night with the rain lashing down and the river threatening to burst its banks.

Follow the road right around the tip of Penton Hook. If you watch the distant scenery or the position of the sun you will see that the road turns a complete semi-circle, before finally making a sharp left turn into the Penton Park estate. At the mini-roundabout (by a post box) turn right over the bridge and out of the estate into Mixnams Lane and past the marina.

At the end of Mixnams Lane is a large roundabout on the A320 Chertsey–Staines road. On the far side of the roundabout is the entrance to the Thorpe Park theme park. Turn right here and follow the main road for just over a quarter of a mile. You may feel safer if you dismount to cross the main road, and there will probably be no objections if you choose to ride along the footway; it is set well back from the busy road.

At the sign indicating 'TASIS' turn left into Norlands Lane. (The absence of a sign indicating 'Thorpe' is presumably to avoid confusion with Thorpe Park.) About half a mile along the lane you will come to a roundabout, off which is an access into the service areas of Thorpe Park. The building directly opposite, once Eastlyend House but now known as RMC House, is the international headquarters of the RMC Group, better known as Ready Mixed Concrete. Their need for raw materials is responsible for most of the large holes in the ground which cover much of the surrounding area.

Turn right at the roundabout into Coldharbour Lane, and continue straight ahead at the mini-roundabout at the junction with Ten Acre Lane. Like Walton Lane in Lower Halliford, the road is mostly lined by brick walls, but the warm red colour is far from off-putting. Pass the restored 17th century brick-built barn on the left – now splendidly and imaginatively doing duty as the Village Hall – and you

come to Church Approach. What a mixture of building styles and materials – brick, timber, tiles, and even a 15th century thatched farmhouse. A signboard on the left tells something of the history of the village and its buildings.

Thorpe: *Given the situation of the village – a major motorway intersection, countless gravel pits, and one of Britain's largest theme parks all lie within a mile – its survival is quite remarkable. It is not so much its physical preservation – although the listing of many of its buildings has helped with that – but the feeling that this is still a living community which enjoys its rich heritage and turns its back on the disfigurement of its surroundings. In the 1930s the noted local writer Eric Parker commented: 'neither Shere, nor Gomshall, nor Thursley, nor Chiddingfold … can surpass Thorpe for richness of peace of ancient homes and quiet brooding over the past.' It has not changed too drastically since then.*

Thorpe

Thorpe village was once owned by Chertsey Abbey, and parts of St Mary's Church were almost certainly built by its craftsmen. The chancel dates from the 12th century, while the chancel windows are 14th century and of good quality.

On the right-hand side of Church Approach is Thorpe Place, now The American School. Opposite, guarding the start of a footpath to Chertsey, is an unusual stile consisting of a large slab of stone about two or three feet high between two side walls. The path, sometimes called the Monk's Way, was once a raised causeway across marshy river meadows. It was undoubtedly used by the monks to reach their church and properties at Thorpe, and suggestions that it may have been built by Abbot Rutherwyk as part of his improvements may not be entirely fanciful.

Some of the meadowland through which the path once ran survived until the 1960s and early 1970s. Now the meadows have gone because of the gravel they once concealed beneath the grass. Artificial lakes now fill the landscape. The path still exists, thanks to its status as an ancient right of way, but as a narrow strip of land between the lakes of Thorpe Park on one side and a water sports centre on the other.

The hectic local roads really cannot be recommended for cycling, so the footpath from Church Approach is the only sensible way back to Chertsey, even if this does mean you must walk for a mile or so. But before leaving Thorpe, do take a ride round the village by continuing to the end of Coldharbour Lane. Note the old cast-iron direction signs outside the Red Lion – 'Staines and London' to the right, 'Virginia Water and Ascot' to the left.

Turn right at the junction and follow the road to its junction with Ten Acre Lane, where another right turn will return you to Coldharbour Lane.

The Red Lion, Village Road, Thorpe. Free house.

③ Thorpe to Chertsey Bridge

From Church Approach lift your bike over the stone stile and set off on foot along the path. Another low stile follows, but made of tubular steel this time. On the left, after the second stile, is Thorpe Farm, one of the features of Thorpe Park. The farm has been restored and is now worked as it was in the 1930s, with unusual breeds of animals. It is linked to the rest of Thorpe Park by the 'Canada Creek' narrow gauge railway which runs parallel to the footpath for almost a mile. Much of the footpath is bordered by hedges, and it is difficult to see much of the surroundings.

There are several links between the two sides of Thorpe Park; first a footbridge crosses the path, then a modern steel bridge lifts the path up over a roadway. The bridge gives an excellent view of St Ann's Hill and the water sports on the lake before you.

The activities inside Thorpe Park may be audible to you, and at one point the smells of cooking food may waft across. (Have a bite to eat before you leave Thorpe village if you want to avoid pangs of hunger.)

However, except for a station on the miniature railway and a water chute, most of the attractions within the Park are hidden from your view. Not only that, but you may well not be able to see any people either, even if you can hear them. The ride can acquire something of a surreal quality as you begin to wonder whether they are hidden from you, or you from them.

Another steel bridge carries the path over a link between two lakes, and from the top you can both hear and see the nearby M3 motorway. As you approach the motorway, the path opens into an overgrown area. Continue along the path right up to the motorway fence, where it becomes a concrete track, and follow it to the left under the road bridge. At the far end of the bridge the footpath turns left and zigzags up to the A320 Staines–Chertsey road above. When you emerge onto the road, turn left and cross the motorway, but stay on the same side of the road. The footpath resumes on the far side of the motorway; another zigzag takes it back down to ground level.

At the bottom of the zigzag the footpath comes out into Staines Lane, once a main road but now a quiet cul-de-sac with mostly modern houses. However, some of the buildings betray the road's historic origins. Staines Lane eventually joins with Windsor Street, the closest that Chertsey has to a High Street. Its many 18th century buildings include the Chertsey Museum. On the left is Abbey Green. Continue along Windsor Street as it curves to the left into the town centre.

Chertsey: *When other nearby towns such as Woking and Staines were modernising themselves, Chertsey seemed reluctant to update itself and began to decay and lose trade. In a way this was very fortunate, for the town was spared the fate of others, where historic buildings were torn down to be replaced by concrete and glass. Now, having undergone a thorough facelift and with much of the traffic diverted away (but not banned) from the heart of the town, its charm has been restored. It even has a modern superstore right in the centre, but it fits in well with the townscape and has been carefully positioned so as not to dominate the surrounding area.*

After problems with its original charter, Chertsey persuaded Queen Elizabeth I to grant it a new one, which remains in force today. There can be few other towns which still use the powers granted in a 400-year-old Tudor charter to regulate parking in its main street! Chertsey does, as the signs in the market place in Windsor Street clearly state.

Chertsey once had two fairs, the Black Cherry Fair on August 6th, and the Goose and Onion Fair on September 26th. Both died out

for many years, but the Black Cherry Fair has been revived in name, if not date, for it is now held in July.

Chertsey's local legend is of Blanche Heriot who saved her lover when he was captured by the Yorkists during the Wars of the Roses. He was condemned to be executed on Chertsey Meads when the curfew bell rang at 8 o'clock the next night. The messenger carrying a reprieve was delayed and was still crossing on the Laleham Ferry when the hour of the curfew came. Blanche climbed the curfew tower and held onto the clapper of the bell, preventing it from being sounded. The curfew bell was saved from the Abbey and is in St Peter's Church. It is still rung nightly between Michaelmas and Lady Day (September 29 to March 25).

Chertsey Museum (☎ 01932 565764) is well worth a visit if you are interested in finding out more about the town and its Abbey. It has a collection of Chertsey tiles and other artefacts, many of which were discovered during gravel extraction. It is open Tue–Sat 2–5, and on Wed, Fri, Sat from 10-1 as well. Admission is free.

Chertsey has many pubs, shops and other facilities, and there is lots to explore in the town, but sadly the historic Porch House, home of Abraham Cowley, Poet Laureate to King Charles II, has long since been demolished.

The Crown, London Street. Youngs. 01932 564657. Open all day. Food C G Rest Acc

Leave Chertsey along London Street, past the Crown, an old coaching inn rebuilt in the 19th century, and the Town Hall which was built in 1852. London Street leads to Bridge Road and thereby to Chertsey Bridge and the end of the ride.

CICERONE GUIDES
Cicerone publish a wide range of reliable guides to walking, cycling and climbing in Britain, and other general interest books.

BIKE GUIDES - UK
THE CHESHIRE CYCLE WAY
THE CUMBRIA CYCLE WAY
LANDS END TO JOHN O'GROATS CYCLE GUIDE
ON THE RUFFSTUFF Cycle routes in northern England
THE SCOTTISH GLENS SERIES 1 - 7

LAKE DISTRICT - General Books
CONISTON COPPER A History
CHRONICLES OF MILNTHORPE
EDEN TAPESTRY
THE HIGH FELLS OF LAKELAND
KENDAL A SOCIAL HISTORY
LAKELAND VILLAGES
LAKELAND TOWNS
LAKELAND PANORAMAS
THE LAKERS
THE LOST RESORT? (Morecambe)
ROADS & TRACKS OF THE LAKE DISTRICT

LAKE DISTRICT - Guide Books
CONISTON COPPER MINES Field Guide
THE CUMBRIA CYCLE WAY
THE CUMBRIA WAY & ALLERDALE RAMBLE
THE EDEN WAY
IN SEARCH OF WESTMORLAND
SHORT WALKS IN LAKELAND-1: SOUTH LAKELAND
SHORT WALKS IN LAKELAND- 2:NORTH LAKELAND
SCRAMBLES IN THE LAKE DISTRICT
MORE SCRAMBLES IN THE LAKE DISTRICT
THE TARNS OF LAKELAND VOL 1 - WEST
THE TARNS OF LAKELAND VOL 2 - EAST
WALKING ROUND THE LAKES
WALKS IN SILVERDALE/ARNSIDE
WESTMORLAND HERITAGE WALK
WINTER CLIMBS IN THE LAKE DISTRICT

NORTH WEST ENGLAND (outside the Lakes
BIRDWATCHING ON MERSEYSIDE
CANAL WALKS Vol 1 North
DOUGLAS VALLEY WAY
FAMILY WALKS IN THE FOREST OF BOWLAND
WALKING IN THE FOREST OF BOWLAND
HERITAGE TRAILS IN NW ENGLAND
THE ISLE OF MAN COASTAL PATH
IVORY TOWERS & DRESSED STONES (Follies)
THE LANCASTER CANAL
LANCASTER CANAL WALKS
A WALKERS GUIDE TO THE LANCASTER CANAL
WALKS FROM THE LEEDS-LIVERPOOL CANAL

A NORTHERN COAST-TO-COAST
   St Bees to Robin Hood's Bay
THE RIBBLE WAY
WALKING IN LANCASHIRE
WALKING DOWN THE LUNE
WALKS ON THE WEST PENNINE MOORS
WALKING NORTHERN RAILWAYS - West
WALKS IN LANCASHIRE WITCH COUNTRY

THE PENNINES & NORTH EAST ENGLAND
CANOEISTS GUIDE TO THE NORTH EAST
THE CLEVELAND WAY & MISSING LINK
WALKING IN CHESHIRE
THE CHESHIRE CYCLE WAY
THE DALES WAY
HADRIANS WALL Vol 1 The Wall Walk
HADRIANS WALL VOL 2 Walks around the Wall
LAUGHS ALONG THE PENNINE WAY
A NORTHERN COAST-TO-COAST
NORTH YORK MOORS Walks
THE PENNINE WAY
ON THE RUFFSTUFF 84 Bike rides in Northern England
THE REIVERS WAY (Northumberland)
THE TEESDALE WAY
WALKING IN COUNTY DURHAM
WALKING IN THE SOUTH PENNINES
WALKING IN THE NORTH PENNINES
WALKING IN NORTHUMBERLAND
WALKING IN THE WOLDS
WALKS IN THE YORKSHIRE DALES (3 VOL)
WALKS IN THE NORTH YORK MOORS (2 VOL)
WATERFALL WALKS -TEESDALE & THE HIGH
PENNINES
THE YORKSHIRE DALES A walker's guide
THE YORKSHIRE DALES ANGLER'S GUIDE

DERBYSHIRE PEAK DISTRICT & EAST MIDLANDS
Star FAMILY WALKS IN THE PEAK DISTRICT & SOUTH
   YORKSHIRE
HIGH PEAK WALKS
WHITE PEAK WAY
WHITE PEAK WALKS - 2 Vols
WEEKEND WALKS IN THE PEAK DISTRICT
THE VIKING WAY
THE DEVIL'S MILL / WHISTLING CLOUGH (Novels)

CICERONE GUIDES
Cicerone publish a wide range of reliable guides to walking, cycling and climbing in Britain, and other general interest books.

WALES and WELSH BORDER & WEST MIDLANDS
ANGLESEY COAST WALKS
ASCENT OF SNOWDON
THE BRECON BEACONS
CLWYD ROCK
HEREFORD & THE WYE VALLEY A Walker's Guide
HILLWALKING IN SNOWDONIA
HILL WALKING IN WALES (2 Vols)
THE LLEYN PENINSULA COASTAL PATH (+ bike)
THE MOUNTAINS OF ENGLAND & WALES
      Vol 1 WALES
WALKING OFFA'S DYKE PATH
THE PEMBROKESHIRE COAST PATH
THE RIDGES OF SNOWDONIA
SARN HELEN Walking Roman Road
SCRAMBLES IN SNOWDONIA
SEVERN WALKS
THE SHROPSHIRE HILLS A Walker's Guide
SNOWDONIA WHITE WATER SEA & SURF
WALKING DOWN THE WYE
A WELSH COAST TO COAST WALK
WELSH WINTER CLIMBS

THE MIDLANDS
COTSWOLD WAY
COTSWOLD WALKS (3 VOLS)
TWENTY COTSWOLD TOWNS
THE GRAND UNION CANAL WALK
WALKING IN OXFORDSHIRE
AN OXBRIDGE WALK
WALKING IN WARWICKSHIRE
WEST MIDLANDS ROCK

SOUTH & SOUTH WEST ENGLAND
CORNISH ROCK
WALKING IN CORNWALL
WALKING IN THE CHILTERNS
WALKING ON DARTMOOR
WALKERS GUIDE TO DARTMOOR PUBS
WALKING IN DEVON
WALKING IN DORSET
EXMOOR & THE QUANTOCKS
THE KENNET & AVON WALK
LONDON THEME WALKS
WALKING IN SOMERSET
A SOUTHERN COUNTIES BIKE GUIDE
THE SOUTHERN-COAST-TO-COAST

SOUTH DOWNS WAY & DOWNS LINK
SOUTH WEST WAY - 2 Vol
THE TWO MOORS WAY Dartmoor-Exmoor
WALKS IN KENT Bk 1 & 2
THE WEALDWAY & VANGUARD WAY

SCOTLAND
THE BORDER COUNTRY - WALKERS GUIDE
BORDER PUBS & INNS A Walker's Guide
CAIRNGORMS WINTER CLIMBS
CENTRAL HIGHLANDS 6 LONG DISTANCE WALKS
WALKING THE GALLOWAY HILLS
THE ISLAND OF RHUM
THE ISLE OF SKYE - A Walker's Guide
THE SCOTTISH GLENS (Walking & Mountainbike Guide)
    Book 1:THE CAIRNGORM GLENS
    Book 2 THE ATHOLL GLENS
    Book 3 THE GLENS OF RANNOCH
    Book 4 THE GLENS OF TROSSACH
    Book 5 THE GLENS OF ARGYLL
    Book 6 THE GREAT GLEN
    Book 7 THE ANGUS GLENS
SCOTTISH RAILWAY WALKS
SCRAMBLES IN LOCHABER
SCRAMBLES IN SKYE
SKI TOURING IN SCOTLAND
TORRIDON A Walker's Guide
THE WEST HIGHLAND WAY
WALKS from the WEST HIGHLAND RAILWAY
WINTER CLIMBS BEN NEVIS & GLENCOE

REGIONAL BOOKS UK & IRELAND
THE PENNINE WAY
THE ALTERNATIVE PENNINE WAY
THE ALTERNATIVE COAST TO COAST
LANDS END TO JOHN O'GROATS CYCLE GUIDE
CANAL WALKS Vol.1: North
CANAL WALKS Vol.2: Midlands
CANAL WALKS Vol.3: South
THE PACKHORSE BRIDGES OF ENGLAND
THE RELATIVE HILLS OF BRITAIN
THE MOUNTAINS OF ENGLAND & WALES
    VOL 1 WALES, VOL 2 ENGLAND
THE MOUNTAINS OF IRELAND
THE IRISH COAST TO COAST WALK

Other guides are constantly being added to the Cicerone List.
Available from bookshops, outdoor equipment shops or direct (send s.a.e. for price list) from
CICERONE, 2 POLICE SQUARE, MILNTHORPE, CUMBRIA, LA7 7PY

CICERONE GUIDES

Cicerone publish a wide range of reliable guides to walking and climbing worldwide

FRANCE, BELGIUM & LUXEMBOURG
WALKING IN THE ARDENNES Castle
THE BRITTANY COASTAL PATH - Castle
CHAMONIX MONT BLANC - A Walking Guide.
   Collins
THE CORSICAN HIGH LEVEL ROUTE: GR20 .
   Castle
FRENCH ROCK Birkett
THE PYRENEAN TRAIL: GR10. Castle
THE RLS (Stevenson) TRAIL. Castle
ROCK CLIMBS IN BELGIUM & LUXEMBOURG
   Craggs
ROCK CLIMBS IN THE VERDON Newcombe
TOUR OF MONT BLANC Harper
TOUR OF THE OISANS: GR54 Harper
TOUR OF THE QUEYRAS Castle
TOUR OF THE VANOISE Reynolds
WALKING THE FRENCH ALPS: GR5 Collins
WALKING IN HAUTE SAVOIE Norton
WALKING IN THE TARENTAISE &
   BEAUFORTAIN ALPS Akitt
WALKING THE FRENCH GORGES (Provence)
   Castle
WALKS IN VOLCANO COUNTRY (Auvergne)
   Castle
THE WAY OF ST JAMES Raju
THE WAY OF ST JAMES CYCLIST'S GUIDE
   Higginson

FRANCE / SPAIN
WALKS AND CLIMBS IN THE PYRENEES
   Reynolds
ROCK CLIMBS IN THE PYRENEES Walker

SPAIN & PORTUGAL
WALKING IN THE ALGARVE Parker
ANDALUSIAN ROCK CLIMBS Craggs
BIRDWATCHING IN MALLORCA Stoba
COSTA BLANCA ROCK Craggs
MOUNTAIN WALKS ON THE COSTA BLANCA
   Stansfield
ROCK CLIMBS IN MAJORCA, IBIZA &
   TENERIFE Craggs

WALKING IN MALLORCA Parker
THE MOUNTAINS OF CENTRAL SPAIN Oglesby
THROUGH THE SPANISH PYRENEES: GR11
   Lucia
WALKING IN THE SIERRA NEVADA Walmsley
WALKS & CLIMBS IN THE PICOS DE EUROPA
   Walker
THE WAY OF ST JAMES: SPAIN Raju

SWITZERLAND including adjacent parts of France and Italy
THE ALPINE PASS ROUTE Reynolds
THE BERNESE ALPS Reynolds
CENTRAL SWITZERLAND Reynolds
CHAMONIX TO ZERMATT The Walker's Haute
   Route Reynolds
WALKING IN THE ALPS Reynolds
THE GRAND TOUR OF MONTE ROSA (inc Italy)
   2 vols Wright
WALKS IN THE ENGADINE Reynolds
THE JURA - Walking the High Route and Winter
   Ski Traverses Reynolds & Evans
WALKING IN TICINO Reynolds
THE VALAIS - A Walking Guide Reynolds

GERMANY / AUSTRIA / EASTERN EUROPE
WALKING IN THE BAVARIAN ALPS Bourne
GERMANY'S ROMANTIC ROAD A guide for
   walkers and cyclists McLachlan
HUT-TO-HUT IN THE STUBAI ALPS Hartley
THE HIGH TATRAS Saunders & Renata
KING LUDWIG WAY Speakman
KLETTERSTEIG - Scrambles. Werner
MOUNTAIN WALKING IN AUSTRIA Davies
WALKING IN THE BLACK FOREST Speakman
WALKING IN THE HARZ MOUNTAINS
   Speakman
WALKING IN THE SALZKAMMERGUT
   Speakman

NORTHERN EUROPE
WALKING IN NORWAY Roos
ITALY & SLOVENIA